Corporate Equalizer

Neil C. Livingstone

THIS BOOKS IS DEDICATED TO
ASSASSINATED FRIENDS

Benazir Bhutto
Ivo Pukanić
JED

CONTENTS

Begin each day by saying I shall
meet with the corrupt, the arrogant,
the deceitful, the envious and the
boastful. This is simply the way
the world is. Therefore I shall not
be unreasonably disturbed by it all.
No more than I am disturbed by the
changes in the weather.

Marcus Aurelius

To a Whisper and a Tsai (Sigh)

INTRODUCTION

In the course of my business career I've had many unique opportunities and experiences. Over the years I've been in the reviewing stand at the French Foreign Legion headquarters in Aubagne on Camerone Day; had a drink on the "Lucky Chest" in Belfast (that missed sailing on the Titanic); been shot at in Guatemala; seen the Moscow to Beijing express, with red flags flying on the front of a massive black steam locomotive, burst through the fog in the Chinese countryside during the Cold War; been arrested, jailed, and interrogated in Libya; had a partner murdered by General Noreiga in Panama; dined at gangster clubs in Moscow and in the back rooms of Georgian and Uzbek restaurants with members of the Russian Mafia; bent an elbow with old lefties and Sinn Fein in the "Kremlin Bar" in the bowels of the House of Commons; ridden a racing camel in the desert; been trapped in Montenegro with a former Navy SEAL with Milosevic hot on our heels; explored the North Korean tunnels beneath the DMZ; stayed in Haiti's legendary Hotel Oloffson and had a drink with Petit Pierre while voodoo drums echoed in the hills above; been stalked by terrorists and Nazis in Argentina; been a guest of a swashbuckling pirate on a yacht full of hookers in Monte Carlo harbor during the annual Grand Prix; been paid in stacks of $100 bills by clients and counted the money with Customs Agents upon my return to the U.S.; been on the run in Colombia with cases of electronic equipment and a 46-foot long antennae; and been subpoenaed, incorrectly, for gun running in Central America and, again incorrectly, for involvement in the Iran-Contra affair.

I've attended business meetings in corporate board rooms high over Wall Street, in dark alleys, aboard private jets, in seedy bars, palaces, bank vaults, on factory floors, and in Hillsborough Castle, the Queen's residence in Northern Ireland. I even went to a business meeting with a six-and-half foot tall pink-eyed albino dressed in white from head-to-foot in a Miami-area motel with the peculiar distinction of having more "floaters" in its pool than any other hospitality establishment in the U.S.

I've met with terrorists in their jail cells in Turkey and over drinks high above Moscow in the Ukraina Hotel and at the Ritz in Paris. I've negotiated for kidnap victims as well as vetted dozens of sleazeballs and terrorists claiming to hold American hostages in Beirut. I've written books, produced television programs, sold a helicopter company and taken another company public.

So if you're tired of business books written by professors that have never met a payroll or made a real buck, ex-military officers who compare business to war but wouldn't know an entrepreneur if there was one in the next foxhole, or even successful but smug Wall Street elitists who have made money while sitting in their offices but never got their hands dirty or took a risk beyond using an iron rather than a wood off the tee, then this book is for you. It represents the sum of what I've learned after more than thirty-five years in business helping corporations, celebrities, heads-of-state, and executives address a wide array of problems ranging from kidnappings to shakedowns, denial of service attacks, mass tort suits, attack journalism, political upheaval, gender and racial issues, industrial espionage, intellectual property theft, internal investigations, missing persons, confidence games, and even murder.

I'm a believer in the school of hard knocks and tough love, of gritting it out in the hard places and doing the dirty tasks, of soaking my aching bones in the tub at a hotel in the Balkans with a gun in the soap dish in case anyone uninvited came through the door. If you believe in corporate motivational speakers who embrace meditation as a methodology for achieving fresh marketing insights or affirm that playing Stanley Kowalski in "Streetcar" at a corporate retreat will make you a better and more caring executive, you may want to stop reading now. Being a bridge master didn't help Jimmy Cayne save Bear Sterns. And don't even mention the philharmonic conductor who maintains that music is the key to corporate team building.

This is a no-holds-barred in-your-face examination about what it takes not only to survive but prosper in a world full of crooks, rapacious competitors, natural disasters, corporate spies, terrorists, accidents, political chaos, wars and revolutions. And I also suggest ways to triumph over stupidity and just plain bad luck.

- 1 -

CORPORATE CRISES

"There cannot be a crisis next week.
My schedule is already full."

Henry Kissinger

THE CASE OF THE MISSING CEO

Your CEO is an unmarried workaholic who has finally met the girl of his dreams. The downside is that she's a twenty-two year old intravenous drug user and denizen of the city's S&M clubs. Within weeks of meeting her, the CEO's behavior has become increasingly erratic. The man who never missed a day of work and stayed at his desk until it was dark every night, now arrives late, leaves early, and can't seem to concentrate while he's in the office. He's losing weight and his appearance has become slovenly and unkempt. He has been spending large amounts of money, and reportedly has leased several apartments in the city for the girlfriend. None of his personal bills have been paid in several months. Those closest to him suspect he is hooked on drugs, too.

Finally, he doesn't show up for work at all. Family members and his personal attorney fear the worst.

Okay, so what would you do?

I was contacted by an attorney with whom I had worked with before, on behalf of the executive's family and company. He explained the situation to me and indicated that the family had not heard from the CEO in weeks. They were afraid not only for the CEO's health and well-being, but concerned that if his situation became public it could have extremely damaging repercussions for the corporation, which was valued at close to a billion dollars.

We knew the situation was deteriorating fast because it was learned that the CEO and his girlfriend had purchased an expensive new luxury car apparently because they couldn't remember where they parked their regular vehicle. The luxury car, it turned out, was subsequently towed by the police to an impound lot because it had been discovered parked in a no parking zone with five outstanding tickets on it. When investigators searched the car, they found someone had defecated on one of the seats.

Our first task, we decided, was to find the CEO and make sure that he was alright, or at least not in jeopardy. Once that was done, we would keep him under surveillance while I located an appropriate clinic outside the United States where we could commit him for treatment. We had ruled out the Betty Ford Clinic and other U.S. facilities for fear that some word of his condition might leak out, with negative consequences for the CEO personally and for his company.

At our suggestion, the CEO's brother phoned the girlfriend's apartment and she answered. She broke down on the phone and began crying. She said they needed help and "that everything was totally out of control." She gave the brother the address of the apartment and then hung up. Our operators (a term we adopted from the Army's super-secret Delta Force, where a number of our employees learned their trade) went immediately to the apartment, fearing that the CEO might have over-dosed. After some coaxing, the girlfriend let them in. What they found shocked even the hardened ex-military men.

The apartment was a total pigsty. According to the after-action report prepared by one of the operators, "There were hundreds of syringes, used and unused, with and without drugs still in them. Bloody tissues, towels and rags were everywhere. Cocaine vials were in purses, shoes, clothes, drawers, literally every place conceivable. Cut off straws, parts of ink pens, and other drug use items were in every drawer in the kitchen. Smut magazines were in the kitchen drawers also (men on men and women on women types). Loose money was just thrown down everywhere, mostly single dollars and change. Someone had puked in the bathtub and on the floor of the bathroom. The oven was at 325 degrees with a piece of pizza in it that had been there a long, long time. A quartz space heater was on full blast, sitting on top of a cardboard file box, and a desk lamp with a 100-watt bulb was hanging from a mirror with silk scarves on it, which were starting to melt. There were sex objects in the closet and on the floor, not to mention her dirty underwear. Some of her clothes had human feces on them. The toilet and wash basin in the bathroom were both clogged with cocaine vials and cocaine. There was so much blood [around the apartment] that it looked like someone had been butchered."

The CEO was in bad shape. He had become physically ravaged by drugs and faded in and out of consciousness. With the family attorney and a physician on hand, the brother went to work to convince the CEO to voluntarily commit himself for treatment at a foreign clinic. A private jet, he was told, was standing by to transport him to the facility. The girl, he was informed, would be taken to a separate facility in the States by private aircraft, accompanied by several of our operators.

The girl, meanwhile, was being detained in another room. She had had a change of heart and was refusing to cooperate with the plan. She demanded that she be allowed to accompany the CEO to wherever he was going, but the attending physician felt that they should be separated so that the CEO could receive treatment away from her influence, which was decidedly negative. Since there was an outstanding warrant for her arrest, the girl relented and reluctantly agreed to treatment at a facility of our choice, with the CEO footing all of the bills.

At this point, I was contacted in Switzerland, where I had just visited another treatment facility to determine its suitability for our purposes. It was just before dawn my time when the phone rang and I was informed that the situation had come to a head earlier than anticipated. Although I was scheduled to leave Switzerland to inspect another clinic that morning, I immediately abandoned my plans and called one of the facilities I had already visited and made arrangements to receive the CEO the next day.

Meanwhile, the operators began sanitizing the apartment. There was enough cocaine on hand to have resulted in serious felony charges against the CEO. The operators filled four five-gallon trash bags with drug paraphernalia and blood products, which they carried out of the apartment and disposed of in dumpsters around the city. The cocaine was flushed down the kitchen sink. "Extreme care had to be taken," said one of the operators, "because there were needles all over the place. They were in the carpet and in every other thing in the apartment."

The car the CEO had used to get to the apartment was also located and cleaned up. "The seats, glove box, and trunk were loaded with syringes and cocaine," observed one of the operators. It took two hours to fully sanitize the car.

The CEO finally agreed to seek treatment. Papers were produced, which he signed, naming his brother his temporary guardian. A guard was posted at the door and the doctor gave the CEO something to help him sleep. A few hours later, the CEO was driven to the airport. Accompanied by the attorney, his sister (since his brother had to stay and run the company), and the physician, the CEO was flown to a European country where the clinic was prepared to receive him.

The last major potential difficulty was getting the CEO through Customs and Immigration. If he indicated to the Immigration officials that he was being coerced or had changed his mind and did not want to seek entry into the country, they would have permitted him to turn around and go home. Although there were some tense moments at the airport, he capitulated to his sister's wishes and allowed himself to be transported to the treatment facility.

The CEO's party and I were converging from two different parts of the world, but so well coordinated was the operation that our respective cars met at an intersection just two blocks from the clinic. It was the only time I've ever had the opportunity to tell a cab driver to "follow that car." We fell in behind the black limo carrying the CEO and we arrived at the clinic moments later. We left the CEO under the care of the very able staff of the clinic and he remained there for a number weeks, until he kicked his addiction and was thinking clearly again. Today, I am happy to report, he's back at the helm of his company.

CORPORATE "EQUALIZER"

Welcome to the world of corporate crisis management. The crisis just described, while unique and deadly serious, was just another day at the office. I'm a crisis manager and the unusual is the ordinary in my world. I get paid to help corporations, and prominent people who can afford my services, tackle one-of-a-kind problems, the sort of problems for which there are few blueprints and little institutional memory. The kind of problems they don't teach you about in business school. This book is about the many kinds of crises and challenges that confront contemporary companies and high net worth individuals in a globalized economy and how they can successfully be avoided or managed before they destroy reputations, market share, share value, or even result in the loss of life.

Some years ago, I was a consultant to the CBS prime-time series "The Equalizer." As a review of the show in *USA Today* observed at the time, "When victims are terrorized and have nowhere else to turn, they call CBS' 'Equalizer'". But what happens when "The Equalizer" gets in a jam? He calls Neil C. Livingstone. Not a familiar household name, but one that strikes fear in the hearts of evil men." I was hired to add authenticity to the show because, as one of the Universal executives put it, "You do in real life what the 'Equalizer' does on the screen."

While "The Equalizer" was purely entertainment, the term "equalizer" is very descriptive and, in many respects, represents the essence of what I do. I'm a corporate "equalizer"; when someone is in trouble they contact me and my colleagues and we try to put things right.

WHAT IS A CRISIS?

A crisis is a non-ordinary event or emergency that may have negative or troubling consequences. Not all problems are crises. Crises lie beyond the scope of a company's or an individual's ordinary activities and often involve a turning point or decisive moment where a misstep can spell disaster. Crises come in every shape and description but most are not as dramatic as the case cited above. Among the kinds of modern crises that a contemporary corporate CEO might have to deal with during his watch are natural disasters, workplace violence, industrial espionage, product tampering, mass tort claims, toxic spills, kidnappings, extortion, product counterfeiting, intellectual property theft, sexual harassment, racial discrimination, fraud, threats, hostile takeovers, unfair competition, media ambushes, and even wars and revolutions.

The first rule of crisis management is that every corporation or prominent individual experiences a crisis at some time. In other words, everyone's parade eventually gets rained upon. If you are a CEO, you hope that a major crisis doesn't happen on your watch. But don't count on it.

The fact that you are confronted with a crisis may have nothing to do with your management skills or crisis avoidance strategies. As the old saying goes, "shit happens." Generally, how prone your company is to crises and how serious they potentially are depends on the size of your company and its global reach. In other words, the bigger your operation, the more vulnerabilities and problems it's likely to have. My late friend and mentor, Admiral Bill Crowe, who was Chairman of our Advisory Board for many years, used to tell the story of the words of advice he received from his predecessor when he was named Chairman of the Joint Chiefs of Staff. "Bill, you're about to take over one of the largest organizations in the world [the U.S. military]," he was told. "Imagine the worst possible thing you can and somewhere, some place in that organization someone is doing it."

In addition, the more countries where you have operations, and the relative political stability or instability of those countries, will have a direct correlation on the likelihood you will have a serious crisis or problem down the road. This is not to suggest that you avoid dangerous countries or unstable regions of the world in your business operations. Often the greatest opportunities exist in those areas. As former Rear Admiral Grace Murray Hopper once observed, "A ship in port is safe but that's not what ships are built for."[1] The same can be said about companies. The day has long since passed where a company can remain in Oshkosh, Cleveland, Dallas, or even New York and expect the rest of the world to beat a path to its door. The pursuit of profits and new markets, as well as raw materials and new production facilities, demands that most corporations have an active international presence. For years, I was extremely dismayed by the absence of Americans in many of the difficult places we worked. I would always see Japanese, Koreans, Taiwanese, and often German businessmen, but rarely, if ever, an American. This lack of engagement with the rest of the world, and fear of taking risks, mirrored the industrial decline of America in the 1970s. Today, I am happy to report, it is hard to find a place where you do not run into American business executives.

The only caveat about doing business in dangerous places is that you must approach these areas with open eyes and take prudent precautions to avoid problems. And should a major a crisis arise, it is imperative that you have crisis management skills and resources available to address the problem, whatever its nature or implications, in

---

1 Grace Murray Hopper (RADM, U.S. Navy, ret.); interview; "Sixty Minutes"; August 24, 1986.

a direct and timely fashion. Such crises can range from airlifting a sick employee to a hospital in Europe to inserting a dozen armed men on the ground in the dark of night to remove company assets before they are confiscated by a radical government or overrun by rebels. If you don't have a tested methodology for addressing such unconventional situations in advance, and appropriate resources, both inside and outside the company, to address the problem at hand, then you could end up in a predicament with money, lives, and even the viability of your whole business enterprise at stake. And if that happens, be prepared to kiss your golden parachute goodbye.

CRISES OF EVERY SHAPE AND SIZE

It's Monday morning. You're a top corporate executive and you just arrived at your desk, a cup of steaming coffee at your elbow, rested and ready for the week's challenges. It will be a busy one, including meetings with your bankers, the opening of a new plant, a review of the next quarter's sales projections, and the kickoff of the company's new ad campaign. You glance absentmindedly down at the newspaper on your desk, see your company's name on the front page, and do a double take. It's one of those holy shit moments.

If you're a Target executive, the article says some of your baseball caps and shorts are imprinted with symbols that stand for "Heil Hitler." The media is demanding an explanation and even the Southern Poverty Law Center, which tracks racist organizations, is involved. Talk about being blindsided; never in a million years would you have expected this kind of problem.[2] Nor did the executives at Beta Shoe Co. which suffered mob attacks and bombings by Muslim extremists in Bangladesh who charged that the company's emblem on its footwear is blasphemous because it is "similar to the written symbol of Allah in Arabic."

---

2 The caps and shorts were imprinted with the number "88" and "eight eight," Apparently neo-Nazi organizations use the symbols to stand for "Heil Hitler since "h" is the eighth letter of the alphabet. According to *The Washington Post*, in addition to being used in White power rock music, the symbols "are commonly used among supremacists in graffiti and is a popular tattoo." See "Racist Markings Spur Target Recall"; *The Washington Post*; August 29, 2002.

If you are a CNN executive, the *New York Post* has just described your company as the "kinky news network" following the arrest of one of the network's top on-air personalities, Richard Quest, at 3:40 a.m. in Central Park with a bag of methamphetamine in his pocket and a rope around his neck tied to his genitals. There was also a "sex toy," according to press reports, in his boot. If you are with the venerable outdoor products company, L.L. Bean, it's the report that the telephone number on the cover of your 2006 fishing catalog goes to a phone sex company.

At Adidas you were taken completely by surprise when one of your limited edition sneakers turned out to have a face on it with buck teeth, slanted eyes, and a bowl-shaped haircut. Asian Americans are irate. What were the designers thinking, you groan. Cingular, of course, was guilty of the same insensitivity and had to deep-six one of its ringtones. The ringtone opens with a wailing siren and then a voice that calls out, "This is la migra," Spanish slang for the Border Patrol. "Por favor, put the oranges down and step away from the cellphone," continues the voice. "I repeat-o, put the oranges down and step away from the telephone-o. I'm deporting you back home-o."

You're a executive at the Caldor department store chain and some dimwits at the company's creative agency have composed an ad showing two smiling boys playing Scrabble with the word "rape" spelled out on the board. Eleven million copies of the ad, which appears in a toy sale insert, have appeared in 85 northeastern cities, producing howls of protest.

For the executives of Matsushita Communications Industrial Co., the article says that a crisis is raging over the disclosure that the company's popular Panasonic mobile phones contain the Republic of China's (Taiwan) phone code in its electronic memory of country codes. Beijing is threatening to halt production of all Panasonic phones made in China, and this has resulted in an eight percent decline in the company's stock value.[3] Take heart, however, because you're not alone. In 2000, Coca-Cola had to pull the plug on Taiwanese pop singer, Ah-mei, who it was using to hawk its products in mainland China, after she sang the Taiwanese national anthem at the

---

3 "Matsushita Faces Phone Ban in China Over Taiwan Gaffe"; *Wall Street Journal*; September 7, 2001.

inauguration of Taiwan's independence-minded new president. Who knew? Two years earlier, Apple Computer fell into the same trap, using images of the Dalai Lama--the very symbol of opposition to Chinese domination of Tibet--to sell its products in Hong Kong. Apparently no one at the company had even the most rudimentary geopolitical knowledge.

If you are the CEO of the Bank of New York, you were just informed that your 30-foot sailboat was sunk by animal rights activists and the dock covered with spray-painted graffiti, all because the bank is involved with Huntington Life Sciences, a British firm accused by animal rights extremists of animal testing.

If you are at the Wal-Mart headquarters in Bentonville, Arkansas, you've just learned that federal agents have raided sixty of your stores and arrested more than 250 illegal immigrants, most from Eastern Europe, working as janitors. If you work for Whole Foods, it's the need to recall two months of ground beef potentially contaminated with E. coli.

If you are from the Bank of Scotland, you're being pilloried for launching what was described as an "innovative joint venture" with American TV evangelist Pat Robertson. The deal envisioned the creation of a bank, targeted at Robertson's followers, along the lines of similar successful ventures in Europe, in which all transactions are conducted by phone. Now Labour politicians, feminists, gays, unions, and the Scottish media are all attacking the bank because of their loathing for Robertson, turning what seemed like such a sound business arrangement into what *The Washington Post* described as "a public relations catastrophe for the Bank of Scotland."

If you work for Marriott, it's a story about Thailand on your world travel web site where the company asserts that "only prostitutes wear sleeveless blouses and/or shorts."[4] Thai officials and women's groups are outraged.

If you're with Texaco, it's reports that company officials have used the "n" word to describe black employees and boasted about keeping "the black jelly beans stuck to the bottom of the bag." The allegations

---

4   "Marriott Apologizes for Web Comment on Thai Women"; *The Wall Street Journal*; September 1, 2001.

have created a firestorm in the media, and Jesse Jackson is on his way to Houston to protest outside corporate headquarters.

If you're a Monsanto executive, you've just learned that Beatle Paul McCartney is rejecting your soybeans in his (now former) wife Linda's sausages because they are bio-engineered.

You're with CBS and have just learned that a work-at-home dad in Bethesda, Maryland, has set up a web site called "Boycott CBS.com" to protest alleged liberal bias in an upcoming mini-series about Ronald Reagan. The network has received tens of thousands of angry emails and phone calls, and advertisers are getting cold feet. Now Fox is on the rampage and you're hearing from your parent firm, Viacom.

And the list goes on and on.

The Eckerd drugstore chain is being sued by an Orthodox Jewish pharmacist who was dismissed after he refused to sell condoms.[5] A Planet Hollywood restaurant in South Africa is bombed after a U.S. missile strike on alleged Osama bin Laden targets in the Sudan and Afghanistan. At the same time, Disney executives are grappling with the issue of whether or not to cancel an appearance by Mickey Mouse and Minnie in the UAE because of security concerns. If you work at Coca Cola, one of your bottling plants in southern India has been attacked by Maoist guerillas protesting the U.S. military action.

And that's far from Coke's only problem: four African-American employees of Coke have sued the company, claiming racial bias in hiring and promotion practices. Now Jesse Jackson has called for a national consumer boycott of the company's products. You don't know it yet, but it will cost the company $193 million to settle the case. A man is arrested in Germany for trying to extort $730,000 from the company by placing contaminated bottles of Coke on supermarket shelves. Even though he's been caught, sales go into a tailspin.

Energy Brands executives have to contend with misspellings and typos on their product labels. Perrier, with a reputation for quality and purity, has to pull its products from the shelves around the world because of contamination problems.

---

5 The suit was thrown out by a federal grand jury who took the enlightened view that there was no way to accommodate the pharmacist's religious views without "hurting customer service."

The U.S. Equal Employment Opportunity Commission joins racial bias suits filed by black Lockheed Martin employees claiming discrimination in hiring and pay, and a hostile workplace, including an open display of Ku Klux Klan materials. Twentieth Century Fox is picketed by Muslim groups who claim that their motion pictures unfairly portray Arabs as terrorists. Environmentalists threaten to launch a boycott against Exxon Mobile because of controversial statements by the Chairman and CEO regarding the Kyoto convention on global warming. A decade earlier an Exxon supertanker, whose captain was legally drunk, ran aground in Alaska's Prince William Sound, producing the most notorious oil spill in modern history.

A Kansas woman sues Denny's over burns she claims she received from cleaning chemicals used to disinfect a toilet seat. McDonald's, on the other hand, is sued by a Dallas Cowboys coaching assistant who alleges he found a dead rat in his salad. On another front, animal rights activists are targeting McDonald's, claiming that the animals used in "Happy Meals" and "Chicken McNuggets" are inhumanely slaughtered. In France, protestors inflict more than $100,000 worth of damage on a McDonald's, which is seen as a cultural interloper and a symbol of globalization. The leader of the attack, Jose Bove, becomes a national hero; more than 20,000 supporters arrive in the rural French village where the attack occurred as Bove goes on trial. In India, Hindus protest McDonald's French fries, maintaining that the company puts beef flavoring in them, violating the Hindu prohibition against eating cows. But McDonald's is not alone. People for the Ethical Treatment of Animals have also taken on Wendy's with billboards sporting images of a Wendy-like character brandishing a butcher knife dripping with blood.

And these aren't even life and death crises like the one in the beginning of this chapter.

MAJOR CRISES

The price of a major corporate crisis is rarely reasonable, and sometimes it can cost a corporation or an individual--think professional football quarterback Michael Vick--everything they've got. A major crisis can be like hitting the wall at the Indianapolis speedway at 180 mph. You may survive it, but you'll never be the same afterward.

A major crisis is one of great magnitude, where human life is at stake or the very company, its share value and reputation are on the line. A good example is the crisis I became embroiled in several years ago.

It was late Thursday afternoon when I summoned to London for a meeting the following night. One of Russia's leading oligarchs, Oleg Deripaska, had been ambushed by a racketeering lawsuit in New York alleging that he employed fraud, death threats, and extortion in consolidating his control of the nation's aluminum industry. The civil RICO suit, filed by accused gangsters, asked for treble damages of $1.2 billion and contained a massive number of scurrilous charges about the oligarch who, only weeks before, had been extolled by *The Wall Street Journal* as "Oleg the Good." The plaintiffs had orchestrated a global media campaign in coordination with the lawsuit and the oligarch was completely blindsided by the attack. In the weeks ahead he would be disinvited to address the World Economic Forum, barred from travel to the U.S., and suffer problems with his banks and foreign allies.

The meeting was held at midnight at the Lanesborough Hotel in a gilded basement room with crystal chandeliers. A reception area outside the room was packed with attorneys and public relations executives eager to win Deripaska's business. When I arrived, I was shown immediately into the meeting room, where a number of men, most of whom were wearing black leather coats, were visible through a thick blue haze of cigarette smoke. When I left two hours later, my colleagues and I had been given the job of coordinating Deripaska's defense against the lawsuit on three continents, a struggle that lasted for more than three years and cost tens of millions of dollars.

The stakes were high. At settlement discussions held some time later in Paris at the Bristol Hotel, the plaintiffs sent not an attorney but a known hit man, code name MacIntosh, with twenty-three confirmed kills. Our team was led by one of our partners, a former East-bloc intelligence official. Both sides had eavesdropping microphones hidden in the room, and when the bargaining began MacIntosh said his side would settle for several hundred million dollars. Our negotiator, the former intelligence official, responded by saying if the plaintiffs dropped the lawsuit and reimbursed Deripaska for his expenses, by then thirty to forty million dollars, a settlement could be reached. Since neither side was prepared to capitulate, both sides parted amicably and the suit proceeded through the courts until it was thrown out on jurisdictional grounds.

This was a major crisis for Oleg Deripaska and, although he prevailed in the lawsuit and became, for a time, Russia's wealthiest man, he is still suffering from the effects today, including damage to his reputation and the inability to get regular visas to the United States. New investigations of Deripaska in both the U.S. and the U.K. were launched in 2007 concerning a $57.5 million wire transfer, and he had serious problems the following year as a result of the global economic crisis, especially as it impacted Russia and worldwide demand for aluminum.

Another example of a major crisis is the 2008 Chinese milk scandal where a variety of milk products and infant formula were adulterated with melamine. Melamine is harmful to the kidneys and made it appear that the product had a higher protein count than it actually did. Hundreds of infants were hospitalized and a number died. Some reports suggest as many as 300,000 people were affected and the scandal spread well beyond China's borders due to the nation's food exports.

Yet another example was the case of sexual harassment of women at Mitsubishi automotive plants in the U.S. The company denied the charges but dozens of women described, in graphic detail on network television, the demeaning treatment they had be subjected to. This included pornographic graffiti, lewd conduct with wrenches and air guns, penises drawn on lockers, and a general environment hostile to women. Despite subsequent attempts by the company to minimize the problem, describing such incidents as "isolated problems," the crisis took on a life of its own and soon it was impossible, according to one Mitsubishi official, to even "drag a woman into a Mitsubishi showroom." Sales and market share plummeted and eventually the company was forced to settle a suit brought by the Equal Employment Opportunity Commission on behalf of 350 women at the Normal, Illinois plant. I later met the deputy chairman of Mitsubishi and indicated that I had heard that the sexual harassment crisis had cost the company $800 million. He laughed and said he would gladly have written a check for that amount to make the problem go away. In addition to lost market share and damage to the company's reputation, he indicated that the issue had cost Mitsubishi in excess of $6 billion.

RISK MANAGEMENT

It is not possible to eliminate all risk, but it is possible to anticipate problems and take steps to prevent them before they occur. And in the event that they cannot be prevented, to make preparations in advance to address any problems that might arise. As former Citicorp chairman and CEO, Walt Wriston, once observed, "All life is the management of risk, not it's elimination."[6]

Any corporation that doesn't try to manage risk is irresponsible, if not wholly deficient in common sense. Remarkably, however, many top corporate managers blithely sail along, not giving any thought to the various risks and downsides associated with their business endeavors, and seem totally surprised when a preventable, or at least predictable, crisis arises. Some of these executives were widely admired before the crisis occurred because of their management styles and other abilities. But as Shakespeare observed, "When the sea was calm, all ships alike show mastership in floating."[7] In other words, it is far easier to look like an effective corporate manager when times are good than when the going gets tough.

During the late 1970s, my partners and I acquired control of Panama's national airline, Air Panama. One evening in Panama City, I was having a drink with the representative of our insurance carrier, Parker Aviation. He knew that we were also involved in the security business and described to me a problem one of their underwriters was having in El Salvador.

In the mid-1970s, it seems, a leading American insurance company had an aggressive sales executive in Central America. He managed to sell hundreds of kidnap and ransom (K&R) policies in El Salvador. Company management back in New York was impressed and rewarded the salesman with generous bonuses. No one at the home office had ever been to El Salvador or had any inkling that the nation was coming apart at the seams. Selling K&R policies, it turned out, was as remarkably easy in view of the deteriorating political climate.

Suddenly it dawned on the company that they had a significant financial exposure. Top management was in a quandary. Then the

---

6   Walter Wriston, *Risk and Other Four-Letter Words*, p.101.

7   William Shakespeare; *Coriolanus*; Act IV, i., p. 17.

man from Parker Aviation and I had a chance meeting in Panama. I was invited to New York and met with a number of top officials from the insurance company.

Over lunch in a private dining room high above Wall Street, one of the vice presidents asked me about Venezuela.

"In what respect?" I responded.

"Well, how stable is it?" the vice president asked. "Politically," he added.

"Why don't you tell me in what context you're asking?" I pressed him.

He explained to me that the company had to make a decision that day on whether or not to insure a five million dollar construction crane at an oil production site in Maracaibo in the Gulf of Venezuela.

"How do you make these decisions now?" I wanted to know. "Do you have a political risk management unit?"

Unbelievably, he responded in the negative.

"You don't subscribe to information about particular countries?" I continued to press him.

"No."

"Surely you must clip the Times?"

"No. But that's a good idea."

"Then for Heaven's sake," I exclaimed, "how then do you arrive at a decision as to whether or not to insure something in a foreign country?"

He dipped his head and averted his eyes. "Well," he began, "we just kind of ask around."

"Ask around?" I replied incredulously. "When you could have a five million dollar exposure. It doesn't sound like a very effective system."

He admitted it wasn't.

I used to believe that most large corporations were well-managed, otherwise they wouldn't stay in business, right? Unfortunately, over the years I've seen so many absolutely inexcusable corporate blunders that I sometimes marvel that many corporations remain in business at all.

I explained to the insurance executives after listening to their story, since they could not cancel the K&R policies without cause, that their only alternative was to manage the risks they had incurred as effectively as possible. And, if they were going to sell new policies, we recommended that their premiums be commensurate with the actual risks, as we defined them, not as they imagined them to be.

We sent teams to El Salvador to do security assessments and to recommend improvements in the security arrangements of each policy holder. In addition, we even provided training to the security details of some of those most at risk. Despite the fact that El Salvador became one of the bloodiest battlegrounds in Latin America during the 1980s, with kidnappings and political assassinations an almost daily occurrence, the insurance company escaped with manageable losses from its ill-considered venture into the political risk insurance business.

Today, we routinely analyze a company when it becomes a client to identify the risks to which it is most susceptible. In this connection, generally any business or activity is vulnerable to two kinds of risks: those that arise from the various activities of the business itself, and those that occur from time-to-time in the environment of the firm. In other words, a company may run the risk of industrial accidents inherent in the manufacture of its products. Such risks are associated with the actual business activities of the company and can, therefore, be anticipated and are, to some extent, under the direct control of the company. Risks associated with the environment in which the company operates are more difficult and elusive. These include such things as natural disasters and political instability. In most instances, a company has only limited control over such risks. It may anticipate them and take steps to protect its employees and assets, but it cannot entirely prevent them.

A few years ago, I delivered an address to the National Ski Areas Association on crisis management. An analysis of the industry suggested that there are a whole host of problems, i.e. risks, that can affect operations, and therefore profits, at the nation's ski resorts. This included avalanches, fires and explosions, attacks on prominent people, injuries and deaths on the slopes (Michael Kennedy and Rep. Sonny Bono to cite just two examples), catastrophic lift failures, forest fires, food poisoning from a resort's restaurants, thefts, bomb threats, toxic substances, workplace violence, sexual harassment, tornadoes, floods, earthquakes, and that most alarming of disasters, no snow. In addition, if the resort operated hotel facilities, one had to also consider the various problems affecting the hospitality industry across the nation: the rape of female guests, security in parking areas, burglary, and other forms of crime. Unfortunately, most of the executives I met that day were very laid back, including the blonde Robert Redford look-alike, the manager of one of the top ski resorts in Colorado, who recommended, "Dude, you should chill out."

In the final analysis, far too many corporate executives regard risk as a four-letter word. This has been labeled the pussy factor. Although it started as a gender-inspired term, the pussy factor can be applied to people of either sex. It refers to wimps and limpdicks, those with small cojones, who are so risk adverse that they are afraid to enter new markets and meet new challenges, to experiment and try new things. They are the reason, in part, that America is losing its competitive edge in the world. This isn't to say that one should take foolish or unnecessary risks, but rather to affirm that almost all risk is manageable.

I once knew a financial guy who used to say, "I want to go with you on one of your cases." But whenever he was invited, he conveniently found a dozen reasons he couldn't do so, most of them the equivalent of having to rearrange his sock drawer. By contrast, we worked with a vivacious blonde who was absolutely fearless and did business in all of the difficult parts of the world, from Beirut to Baghdad to Tripoli and beyond. In Baghdad she carried an MP5 sub-machine gun and lived outside the "Green Zone." She could also maximize her femininity when it served her purposes. She once introduced me and a colleague to the right hand man of one of the Russian oligarchs. When we arrived at the meeting, she greeted us wearing a tiny black dress with a plunging neckline that barely covered the essentials at either the top or the bottom, over-the-knee boots with spike heels, and large, dramatic jewelry. My colleague, who was hyperventilating, turned to me and said, "That's the most unprofessional outfit I've ever seen on a woman in a business meeting." Nevertheless, it worked for her and to this day I have nothing but respect for her "cojones."

EXPECT THE UNEXPECTED

Some crises are easy to anticipate. My friend, Ricardo, tells the story of being at a lavish party in the hills above Medellin, Colombia. Men in expensive Italian suits and beautiful women in glittering jewelry and skin tight dresses were enjoying drinks around the pool when they were startled by the sound of a helicopter overhead, whup, whup, whup. The chopper hovered over the pool for a few seconds as everyone stared up at it, wondering what it was doing. Then the side door opened and a coffin was pitched into the pool, splashing many of the guests with water. The uninvited guest departed and the coffin was pulled from the pool. Inside was a note with the host's name on it.[8] One didn't have to be a genius to understand the message that had just been delivered.

By contrast, there are corporate crises that are just plain hard to predict. I seriously doubt if Michael Eisner, the former Chairman of Disney, would ever have imagined that some fundamentalist religious groups would criticize his company for allegedly hiding obscene or suggestive messages--in a dust cloud--in the animated hit, "The Lion King." In this same vein, it is hard to imagine that anyone at Procter and Gamble could have divined the nationwide campaign against the company accusing it of Satanism, based on its long-time corporate logo. The murder of Italian designer Givanni Versace also fits into this category. Perhaps an even more far-fetched crisis, at least from the standpoint of the people on the ground, was the bombing of Pan Am 103 on December 21, 1989. I'm sure that no one in the Scottish village of Lockerbie ever lost a moment's sleep worrying over the possibility of a wide-body jetliner one day exploding in the sky over the peaceful village, raining down debris, setting numerous buildings on fire and killing eleven people on the ground, all because of a conflict thousands of miles away and because the plane had departed from its normal route because of extremely strong headwinds.

Sometimes even the most obvious potential problems are neglected or ignored because of tunnel vision on the part of those making the assessment. In 1998, Rome's National Gallery of Modern Art was robbed of two van Goghs and a Cezanne. Afterward, Italian Minister of Culture Walter Veltroni tried to make excuses for obvious security oversights. "The security system was adequate," said Veltroni, "but it did not foresee an armed robbery."[9] In other words, only a burglary had been anticipated.

In a similar vein, former Secretary of State Condelezza Rice described the 9/11 attacks on New York and Washington as "unforeseeable." This, of course, is nonsense.

---

8   Ricardo Bilonick, "Inside Dope: My Life in the Medellin Cartel," book proposal (unpublished), p. 1.

9   Walter Veltroni; quoted in *Newsweek*; June 1, 1998; p. 29.

During the summer of 2001, MSNBC assembled three terrorism specialists, including this author, and two popular novelists, and asked them on camera, as part of a one-hour special report, if there would be a terrorist attack on the United States itself (CONUS). We unanimously replied "yes." Where, we were asked, would it take place? New York City, we responded. What would be the target? The World Trade Center towers, we answered, and we predicted they would knock both towers down. Finally, the correspondent wanted to know who would be behind this horrendous attack? Osama bin Laden, we once again responded in one voice. The only thing we got wrong was that we believed the attack would be carried out with explosives instead of hijacked jetliners.

The show, which was to air shortly after 9/11, was pulled because of obvious network sensitives in the wake of the national tragedy that had just occurred, but the network decided to revisit the subject the following summer for a special that aired that Fall. MSNBC assembled the same group and the correspondent wanted to know why were we so prescient and everyone else, including the nation's spy agencies, appeared to be oblivious to the threat? The warning signs were apparent to anyone who was paying the slightest attention to Al Qaeda, we answered, including the attacks on the U.S. embassies in Kenya and Tanzania and the attack on the USS Cole, not to mention to the threats that top Al Qaeda operatives, including Osama bin Laden, were making on an almost daily basis. The warning signs were there for anyone to see.

In the chapters that follow, I will explore the causes and nature of many of the crises confronted by corporate executives, celebrities, and government officials in our contemporary world, which is characterized by an increasingly globalized economy, unfettered competition for resources and markets, and a near-permanent state of conflict. Finally, I'll offer insights and suggestions regarding how to avoid or manage crises and even discuss problems with clients who don't listen to advice, no matter how good or succinct.

- 2 -

WORKING THE HARD PLACES

"This world is like Noah's Ark,
In which few men but many beasts embark.

Samuel Butler

I arrived in Monrovia on a sweltering summer day as rebels closed their grip on the city. It was the only national capital in the world without running water, electricity, or garbage collection, and from time-to-time mortar rounds fell on the edge of the Liberian capital, sending a clear and deadly message to the country's embattled president, Charles Taylor, that time was running out.

The city was breathtakingly poor and packed with refugees. Militias patrolled the streets, many in battered jeeps with .30 and .50 caliber machine guns on swivels. My favorite pro-government unit was the so-called "Butt Naked Brigade" (also known as the Buck Naked Brigade) led by "General" Butt Naked himself. Members of the unit sported combat boots and wrap-around shades and nothing else but juju beads hanging from their genitalia to ward off bullets and other misfortunes.

I had come on business, accompanied by my client, a good friend from the Washington area, and we were scheduled to meet with Taylor the following day in his largely burned-out palace. Our trip couldn't be postponed, despite the circumstances, since my client was one of the few Westerners still doing legitimate business in the country. There were, to be sure, arms merchants and traders in blood diamonds, mostly Lebanese and Syrians, but nearly all Western businessmen had long ago given up on the country, after nearly two decades of civil war and chronic instability. There was a word the locals had for it: wawa, meaning West Africa wins again.

23

In the meantime, I was staying at the Monga Point Hotel, the only hotel still operating in Monrovia, a small, unpretentious place owned by an Irish couple with creaky overhead fans and an old dog sleeping in the entryway that guests had to sidestep. The hotel had a white-washed stucco exterior, adorned with Christmas tree lights, and was surrounded by a high wall. Guards were posted at the front gate, which opened up onto a road that ran parallel to the front wall. There was a narrow beach, dotted with palms, on the other side of the road, which sloped down to the ocean. The roof of the hotel was partially collapsed from shelling, but all-in-all it was a remarkably clean and orderly oasis in the midst of the filth and chaos of the Liberian civil war.

I'd already had dinner with my client and one of his colleagues at a small villa they leased a short distance away but the sun had not yet set and I wanted a cigar. I found the hotel bar at the top of the steps on the second level. When I appeared in the doorway all conversation abruptly stopped as the half-dozen or so boozy ex-pats all turned to stare at the newcomer as they nursed their iced drinks. They didn't see many unfamiliar faces: tourism had long ago ceased and most business in the country had come to a halt. I gave fleeting consideration to just retiring to my room and turning in, but it was too early. Nevertheless, I was not eager to be quizzed about who I was or why I was in town, so I passed through the bar and out onto a terrace overlooking the sea a short distance away.

A soft breeze was blowing from the sea, rustling the palm trees and dispersing the smoke from cooking fires and the stench from the teeming city. I sat down at a table and pulled out a Monte Cristo Number Three. At that moment, I was jolted by a sharp, rasping voice next to me.

"Hello. I'm fine. Hello."

I turned sharply and found to my amazement a large green parrot had alighted on the table near my right elbow.

"Hello. Hello. I'm fine."

I glanced over my shoulder and spied a large cage in the corner with its door open. Obviously the parrot belonged to the hotel.

A waiter materialized and asked what I wanted. He ignored the parrot, which continued to mutter its salutations and didn't seem to be going anywhere.

"I'll take three cognacs," I answered, and then glancing down at my little green friend, added, "and buy the parrot dinner."

"As you wish."

The waiter reappeared a short time later with three identical brandy snifters, each with a healthy shot of cognac, and set a plate of fruit down in front of the parrot.[10] The parrot immediately dug into the repast while I lit up my cigar and brought the first cognac to my lips. As I gazed out at the darkening sea, I marveled not just at the absurdity of the scene, sitting with a green parrot on the deck of a shattered hotel in a war-torn city, cradling a cognac and smoking a Havana cigar, but on the lengths some of us go in our contemporary world, traveling to places where our fears and our hopes merge, to--simply put--make a buck. For me, it was just another day at the office, as I've said before, and it filled me with a strange revelry.[11] For others, uncomfortable with globalization and the need to leave the security of their families and tidy suburban enclaves, I knew it was a nightmare.

There once was a time when U.S. business could ignore the rest of the world. The U.S. was a huge market and its citizens had the most purchasing power of any people on earth, and with the exception of a few key minerals, chromium being one example, and commodities like rubber, nearly everything Americans needed to sustain their thriving

---

10 Dinner with the parrot brought back memories of a small monkey I used to feed on a postage-stamp sized island called Por Venir off the coast of Panama in the San Blas chain. It was leashed to the railing of the restaurant and whenever it saw me coming performed flips in anticipation of fat times ahead.

11 The following day, my client picked me up and we were drove to the Presidential palace. Most of the building's floors had been destroyed in the fighting, but one floor was intact and we were escorted down a long hall. Heavily armed guards were everywhere, leaning against the walls, slumped in the chairs, all wearing dark glasses. We halted just beyond a set of heavy doors and our escort knocked. A moment later we were ushered into the presidential office, where we were greeted by Charles Taylor, the Liberian president, a wail war and was accused of a litany of human rights violations and for being one of the chief purveyors of "blood diamonds."

He was a short but trim man, immaculately tailored in what appeared to be a custom-made Italian suit. "Come in, come in," he said graciously, extending his hand. "We don't get many visitors these days. I feel I should decorate you just for coming."

"Feel free, excellency," I replied.

economy was available here. It was the perfect example of an autarky: a nation with a self-sufficient national economy.

Consequently few Americans grew up with any real sense of the outside world or command of foreign languages. For most, the first and only time they had ever ventured abroad was as a member of military, especially in the First or Second World Wars. Similarly, many large American corporations were detached from the rest of the globe, or only active in foreign locations like Canada and Western Europe. There were, of course, exceptions like Coca Cola and United Fruit, which became synonymous with what some saw as the march of American imperialism, but to many U.S. CEOs most of the globe was as remote and unknowable as the dark side of the moon.

ARRESTED OVERSEAS

For my money there is nothing in the world more terrifying than a rural checkpoint manned by a stoned fourteen year old with an AK-47. The next worst thing is being arrested in a foreign country, especially a military dictatorship. This happened to me many years ago.

I was walking along a major street in Tripoli, Libya, near the old seawall, when a man in a uniform jammed a sub-machine gun into my ribs and ordered me to come with him. And so began an odyssey that ended up with me being expelled from Libya on an unscheduled Sudan Airways flight three days later. In the meantime, I was held in four different locations, including in the basement of the Aziziyah Barracks compound, which served as Libyan leader Muammar Qaddafi's home and headquarters. Ten years later the compound was bombed by the U.S. in retaliation for Libyan terrorist attacks in Europe.

While in the labyrinth of the dark cells underneath the barracks, I was for a short period of time with another prisoner who spoke with a British accent. The cell was pitch black, and it took some time for my eyes to adjust to the darkness, and I didn't realize at first there was anyone else in the cell until he spoke. "Hello," he rasped, "what are you in for?" Our conversation was cut short by one of the guards who entered the cell and pressed the man's nose hard with a sub-machine gun. After that he didn't say anything else and I was soon moved to an interrogation room.

There I was seated across a table from a severe-looking young man dressed in a white short-sleeve shirt, dark slacks, shiny black shoes and white socks. His haircut was high and tight and gave him every appearance of a military man. The translator, by contrast, was an older man with a gray brush mustache attired in an elegant three-piece Savile Row suit. He had a cordial demeanor and treated me with politeness and deference even as the interrogator's tone became sharper and sharper in response to my answers to his probing questions, especially his demand to know why I was in Libya. I kept pointing out that I had a visa that had been issued in Washington and that I was exploring business opportunities. The interrogation went on for more than six hours. Finally, he raised up, hands braced on the desk, and leaned across at me. "I'll ask you one more time," he announced threateningly, "what are you doing in Libya?"

Before I traveled to Tripoli one of my Arab friends had advised me that if I ever had a problem in Libya, I should always remember that they, meaning the secret police, had "small minds." His advice came back to me at that moment and I thought, what the hell, I'm not getting anywhere with my present strategy, perhaps I should try something else. "The reason I came to Libya," I began tentatively, "is that the Zionist-controlled American media has hidden the truth about Libya and the great success of its revolution and I wanted to see it with my own eyes."

The translator gave me a very slight nod and then told the interrogator what I had said. For the first time that day a faint smile spread along his thin lips and he began to write furiously. It can't be this easy, I told myself. They can't be this stupid. But I was wrong; they were that stupid.

The translator told me to continue and for the next forty five minutes I waxed on and on about how shabbily the Arab world was treated in the American media, and why every American should be inspired by the leadership of Libyan strongman Mummar Qaddafi. But topping it all in the bullshit category, I even described how inspired I was by a banner I had seen in a traffic circle proclaiming in English that, "Revolution is the citadel of revolutionaries." There were signs and banners all over the city with insipid slogans and truisms in a multitude of languages.

As the session drew to a close I was asked to sign the statement written by the interrogator, purporting to be an exact rendering of my words. Now this posed a dilemma since the statement was written in Arabic and could, for all I knew, be a confession stating that I was a CIA operative and had come to Libya to assassinate Qaddafi. I realized, however, that if I didn't sign the statement that the interrogator would not be happy and I'd be back at square one again. I figured that the odds were about equal either way, so with a nod of encouragement from the translator I signed the document and the interrogator and the translator quickly departed. Perhaps forty-five minutes later, several guards came for me and I was escorted up to ground level and through a massive gate, where I was pushed out onto the street with the gates slamming shut behind me. They had kept my passport and Minox camera and told me to return to my hotel and not to leave, that I was effectively under house arrest.

A day and a half later I was summoned to the lobby of the hotel and told I was being expelled from the country on an unscheduled Sudan Airways flight to Cairo. My passport and camera were returned to me and I was driven to the airport where I boarded the flight, which had apparently been diverted to Tripoli to pick me up.

I had another tense trip nearly a quarter century later when I arrived in Podgorica, the capital of Montenegro, with my colleague, Gary Stubblefield, the former commander of SEAL Team Three. Gary sported a shaved head and mustache, and claimed to have perfected the look long before Jesse Ventura, the former SEAL and ex-Governor of Minnesota.

Tensions between Serbia and NATO were running high and we had come to advise the government of Montenegro, which was technically still part of Yugoslavia along with Serbia, how to put some distance between them and the Milosovic regime in Belgrade, especially if it came to war. Our actual client had been unjustly charged with violating U.N. arms sanctions, following an incident where Serbian troops had pulled Croats off a train and shot them next to the tracks. The Montenegrins were horrified and wanted to make it clear that they were not responsible for the barbarous act, so our client had purchased new uniforms and web gear for their soldiers and police. A corrupt Western ambassador in Belgrade, who was on Milosovic's payroll, had succeeded in getting the U.N. to regard the benign act as a violation of the sanctions that had been put into effect to keep the Serbs from acquiring new weapons.

On our third day in country, we drove with our client down to the coast, planning to spend the night near Hercegnovi on the Adriatic and then slipping across the Croatian border the next day at Dubrovnik. We stayed at an decrepit old hotel, an ugly pile of communist masonry bereft of charm or guests, thanks to the political problems in the country. As one of the desk clerks showed us to our rooms, a hotel maintenance man walked ahead of us screwing bulbs into the lights in the hallway; apparently they were stolen if left in the light fixtures.

That night, thanks to our client, we were invited to a masked ball at the hotel, which gradually came alive as hundreds of party-goers descended on it, trying to put the conflict raging around them out-of-mind, if only for an hour or two. Gary and I were the only two outsiders at the event, and our client had reserved a long table near the stage for his friends. We were not really in a mood to party and knew we needed to keep our wits about us, but our client insisted we attend and so around nine we arrived at the ballroom, sans costumes. By contrast, nearly everyone else had costumes; there was a bull labeled "Serbia" and a matador labeled "Montenegro," cowboys, pirates, bumblebees, princesses, a Mexican mariachi band, a Soviet Commissar with a long cigarette holder, and even terrorists in black ninja-like outfits. The hit of the evening, however, was a couple with large expertly-made paper mache heads of Bill Clinton and Monica Lewinsky resting on their shoulders. Monica was wearing a blue dress with white spots on the front. As the evening wore on, Bill opened his jacket, revealing a three-foot long cloth missile with fins and a pointed nose protruding from the front of his pants. A few moments later, he tugged on the missile, which slipped off leaving an anatomically correct penis. Monica promptly went down on the penis in the middle of the ballroom floor.

"Makes you really proud to be an American," groaned Gary, leaning over and shaking his head.

More than a dozen young women had zoned in our table and were trying to catch our eye, each one more lovely than the next and all of them in short, tight dresses and with come-hither looks on their faces. We had no illusions: they saw us as plane tickets to a new life in America, far from the threat of war and the scarcities they had known all their lives. The band was great but Gary and I took our leave and headed up to our rooms. Even if we had wanted to take a friend, the rooms didn't have beds but only cots with a couple of thin blankets.

The next morning we learned that the border crossing to Croatia was closed; apparently the Serbs had gotten wind of our mission and were actively looking for us. Gary suggested that we hike over the mountains but there was a good deal of snow at higher elevations and I was dressed in a suit, a light overcoat, and dress oxfords. Ultimately, we decided to return to Podgorica and take a flight to Belgrade, thinking that that would be the last place they would expect us. There were only a few JAT flights still flying since war was imminent, and we took a nearly empty plane to a deserted airport in Belgrade, where we found an old man, with a rattletrap cab, grateful to have a fare. There was snow on the ground. Everything was in shades of gray, from the ground to the sky; it was like being in a black and white movie.

Our hotel had little heat and almost no food. We found there were two JAT flights the next morning, one to Athens and the other to Switzerland. We knew they were looking for two men traveling together, so we decided to split up. We flipped a coin and I got Athens, which at least promised to be warm.

I held my breath while the security people at the airport looked me over carefully but eventually they waved me into the jet-way. Apparently they didn't have our names and didn't really expect us in the belly of the beast, Belgrade. I was met in Athens by the son of a late friend who wanted to do business with us. He was bearded, in his fifties, and dressed in an English suit and a long, heavy coat. I soon discovered he was a walking office; the coat had special pockets inside for a multitude of cell phones and other gadgets, including a laptop computer, a fax machine, and a copier.

Lots of things can happen to you when you travel abroad, not all of them good, especially in military dictatorships where the rule of law doesn't exist. As one of my professors of international law once observed, "The Constitution doesn't travel." In other words, one should not expect all of the rights and privileges that an American citizen is normally entitled to when beyond the borders of the U.S.

FOREIGN PRISONS

One day I was visiting Dr. Roger Lafontant, the Haitian Interior Minister and head of the infamous Tonton Macoute, in Port-au-Prince, Haiti, in the basement of his headquarters. The organization had been created under Papa Doc Duvalier as a private praetorian guard, and its members were the regime's "enforcers," with a reputation for torture and systematic terror. In voodoo lore which permeates the culture, the name, Tonton Macoute, was synonymous with a "boogeyman" who roamed the streets at night kidnapping children who stayed out too late.

Under the rule of Papa Doc's son, President-for-Life Jean Claude Duvalier or "Baby Doc," the Tonton Macoute were called by the more innocuous sounding name Volunteers for National Security (VSN). Nevertheless, its members continued to be the regime's private security force and still wore their trademark loud shirts and wrap-around dark glasses.

Haiti's prisons were notorious throughout the hemisphere for their overcrowded conditions, lack of sanitation and miserable food, and the torture and abuse they inflicted on prisoners. Often people simply disappeared once they entered one of the country's prisons and were never heard from again. One of Lafontant's predecessors, Madame Max Adolphe, known more commonly as just Madame Max, had been warden of the notorious prison, Fort Dimanche, called the "Auschwitz of Haiti," and then become head of the Tonton. During her tenure at Fort Dimanche she had spent a good deal of time locating just the right paint to match the dried blood stains in the cells, so that they wouldn't have to be repainted after each interrogation session to hide their crimes. Hundreds, if not thousands, of people were shot outside the walls of Fort Dimanche, and their bodies were buried in mass graves, now covered with weeds.

The basement where Lafrontant's office was located was a short distance from the cells that held political foes of the regime. On the day I was sitting with Lafontant in his office, I was startled by screams in the hall behind me. Two Tonton interrogators were on either side of a man they were dragging down the hall, who was trying to dig his heels into the stone floor as they pulled him along. Lafontant, without any acknowledgment of the commotion in the hallway, simply got up from behind his desk and shut the door, drowning out the noise.

If there is one thing to remember about foreign prisons it is that, with the possible exception of a few Scandinavian hoosegows, you never want to be in one. Many Americans still remember the chilling depiction of the brutality and suffering inflicted on a young American in the film "Midnight Express," which ostensibly was based on a true story and took place in Turkey. The American had been attempting to smuggle drugs back to the U.S. when he was arrested. I handled a similar case when I worked on Capitol Hill. A Kansas woman contacted her senator, my boss, about her son who had been imprisoned in Morocco for attempting to smuggle hashish. The kid had been incarcerated for more than a year and was suffering from malnutrition and various physical ailments. But the worst part of his imprisonment was that he was beaten on the soles of his feet with a rubber truncheon every few days so that he could not walk   and, therefore, to make it harder for him to escape. It took some time, but we were ultimately successful in securing his release.

In many of the world's prisons rape, unprovoked violence, torture, HIV, drugs, gangs, disease, overcrowding and malnutrition are commonplace. Inmates in many Third World prisons must purchase their own food, medical care, soap, and other necessities, and without someone on the outside bribing guards and prison officials to deliver such items a prisoner is unlikely to live very long.

Some of the worst prisons in the world are in Brazil, Syria, Venezuela, Turkey, Cuba, Mexico, Iran, Haiti, Pakistan, Thailand, North Korea, Russia, and virtually any place in Africa. As one report says of Nairobi Prison in Kenya, "Inmates here tend to be naked and infected with horrible diseases that kill them slowly."[12] Perhaps the most notorious prison in Africa is Black Beach, located on the island of Bioko in Malabo, the capital of Equatorial Guinea, where the average life expectancy is less than ten years. Many prisoners are shackled twelve hours a day, denied medical care, and given only the most meager of rations. Among the best known prisoners at Black Beach were Simon Mann, the British mercenary, and a number of his men, who attempted an unsuccessful coup in 2004. Other Western prisoners paint a grim portrait of life in Malabo's other jails as well. According to one account, cells at the city's police headquarters were so overcrowded that prisoners were forced to stand up, "rats scurried about and a solitary bucket overflowed with excrement."[13]

Even France has an infamous prison known as La Sante, where "(m)attresses are infected with lice, and because prisoners are only allowed two cold showers per week, skin diseases are common. Overcrowded cells, rat infestations, rape, and the humiliation of prisoners' families were also common."[14] I once was able to secure the dawn arrest of a Russian gangster in Paris who was rudely pulled out of

---

12 "The List: The World's Most Notorious Prisons," *Foreign Policy*, January, 2009.

13 David Lister, "I Was Held in the Notorious Black Beach Jail," *The Times of London*, Feb. 1, 2008.

14 *Ibid.*

the bed he was sharing with two hookers, in a suite littered with champagne bottles and taken directly to the Sante. He spent six weeks there and was far more amenable to reaching a settlement with my client after his experience as a guest of the French government.

If you are arrested or detained in a foreign country, you should get word to someone on the outside, especially the U.S. embassy, if at all possible, and let them know your situation. Hiring local counsel is a hit and miss proposition and in many Third World countries attorneys are good at fleecing their clients but provide little real representation. Often the justice system is stacked against the accused and trials are not really a method for determining guilt or innocence but rather simply a forum for pronouncing sentence on the defendant. The Napoleonic Code, of course, presumes someone charged with a crime is guilty unless proven innocent. The only real chance many foreigners have when confronted with imprisonment in some Third World countries is to cultivate friends in high position, which may also mean bribing them.

Above all else, don't panic. Remain cool, calm, and collected and keep your wits about you. Conserve your strength because you will need it later. Don't call attention to yourself or make threats. If you need certain medications, let prison officials know and inform the U.S. embassy or your outside contact. If you are dependent on eye glasses, make certain that someone gets you a spare pair in the event that the primary pair is broken.

Remember that you are extremely vulnerable in a foreign prison, especially if you are a foreigner. Prison guards, as well as other prisoners, are likely to try and shake you down for money, protection, or even sex. Incarceration also gives your enemies an opportunity to lean on you hard as in the case of the American con man who fled the U.S. to escape prosecution for a massive fraud he had conducted. He was arrested in a Latin American country and fought extradition tooth and nail. He also refused to disclose the whereabouts of the money he had stolen. His victims grew impatient and decided to take matters into their own hands. First, they paid the prison warden to withhold the man's medications and to serve him small portions of rancid food, which one of the guards urinated on some days. He continued to hold out and the victims decided to ratchet up the pressure. The con man was moved into a cell with a six-and-a-half foot tall roommate who had been incentivized to sodomize his cell mate every day, preferably more than once a day. The con man quickly withdrew his opposition to being extradited, but now, in a total switch of positions, the victims paid off the Justice Minister to delay any action on the U.S. request, prolonging the con man's agony. It didn't take long for the con man to break and he cut a deal with attorneys for the victims, giving up the foreign bank accounts where he had hidden his ill-gotten gains.

If you have enough money and physical presence it's possible to turn prison in some parts of the world into something, if not exactly luxurious, then certainly tolerable. A few years ago, I had a client from the Balkans jailed in northwest Greece. When his Greek attorney and I arrived at the remote prison, we were warmly greeted by the warden, who ushered us inside and insisted that we use his office to meet our client since "it would be more comfortable." When our client appeared, he was wearing a designer jogging suit and obviously hadn't missed any meals, which we later learned were being brought to the prison from a nearby restaurant. He was also working out regularly and, frankly, appeared to be in better health than the last time I'd seen him in his own country. He had obviously greased the warden because the warden ordered up drinks and snacks while we sat with our client and discussed developments regarding his case.

Over the years my companies have secured the release of numerous Americans from foreign prisons. In some cases it is a matter of political pressure or bribes, and in other cases we have actually smuggled prisoners out of the country. In one case an American businessman had been arrested and detained for many months in a Middle Eastern country after a falling out with his local partner, who was attempting to extort a great deal of money from him. We compromised a corrupt official who said he would permit the businessman to "escape" from prison, but after that he was on his own.

When the businessman emerged from the prison, he was picked up immediately by our operatives in a nondescript truck. The truck had false panel behind the cab, leaving a small crawl space between the cab and the cargo area that no one was likely to notice. Although the crawl space had little ventilation and was like an oven inside, the businessman survived a twelve-hour drive to a neighboring country where he safely boarded a flight back to the U.S.

KIDNAPPING

Kidnapping remains an endemic problem in many parts of the world and a serious issue for companies doing business in those places. There are more kidnappings in Latin America than anywhere else, although it is also a problem in parts of Asia, Africa, and the Middle East. In places like Mexico and Colombia, kidnapping is a virtual industry, generating tens of millions of dollars annually for its perpetrators, who often work in teams, each with a different expertise. This kind of division of labor is done "in part to ensure that members of one team would never know the identity of members of another."[15]

There are two kinds of kidnappers: those who do it purely for profit and those who carry out kidnappings for political reasons or to support revolutionary movements. Whatever their motivation, if you are kidnapped there is one immutable rule: don't depend on your government to get you back. Times have changed since Secretary of State John Hay called for "Perdicaris alive or Raisuli dead," after a Moroccan bandit seized a Greek of dubious nationality who claimed to be an American citizen. All the U.S. can really do in most countries is to encourage the local authorities to resolve the situation satisfactorily. Hence, U.S. citizens are, for the most part, are on their own if they are kidnapped in foreign lands.

Many kidnap victims later say they never dreamed it could happen to them, and therefore they didn't take adequate security precautions. Indeed, mid-level executives who have been kidnapped often explain that they felt they were not important enough to be targeted. Former Brig. General James Dozier was one of those who thought he was too low on the leadership chart to be a kidnapping target. He was seized at his home in Naples in 1981 and held for six weeks until rescued by Italian commandos.[16]

Executives working or traveling to foreign countries in many parts of the world should consider a number of responses to the threat of kidnapping. First, do not invite a kidnapping by an ostentatious show

---

15 Ann Hagedorn Auerbach, *Ransom*, (New York: Henry Hold & Company, 1998), p. 33.

16 Dozier was selected because he was under surveillance by the Red Brigades and was observed talking to a top officer in the Carabiniere, giving him what appeared to be orders and directions. In reality, Dozier actually was giving him directions to his Thanksgiving party.

of wealth or by behavior that suggests an apparent disregard for good security. Nor do you want to do totally dumb things, like several kidnapped U.S. agronomists in Ecuador, who were wearing tee-shirts saying "CIA" when they were taken hostage. In their case, the letters CIA stood for Committee Institional Agriculturas, but the kidnappers were certain they were members the U.S. spy agency. One has to be a total moron to dress in a tee-shirt like that in a jungle inhabited by anti-government guerrillas.

Second, you may want to have full-time security, with the proviso that any detail must be properly trained because poorly-trained guards without adequate experience are often more of a threat to the protectee rather than kidnappers and other malefactors.

Third, a threatened person might want to consider going through an anti-terrorist training program where he or she can learn the elements of good security including defensive driving, weapons safety and marksmanship, and threat avoidance.

Finally, there is the issue of whether or not to purchase kidnap and ransom insurance, known in the trade as K&R insurance. Only about two percent of all victims are insured, according to Ann Auerbach, and if there is a policy it should be kept secret so as not to serve as an incentive to kidnappers, who might find the policyholder a more attractive victim because they can be certain that there is money available in exchange for his life. Also, most K&R policies come with the support of companies like Control Risks of London which have professional negotiators who can facilitate the ransom negotiations and exchange. More than once non-professionals have tried to make a ransom exchange only to be robbed of the money. Later, the kidnappers claim to know nothing about the theft and tell the negotiators that they are still waiting for their money, forcing the family or company of the victim to raise an entirely new ransom.

In the event you are kidnapped, some of the things you should remember are the following:

ABDUCTION PHASE

1. If you resist, you may be killed. Nevertheless, you are worth far more to the kidnappers alive, than dead;
2. The experience will be extremely unpleasant, at least initially. Expect to be treated roughly, and you may be drugged,

blindfolded, have a hood put over your head, or bound with duct tape. You may be stuffed into the trunk of a car;

3. Remember sounds, scents, distances, road surfaces and other things that later might help the authorities discover the terrorist hideout; and

4. If you need medications, tell your captors at the first opportunity.

CAPTIVITY PHASE

1. Try to develop rapport with your captors. It is much harder to kill or abuse someone with whom you have a personal relationship. During the siege of a Dutch train, one of the captives was told by the terrorists that he would soon be executed because the authorities had not met their demands. The soon-to-be-victim requested a few moments to leave a message for his family. By the time the terrorists had listened to the man's story of his troubled life and failings as a husband and father, they were so emotionally involved that they found it impossible to kill him. He had transcended the role of a hostage and had become, in their eyes, a human being;

2. Don't offer advice to or threaten the kidnappers, and don't assume you can reason with them. Always maintain your dignity and generally cooperate with them;

3. Behave as though you are always under observation. Accept the loss of privacy and learn to live with it;

4. Eat everything you are given because you will need to keep your strength up. Try to exercise regularly and adapt to your environment, no matter how challenging;

5. Inform your captors about any health problems. Hostages are a burden to care for, and kidnappers know that a healthy hostage is much easier to take care of than a sick one;

6. Don't try to be heroic and, generally, don't try to escape unless you believe your captors are going to kill you or, in the case of several hostages working for California Microwave who were taken captive after their light plane went down in Colombia, it becomes clear that the kidnappers are prepared to hold you indefinitely.

In the final analysis, no one wants to be kidnapped, but in the event you are remember that the great majority of all victims eventually are released, especially if you follow the suggestions above.

PLANES, TRAINS, CARS, & BUSES

There are always risks involved in traveling, whether by car, bus, train, or plane. These risks increase significantly in the developing world, especially in the "hard places" like Africa, Latin America, and parts of Asia. I was stranded in an African nation at a crumbling sun-baked airstrip when the twin-engine aircraft that was supposed to carry me out of the country developed mechanical problems. A rusting old Antonov transport was subsequently diverted from Sierre Leone to pick me up. The plane had six rows of seats and behind that cargo was stacked up from the floor to the ceiling. All of the Russian language signs had been stenciled over in English using white paint, and the side door was pulled shut by a rope.

There was only myself, the crew, and one other passenger, an African dressed in a dark suit who acknowledged my presence with a nod but didn't say anything throughout the trip. Although there was a good deal of turbulence, once we were up at altitude, I began to relax; if all went well, I'd be on the ground again in two hours and soon thereafter on my way to Paris. As I dozed off, something rolling across the floor struck the back of my shoe. I reached down to see what it was but the plane lurched to one side because of the turbulence and the object rolled away. A few moments later it hit my shoe again, and again I missed it before it rolled away. Finally, on the third attempt, I was able to grab the object and much to my distress it was a pineapple style hand grenade, probably a Russian F1, fortunately with the pin still in it. I unbuckled my seat belt and carried the grenade up to the cockpit, the door being open, and handed it to the first officer, who took it without comment. Apparently, unsecured cargo of the lethal variety was not unusual.

Over the years I've been on planes so corroded that water ran down the fuselage and dripped on passengers (and umbrellas were handed out inside the plane), where passengers with livestock were given priority seating, where armed men boarded the plane on the ground and walked up and down the aisles intimidating passengers with their weapons, and where the flight attendants, all female, openly propositioned passengers in the event they were interested in a little intimate companionship when they arrived at their destination. I've also been on flights where the landing gear didn't work and where we lost engines, requiring emergency landings at strange airports. Once I was even on plane with a six-and-a-half foot tall guy seated next to me in a full gorilla suit (he was on his way to meet his grand-kids for Halloween and wanted to surprise them).

If anything looks amiss when I begin to board a flight, I leave and take another flight. This has only happened to me twice but I'd rather be safe rather than sorry. The first time it was because of the torrential rain that began pounding a Colombian airport as we boarded and the second time because there was a threat against the flight and against me specifically. I had just wrapped up a trip to Istanbul, after meeting with the military government and visiting a prison to review the conditions under which several Dev Sol terrorists were incarcerated, when apparently details of my presence and my flight were leaked to government opponents and, subsequently, to the Dev Sol. Rather than take the original flight on which I was scheduled, I opted for another at the last moment, flying to London and then on to the U.S.

When one of my former firms was in charge of logistics and security for YoYo Ma on his Silk Road Tour in Central Asia, we had wanted to take him and his ensemble aboard a private charter of our choice. But one of his political hosts insisted that we use his charter company, which operated old Soviet-era Yak-40s, which was not reassuring. Faced with a difficult situation, we requested maintenance information on all of the Yaks and ultimately selected the one with the lowest hours on its engines and the shortest time since its last major overhaul. The trip was completed without incident but I was always glad we took the extra time and effort to locate the best aircraft available under the circumstances.

I continue to be annoyed at people who drive far too fast for the road conditions, often at speeds of more than a hundred miles an hour. This is particularly true of gangsters and oligarchs in CIS countries, who often have their cars outfitted with flashing blue lights and sirens. In 1999, I was being transported between two cities in Central Asia in a long black Mercedes. While there was little traffic in those days on this particular highway, there were people sitting along the roadside and animals, especially goats, wandering in the roadway itself. We were traveling at more than 120 miles an hour when a policeman stepped out of a small shack and held up a paddle saying "Stop!" The driver made an obscene gesture at the cop and stepped on the accelerator even harder. Since the traffic police had no cars, he knew that pursuit was impossible.

On a number of occasions, I was met at the airport in Guatemala City by a man known as "Blowtorch," who worked for one of our clients. He was thin, with coal black, slicked back hair, and a thick black mustache, and he always wore dark glasses, day or night. To show his open disdain of the terrorists in his country, he drove a convertible. But the backseat was full of assault rifles, pistols, a .30 caliber machine gun, ammo belts and even an RPG (rocket propelled grenade). There was shotgun under the dash and grenades in the glove box.

On one particular trip, I had arrived with four other people, all of whom were loaded into a hardened Suburban while Blowtorch took me in the convertible. This had been a daytime flight, and the trip into the city was uneventful. By contrast, most flights into Guatemala City arrived late at night, often after midnight. Driving into the city late at night was a security nightmare; we'd occasionally see a body alongside the road or, once, hanging from a streetlamp. We were always on guard for guys on motorcycles who would come up fast behind us, fearful that they might open fire on our car or toss a grenade underneath it. We only slowed up for red lights and then kept moving through the intersections. If there was a suspicious car or motorcycles, the bodyguards would hang their guns out the windows as a warning to keep their distance.

HOTELS

In 2008, we were contacted by the representative of a leading rock and roll figure who asked us about security in Mumbai, India, where a Live Earth concert was going to be held. According to the representative, former U.S. Vice President Al Gore had assured the rock and roller that India was "absolutely safe" and that he should not be worried at all about his security. We told the representative, by contrast, that India had many security problems and that there was no absolutely safe hotel in the country. The representative said that Gore had recommended staying in the Taj Mahal Palace and Tower or the Oberoi Trident. We counseled against going to Mumbai without special security, especially given the rock and roller's international fame and the potential threat of terrorism. A week before the Live Earth

40

event, Islamic terrorists carried out bloody attacks across Mumbai, including at the Taj Mahal and Oberoi hotels, resulting in 173 dead and almost 400 wounded.

When it comes to selecting a hotel, either in the U.S. or overseas, there are certain issues that should be taken into consideration. To begin with, the location of the room is extremely important. Rooms in the back of the hotel are often less risky than those in front, as in the bombing of a Marriott Hotel in Islamabad, Pakistan, in 2008, which killed 53 and injured more than 250. Similarly, in attacks on three hotels in Amman, Jordan, in 2005, by suicide bombers, the entrance of the Grand Hyatt was destroyed, the lobby of the Radisson SAS was heavily damaged, and a restaurant in the front part of the Days Inn was hit.

Your room should neither be on the ground floor, where access from the street or a garden may be too easy, or too high up, where it may be beyond the reach of fire truck ladders. Rooms that share balconies should be avoided and the identity of guests in the adjoining rooms should be examined by your security team with the hotel's security chief. Although it's more difficult in the aftermath of 9/11, many hotels still protect the privacy of their celebrity or political guests by registering them under other names.

FOOD

It was one of the original clubs for the elite of Russia's criminal underworld. Located near Red Square, it boasted, naturally, red and gold decor, swarms of security men at the door, and an array of stunningly beautiful hookers at the bar, mostly long-haired blondes in dresses so short that they left little to the imagination. The menu was French, Russian, and Kosher, and the wine list was extensive and expensive, providing ample opportunity for high-rollers to show off by purchasing thousand dollar bottles for their guests. Heavy-set men with sausage fingers clustered around the tables, smoking and speaking in hushed voices to one another.

The club was like the set from a B-grade Hollywood gangster movie; it represented someone's notion of how such a club, frequented by a certain clientele, should look. It was not subtle but, then again, it wasn't it-your-face; it lacked the loud music, strobe lights, and the TGIF Friday inspired cuisine boasted by so many other places in Moscow at that time.

And if the mobsters didn't want to go to the club, there were always Uzbek or Georgian restaurants, with nostalgic menus and booze that brought back memories of other times in other places.[17] For a number of years in the nineties and early 2000s, the Mafioso were the rock stars of the new order that emerged after the collapse of the Soviet Union. They would sweep into a restaurant, surrounded by bodyguards invariably dressed in black leather jackets, and follow the fawning proprietor to their table in a back room, where the muscle would take up positions outside to intimidate anyone unknown or trying to get too close to the great man.

Today, in Putin's Russia, things are more orderly, there's more outward decorum, and the Mafia is less visible although still a presence. And the gangster clubs have been eclipsed by some of the most over-the-top restaurants in the world, the most extraordinary being Turandot, a restaurant in the round, three floors of gilt and gold leaf, crystal chandeliers, a staff of 600, with some of the finest Asian cuisine in the world served on English porcelain. A chamber orchestra composed of women in powdered wigs and dresses from the court of Louis XIV plays on the first level. Turnadot reportedly cost $60 million to create.

Food, however, can be problematic in many countries, especially in the developing world outside major cities. Many intestinal problems can be linked to fruits and vegetables, in some cases no matter how well they were washed and prepared because their roots absorbed polluted water during the growing cycle. Cholera and hepatitis A are both caused by unsanitary conditions. One prominent businesswoman says her rules for staying healthy include not drinking tap water east of Athens or below the Mediterranean, avoiding all vegetables that grow underground, and all fruits and vegetables that grow above ground unless they can be peeled.

While many seasoned travelers understand the need to avoid local water and use bottled water instead, there is no guarantee that it is pure. Many overseas restaurants refill bottles with local tap water or, if you're lucky, filtered water. It's always a good idea to order a name brand and ask the waiter to crack the cap at the table in front of you. And beware of ice cubes as well. Most are made with local water and will contaminate your expensive bottled water.

---

17 Uzbekistan is the only Muslim nation that distills vodka.

Business travelers should be mindful of the religious customs and prohibitions of the regions to which they travel. Observant Jews and Muslims, of course, don't eat pork, and Muslims also avoid alcohol. Hindus regard cows as sacred.

Another issue for travelers is the fact that what might be considered a delicacy in one country could be viewed as revolting in another place or culture. In Asia it is not uncommon to see dogs, even young puppies, and cats for sale in food markets. In 1987, the U.S. provided the South Korean government with ten bomb-sniffing dogs for the upcoming Olympics. Each dog was worth $25,000 and after the Olympics the U.S. expected the dogs to be returned. Unfortunately, there were no dogs because the Koreans had eaten them. The incident was hushed up before it became a major problem in U.S.-South Korean relations.

In Arab nations the honored guest is often given the choice of a cooked lamb's eyes or its ears. Former CIA Director Jim Woolsey said he was advised by aides at the CIA to go for the eyes because they could be thrown down one's throat and swallowed quickly like raw oysters whereas the ears are quite "chewy." Although I'd rather dine at Turandot or Rostang's in Paris, on business trips I've eaten snake, sheep's eyes, alligator, roasted monkey on a stick (washed down by warm Coca Cola), omelets made of giant iguana eggs, cow testicles, sheep testicles, and even been served a breakfast of Cognac and horse meat. And I'm none the worse for it.

There are some things, however, that are just too disgusting and unhealthy to eat. During a visit to Tashkent one of the restaurants featured two lard dishes on the menu: pork lard with salt and pork lard with pepper. Some older Russians still purchase little tins of lard, packaged like canned sardines, with a lid that one rolls back with a key and a plastic spoon taped to the underside of the tin. Apparently before the introduction of Western candy and snack foods, tins of lard were very popular and considered a delicacy. Along with vodka, lard consumption may have something to do with the fact that the average life-expectancy for a man in Russia is only fifty-seven years.

One thing I won't do in Russia and the CIS countries is try to match my hosts drink for drink as they throw back shots of vodka, one after the other. It is not uncommon to see each man at the table with a bottle of vodka at his elbow and for the bottle to be empty before the dinner is over. I've seen Western businessmen fall face first into their plates even before the main course was served because they tried to keep up with their Russian hosts, who consume vodka like water. During my first visit with one of Russia's mafia kingpins I rejected vodka in favor of wine and a cognac after dinner. While he joked that I drank like a homosexual, I ignored his ribbing and in subsequent meetings he orders wine for me even before we sit down at the table. I found that he, like many people in hard-drinking cultures, had a grudging respect for those who are measured in their drinking and don't allow themselves to be bullied into over-indulging.

Some years ago I took a number of our key security specialists, including former Navy SEALs and Delta veterans, to lunch at the Washington Palm. The conversation somehow arrived at the subject of what was the worst thing the men had ever eaten. As we went around the table and each man described his worst culinary experience, a nearby table of women was clearly eavesdropping. When the last member of the group, a former Delta shooter, recalled a meal of rice in West Africa where the maggots crawled up his arm as he reached into the bowl, one of the women bolted the dining room covering her mouth with her hand.

MEDICAL ISSUES

I was met at Sheremetyevo Airport, 18 miles from downtown Moscow, by a tall blonde in a full-length fur and stiletto heels. She explained that she represented the V.I.P. travel service that would expedite my trip through Customs and Immigration. She did her work efficiently and we were soon at the hotel, where she escorted me to reception. As I checked in she asked if I wanted her to stay with me during my visit to the Russian capital. I demurred but the temptation was certainly there, as it was on another trip to Moscow when I was informed that a "special surprise," courtesy of my host, would visit my room after dinner. I told the bodyguard to thank his boss but that I was in Moscow on business and not to play. After a four-hour dinner with the man I had come to see, ending at 2 a.m., my three traveling companions and I retired to the bar for a drink and to recap the evening's meeting. My present, it turned out, was waiting in the bar. She was one of the most striking women I have ever seen, a little over five feet tall, blonde of course, wearing over-the-knee boots and a short, tight little bondage dress with laces up the front and along the sleeves. She wasn't going to give up easily for fear of not getting paid by my host, but I made it clear to her that as much as I appreciated the gesture I wasn't interested.

The days when servicemen lined up for a shot of penicillin before going on weekend liberty in anticipation contracting syphilis or the clap now seem like quaint stories from the past. Today AIDS is a disease from which there is no cure or reprieve, and this should give pause to every businessman who might consider a fling with a hooker or b-girl during his travels. The disease is rampant in Africa, Russia, and many other parts of the world. And it is just one of many illnesses that a person can contract while traveling. While no one wants to be taken ill or suffer a medical emergency overseas, such problems can be far more serious and even catastrophic in parts of the developing world.

A close friend of mine had a major heart problem in Tashkent. The last thing he remembers in Uzbekistan is being on a hospital gurney in the emergency room with a dozen people standing around him smoking, a blue pall of smoke hanging in the air, and a clothesline strung over him with disposable latex surgical gloves, attached by clothespins, which had been washed so they could be used again. The next time he woke up was a month later in a Finnish hospital, having undergone life-saving surgery and being put in an induced coma. Initially disoriented and believing he was in Rome, he told the nurse to get the hotel manager, and be quick about it, because the room was not up to the hotel's usual standards. It took him a little time to finally realize where he was and what had happened, and today he knows he survived only because of the resourcefulness of his son and various friends who had spirited him out of Uzbekistan to the nearest medical center capable of providing him with the kind of care he needed.

The contemporary world is full of hazards and health challenges. One of my former employees woke up one day after a trip to Africa and found he was nearly deaf in one ear; his doctor subsequently removed a large beetle from his ear canal. Western businessmen are killed and injured virtually every day on motorbikes in Southeast Asia. A television news producer shattered her kneecap when getting out of a boat in the Republic of Georgia when the boat drifted away from the pier and she fell against the dock, smacking it with her knee. The host of a well-known travel show tumbled off a camel in Central Asia and cracked his head on the pavement and dislocated his shoulder. Any number of Western travelers have overdosed on narcotics overseas because they are available in much purer, and therefore stronger, form in some countries like Thailand. In the U.S., narcotics have usually been "stepped on" three to five times by the point they reach the consumer. An Israeli diamond merchant was stricken with Black Water Fever in Africa while on a buying trip and almost died. Then there are the thousands, if not millions, who come down with exotic fevers and intestinal problems every year. And this does not even take into account terrorist attacks, airplane crashes, car wrecks, and natural disasters.

To those fortunate enough to live in one of the more pristine Western nations, who haven't built up resistance to many of the health scourges so prevalent today in some less developed countries, and unaccustomed to local food and poor sanitary conditions, great care should be taken when traveling overseas.

No business executive desires to be the victim of Third World medicine, except in an absolute emergency. Many hospitals in developing countries lack the hygiene and modern technology that we take for granted in the U.S., Western Europe, or parts of Asia. Moreover, their physicians often have inferior training by Western standards, including ex-pats working in foreign hospitals. The horror stories are legion about sweat-stained ex-pat doctors with alcohol on their breath and shaky hands encountered at Third World clinics and hospitals, some of whom probably lost their licenses to practice medicine in their home countries because of incompetence, substance abuse problems, or criminality.

Many Third World hospitals, moreover, recycle syringes, purchase counterfeit or adulterated medications, and have few, if any, private or even semi-private rooms. During a recent outbreak of dengue fever in New Delhi, local hospitals "reported four patients to a bed."[18] Often there are just open wards, lacking air conditioning in the tropics or heat in some of the former CIS countries, where the lights are kept on twenty-four hours a day and all patients, including those with infectious diseases, share the same space, sanitary facilities, and overworked staff. Some hospitals have no food service and depend on family members to bring food and liquids to their relatives when they are in the hospital. Depending on the country and the facility a little cash to hospital workers, and even doctors, can secure you better care and medications.

---

18 Jason Overdorf; "The Games Just Started, but India Has Already Lost"; *The Washington Post*; October 3, 2010; p. B3.

I worked on a film overseas where the male star, an iconic action hero, brought a supply of his own blood in case he was injured during the filming.

Dentistry is also a serious challenge in many developing nations. I always remember the roadside dental chair I saw in Pakistan and the smiling dentist, with only two teeth himself, waving a pair of pliers at passing cars.

It is recommended that all travelers to less developed countries carry a medical kit and consider enrolling in one of the medical evacuation programs that have consulting doctors and will fly you out of a country with inadequate medical services to get needed care. The medical kit should contain, at the very least, diarrhea medication, flu medication, an antibiotic, water purification tablets, and some basic first aid items like bandages, tape, and gauze. Some firms actually offer emergency medical kits designed for those involved in extreme sports and adventure travel, which can be very valuable in remote and rural areas. Such kits contain splints, bandages and dressings, wound closure strips, gauze, tape, syringes, EMT shears, heat packs, blister and burn medications, a temporary cavity filling mixture, a stethoscope, a thermometer, antacids, bite wipes, eye wash, Ibuprofen, oral re-hydration salts, a scalpel, sunscreen, Providone Iodine, antibiotic ointment, and a first aid book. It is also recommended that before traveling to less developed countries that one investigates what vaccines or medications are required or recommended (especially Yellow Fever and Malaria), including a current tetanus shot (it is recommended that adults get them every ten years).

I have also carried Percocet (Oxycodone) with me ever since I threw my back out in the Balkans and spent the entire night in a hot bath at my hotel, nursing a bottle of cognac, trying to reduce the spasms and pain, with a pistol in the soap dish since I feared we had offended some very powerful people in the country who might want to eliminate the problem, namely me. They had already made an attempt to stab one of my colleagues in the back as he walked through a city square (and he would later be murdered when a bomb was wired to the ignition of his vehicle). I vowed afterward never to be helpless again when confronting a threat (or a natural disaster), and I've found that a good pain-killer, which should not be abused, is an absolute necessity.

CONCLUSION

Of all the terrible places I've been, none was worse than Kano, Nigeria. As noted earlier, I spent a lot of time in Haiti, I was in Liberia's chaotic capital before it fell, I've seen the wretched slums of Bogota, Cairo, and Manila, not to mention the grinding poverty of the Chinese countryside more than a quarter of a century ago, but Kano takes the crown when it comes to just plain bad places. A city of nearly four million people, there are only a handful of real buildings, including the Emir's palace, the governor's palace, and the Bank of the North. Virtually everyone else lives in cinder block shacks with tin-roofs and no glass in the windows, next to fetid brown rivers or canals full of filth, abutted by snowdrifts of garbage crawling with insects that have been picked over again and again by children desperate to find anything of value. There are open sewers in the streets and few of the street lights at intersections work.

The streets are teeming with people, who share the right-of-way with mopeds and motorcycles, beat-up rusted cars missing tail lights, often with a single headlight, and a few old trucks. Legless men scurry around on small platforms with roller skate blades underneath. I did not see a single dog or cat; presumably all have been eaten. There's little electricity, and what there is comes mostly from generators, and if you fly in after dark, as I did, given the paltry number of lights it appears that Kano is a small town or village with only a few thousand people.

Billboards exhort residents to "Dress Modestly," and there are no real shops or restaurants, branded products, or even hotels. The "Allah is the Greatest" store appeared to be selling used motor parts and gasoline in plastic jugs, and just a few doors away was the "God is Able" restaurant, which had dead fish on a blanket displayed out front. It seemed as if every street corner was jammed with beggars and cripples, many covered with warts and lesions, selling lottery tickets. Since there were no hotels, I stayed in a guest house made of cinder blocks, which was advertised as "Serene and Luxurious," which was serene and luxurious only by comparison to the tin-roofed huts that sheltered most of the people in Kano.

Despite all of the negative incidents and places I've described, however, I still believe that no American should hesitate to experience different countries and cultures. As Lord Chesterfield wrote to his son, "The world is a country which nobody ever yet knew by description.

One must travel through it one's self to be acquainted with it." For every Kano there are a dozen places that you will be richer for having visited.

- 3 -

TAKING SECURITY SERIOUSLY

"Only those means of security are good,
are certain, are lasting, that depend
on yourself and your own vigor."

Niccolo Machiavelli

He travels in a hardened, or armored, SUV wherever he goes. A crash car runs interference in front and another car, full of gunmen with shotguns and assault rifles, follows close behind. His house is a virtual fortress, surrounded by a high wall imbedded with glass, and protected by massive iron gates, CCTV cameras, vicious dogs roaming the grounds, and armed guards. There is a pistol or rifle in every room of his house, on the credenza, the dresser, the dining room table, and even on the back of each toilet. He no longer eats out or plays golf. When he does go out, he never leaves the house without several bodyguards. He is a virtual prisoner in his house and office.

Terrorists have tried to assassinate him three times. Although he graduated from an Ivy League school and writes poetry, he muses that, "After the first time they try to kill you, you're no longer a liberal."

His greatest source of resentment against his foes is that they have forced him to become like them. Two women came to his house disguised as nuns, and his wife invited them inside. They turned out to be leftist terrorists intent on kidnapping her, but there was a shootout that left two members of the household dead and the bogus nuns fleeing with his sister as a hostage. He eventually paid a ransom to free the sister and then systematically hunted down the terrorists and killed them, one at a time.

Who is this man? Why must he live this way?

Ironically, he's not a politician or a public figure. He's merely a successful self-made businessman who lives in a country that has, for the better part of six decades, been periodically wracked by political instability and violence.

Business executives have increasingly become targets of kidnappers, terrorists and assassins in recent years. During the U.S. occupation of Iraq, American, British, South Korean and other contractors and businessmen were victims of bombings, shootings, and even beheadings. This was also true of U.S. contractors in places like Saudi Arabia, where Lockheed Martin employee, Paul Johnson, was abducted by terrorists allied with Al Qaeda and later beheaded. Johnson, ironically, had a great affinity for the Muslim culture and had lived in Saudi Arabia for a decade. To his murderers, however, he was simply a convenient representative of the American presence in Saudi Arabia, whose murder could be used to make a political statement and attract recruits and money to the jihadist movement.

But it's not just businessmen in Russia, the Middle East, and unstable countries in the developing world that are victims of violence. The Unabomber, after all, killed and maimed businessmen in the U.S. whom he considered enemies of the environment and the Luddite society he espoused. During the 1970s and 1980s, business leaders in Western Europe were regularly assassinated and kidnapped by left-wing terrorist groups like West Germany's Red Army Faction and Italy's Red Brigades. Countless business executives and their family members have been kidnapped by criminal groups and brigands whose main goal is to collect ransoms. Other business executives have become targets because of actions or policies of their companies, as in the case of BP chief executive Tony Hayward, who received dozens, if not hundreds, of death threats during the catastrophic BP oil spill in the Gulf of Mexico. Hayward, who few people had ever heard of prior to the incident, was forced to implement around-the-clock security for himself and his family. Georgian oligarch, Badri Patarkatsishvile, who died of a heart attack in 2008, so feared for his life that he reportedly had 120 bodyguards.[19]

Executives at many of the Wall Street companies involved in the Great Recession received death threats like the chilling email sent to

---

19 Suzanna Andrews, "The Widow and the Oligarchs," *Vanity Fair*, October, 2009, p. 263.

AIG executives warning, "Get the bonus, we will get your children." The email was signed "Jacob the Killer." Because of the enormous financial losses incurred at Lehman Brothers and Bear Stearns, executives at both companies also received threats against their lives. Even seemingly trivial matters like the decision by NBC to get rid of Conan O'Brien and bring Jay Leno back allegedly resulted in death threats against network chief Jeff Zucker.

As noted in the opening paragraphs, family members are often targeted by kidnappers if they can't reach the principal because he or she has such good security. In one case a mid-level American auto executive based in Latin America came home to find his wife with her throat slit and a note pinned to blouse saying that more children and spouses would be killed unless the company shut down operations in that particular country. The company subsequently sold its factory to a competitor and left rather than risk any more casualties.

SECURITY AS AN EGO TRIP

Some businessmen don't really need security but have it anyway because it suggests a person of importance and confers a special status on the protectee, rather like a celebrity's "posse." It almost always guarantees a good table at a restaurant where you're not known since the maitre'd will naturally assume that anyone significant enough to lead a threatened life is not to be trifled with and is probably a good tipper to boot.

But a lot of the security one sees is not very good, and in some cases more of a threat to the protectee than to the bad guys. You know a protectee's security isn't top notch when his bodyguards are kidnapped instead of him, which happened in Colombia in 2003 over Easter. In the security business, incompetent bodyguards are derisively referred to as Big Samoans, knuckle draggers, palookas, and worse. They are the big-of-shoulders, weak-of-mind bodyguards you often see with celebrities and prize fighters. These are the guys who will take unnecessary risks or, even worse, shoot the client in a panicky effort to fend off an attack or kidnapping.

One Hollywood action hero used to travel around with two bogus Navy SEALs often dressed in Italian suits, black shirts with light-colored ties, and pointed toe shoes like they were refugees from an old

George Raft movie.[20] The star, not one of his industry's brightest lights, had met them while bodybuilding and the two bodyguards insisted on standing next to him wherever he went like they were Siamese triplets. A studio chief that was our client one day asked why my men, by contrast, hung in the background and never stood near him unless he was moving through a crowd. I replied that the star's bodyguards were so obvious that anyone wishing to carry out an attack would shoot both of the bodyguards first and then the star. My men, I explained, were not so obvious and were watching the room instead of basking in the reflected glory of the star. He then raised another point that had always troubled him. My people, he observed, were not big muscular guys like the star's bodyguards, but were quiet, compact men that didn't throw their weight around. Surely, he asked, you want bodyguards that are intimidating? I responded that my guys were former Delta Force shooters, men who had seen the bear and heard the hoot owl. They were in superb physical condition, I continued, like coiled springs prepared to go into action whenever the situation called for it. Their job, I told him, was first and foremost to out-think adversaries, not out shoot them, though they were certainly capable of that. They were not knuckle-draggers but trained professionals whose first responsibility was always to avoid trouble rather than cause it.

Poorly trained security men and women, who exhibit bad judgment, can be more of a threat to the client than to adversaries. Princess Diana's death was a tragedy, but it also was a preventable tragedy and illustrates how bad choices and inadequate oversight of the security function can lead to disaster. The Princess, accompanied by playboy Emad "Dodi" Fayed, left the Ritz Hotel in Paris late one night after a quiet dinner in the Imperial Suite. Accompanied by Fayed's personal bodyguard, they set off in an S-280 Mercedes sedan, driven by the hotel's deputy chief of security, Henri Paul. The hotel, incidentally, was

---

20 When we checked out their backgrounds we found that neither was a veteran of the U.S. military, much less a Navy SEAL, and that one of them had been a police officer for a year and a half until he was fired for cause. When we informed the star what we'd learned, he said they had already warned him that anyone without the highest level clearances, "code word only," would be unable to confirm their government service because they had worked on such sensitive and secretive projects. The star refused to listen to reason and fire the two bogus SEALs; a few months later we caught the two men stealing plywood on one of the movie sets and selling it out of the back of a truck.

owned by Dodi's father. Tests later confirmed that Paul was legally drunk, with over three times the legal alcohol limit in his blood, along with traces of an anti-depressant.

In an effort to escape the ever-present paparazzi, who were eager to take photographs of the princess and her lover, Paul apparently was driving at a high rate of speed when he lost control of the vehicle and crashed into a tunnel abutment, killing himself, the princess, and Dodi Fayed. Only the bodyguard, Trevor Rees-Jones, survived.

In retrospect, there are many lessons to be learned from this unhappy episode. First, good security is predicated on good planning. Despite the constant problem posed by the paparazzi, there appears to have been little or no thought given in advance to the couple's departure from the Ritz around midnight. By all accounts, Dodi Fayed and Rees-Jones hastily improvised the journey to Fayed's apartment near the Arc de Triomphe, deciding at the last minute to send Fayed's Mercedes S-600 away as a decoy from the front of the hotel. Dodi Fayed and the princess then slipped out through a rear entrance, where the S-280 was waiting for them. Since they were accompanied by only one bodyguard, Paul was summoned at the last minute to drive the S-280. Even though he had been drinking, Paul did not protest or decline the task, no doubt fearful of antagonizing his employer.

Rees-Jones, the security man, must also be faulted for his performance that evening. He was either unaware of the fact that Paul was impaired, or chose to ignore it. Despite the fact that the car was obviously traveling too fast, there is no evidence that Rees-Jones protested or tried to get Paul to stop. Most serious of all, he alone in the car was wearing his seat belt, which probably saved his life. Why hadn't he insisted that Dodi Fayed and the princess wear their seat belts? Especially if they were going to try and outrun the paparazzi? Even if Fayed and the Princess had refused to strap themselves in, why wasn't the driver required to wear his seat belt? If they had been attacked by kidnappers or terrorists, instead of the paparazzi, the driver--even if he wasn't drunk--was violating a basic rule: you must always wear your seat belt, especially if you are going to attempt any of the more dangerous evasive-aggressive driving moves in an attempt to escape attackers.

A second lesson to be learned is that Dodi Fayed and the princess both exhibited terrible judgment when it came to questions of their personal security. You must always be engaged in your own security planning, not in all of the details, but in the basic decisions about the people you hire and ensuring that they carry out your wishes in a professional and prudent manner. This is not something that can be delegated. You do so at your own peril.

Diana, it turned out, had earlier rejected a proposed protective detail from Scotland Yard. Had she accepted the Scotland Yard detail, she might still be alive today. Instead, she relied on Dodi Fayed's security. But Fayed, who had little education or managerial experience, and certainly wasn't the sharpest knife in the drawer, seems to have been surrounded by unreliable people of questionable judgment.

So, what should they have done that evening?

First, there was no need to have driven at an excessive rate of speed to escape the paparazzi. The paparazzi knew the location of Fayed's apartment and would have shown up there eventually. If Fayed and the princess didn't want photos taken of them en route, the car should have been equipped with curtains or screens to give them some privacy in the back seat. Then the driver could have driven at normal speed to the apartment.

Secondly, the al-Fayed family was extremely wealthy and it was inexplicably shortsighted to have only one security man present. A full security detail of three or four man would have alleviated the necessity of summoning Henri Paul to drive the getaway car. A full detail could have mapped out the couple's retreat from the Ritz and been prepared when it came time to depart.

Finally, there should have been at least one chase car, preferably two, to keep the photographers at bay. It also appears that the decoy car wasn't an effective ploy. Nor is there any evidence that either Dodi Fayed or the princess ever considered disguising their features in order to make a clean escape. In the end, one can speculate that the two lovers viewed their brushes with the paparazzi as a kind of game, rather like hide-and-seek. Since they were both irresponsible and extremely disengaged with respect to their security, it was perhaps inevitable that some kind of tragedy would occur. And it goes without saying that they could simply have stayed at the Ritz that night rather than give the paparazzi another opportunity to take photos.

Predictability is the enemy of good security. Whatever you do, vary your routes and your routines. In the late 1980s, I had a client that was kidnapped in Great Britain. An Arab of immense wealth with a controversial past, he was driving himself to his palatial home in central

London.   Unfortunately, there was only one road into his neighborhood, and to his house, and one road leading out; both were one-way streets. Anyone wanting to kidnap him or do him harm could simply wait for him on one of the roads with the certainty that there were no alternate routes.

One day a car pulled out of a side street and struck his fender. He stopped and got out of his car to inspect the damage, and a policeman standing nearby approached and offered to take his statement so he could be on his way. Since it was raining lightly, the officer suggested they seek shelter in the car and he opened the rear door. The Arab climbed in and as he did so, he officer followed. Suddenly another man appeared and jumped behind the wheel of the car. The policeman pushed the Arab to the floor with a gun to his head and a third man slid into the backseat, hemming the victim in on both sides. The car sped away and soon rendezvoused with a van on a side street. The victim was then transferred to the van and wrapped in duct tape from head to toe by a second set of kidnappers. Finally, he was turned over to a third set of "keepers" at an isolated country house where he was held until he was released.

Four U.S. auditors working for Union Oil Co. in Pakistan on temporary assignment were also victims of their predictability. They were shot to death by two gunmen on motorcycles when their car became stalled in heavy traffic. The driver was supposedly trained in anti-terrorist driving tactics but it was subsequently determined that he had received no training in evasive-aggressive driving and took the same route every day after picking up the auditors in the morning. The company, moreover, operated the only Nissan Cedrics in the country, thus the car being used to transport the auditors was highly recognizable. The company claimed it made them less likely targets of carjacking since their cars were so identifiable. Finally, the driver wore eyeglasses with coke bottle lenses and witnesses say his vision was so bad that it was not uncommon for him to sideswipe parked cars.

Some executives, like the Arab kidnapped in London, don't like having a security detail, or even a driver trained in anti-terrorism tactics, because they see either as an intrusion on their privacy. Years ago we met with a wealthy Latin coffee grower to discuss providing him with a security detail. When we sat down with him he explained that he wanted the detail with him all the time with the exception of Tuesday and Thursday afternoons. It was obvious that he probably met his mistress at those times and didn't want anyone to know. When I confronted him with my suspicions, he reluctantly admitted that I was right. "If someone wants to kidnap you or kill you," I argued, "they're sure to have you under surveillance. Don't you think they'll recognize that your security detail doesn't accompany you on Tuesday and Thursday afternoons? Since those are going to be your most vulnerable times, why would they attempt to snatch you anywhere else or on any other days? If they come after you on a Tuesday or Thursday afternoon they won't have to contend with a well-armed and highly professional security detail."

After some thought, the coffee planter saw that we were right and permitted a security detail to accompany him everywhere, even to his mistress' apartment. This probably saved his life. Over the years, moreover, we have had a number of cases where the mistress set up her lover either to be killed or kidnapped. In one case, in Colombia, the mistress was also the victim's secretary, and she had complete knowledge of his schedule and whereabouts. She belonged to a fringe religious group and was able to recruit some of her coreligionists to carry out the actual kidnapping, whereupon the victim was then sold to a group of brigands with ties to the Colombian guerrilla organization known as the FARC. The victim was subsequently killed by government troops when they ambushed a rebel column and didn't realize that several of those with the rebels were hostages on their way to being exchanged for ransoms.

Gay clients also present problems in terms of their often obsessive desire for secrecy, since many of them are still in the "closet" and don't want anyone outside their immediate circle of acquaintances to know their proclivities. We had a client from a dangerous country overseas that believed no one knew he was gay, though it was widely suspected in his country, and would permit his security detail to stay with him throughout the day and drive him home at night, ostensibly so he could get some sleep. In actuality, a short time after returning home he would slip out most nights and drive, without anyone from his security detail accompanying him, to a friend's house or a gay nightclub where he was totally without protection.

Another business executive in Europe was a transvestite and would not use his security detail when he was wearing women's clothing. On one of his late night carouses he was mugged and seriously injured, which probably wouldn't have happened if he had been accompanied by his security detail.

Many prominent leading men in Hollywood are gay and must adhere to the fiction that they are not, especially when it comes to their female fans. Often their security details are the only thing that stands between them and exposure in the tabloids, for example, in cases where there has been a noisy altercation with a lover, an ill-advised effort to pick up a he-she or male prostitute, or medical complications from certain sex acts. A good security detail will be absolutely loyal to their client and shield the client from prying eyes and compromising situations. This is also why it is important to have low turnover on a security detail, where the client has a bond with his protectors and knows their names and family histories. A client who is abusive to his detail or to other people in front of his detail may not command their respect and they may be tempted to reveal sensitive information to the paparazzi or tabloids if offered enough money.

The best security details are composed of ex-Secret Service agents or highly trained former military or law enforcement veterans in top physical shape that have served together as a unit for some time, have a good working relationship with the client, are trained in executive protection skills and tactics, and operate with clear rules of engagement (ROE). Rules of engagement pertain to the circumstances when and how a member of the security team is permitted to use any kind of force, especially deadly force. This was never better illustrated than when I had a prominent Hollywood client who had just purchased a new $14 million home in Bel Air and sent me over to perform a security assessment of the house and its surrounding acreage. When I arrived I found a fat, moon-faced, slow-witted security guard who had apparently been transferred, along with the property, to the new owners as part of the sale. He was armed and proud of it, sporting a 9mm Glock pistol high on his hip. I asked him what his rules of engagement were and he looked quite baffled, explaining that he'd never heard the term before. I rephrased my question, inquiring as to what rules, if any, he had for protecting the property. He replied that no one had ever briefed him as to their expectations and that he just used his own judgment, which was not reassuring.

Continuing to press him, I asked him to describe his duties. Well, he said, he patrolled the property and kept the "bad guys" out.

Describe the "bad guys" to me, I told him. He stared at his shoes for a few moments, then sidled up to me and said, "You know."

"No, I don't," I said. "Tell me."

He cleared his throat. "Black guys. Mexicans," he replied, looking at me like I was a total dimwit.

"Have you met the new owners?" I shot back.

"No. Not yet."

My client was trim and athletic, but decidedly swarthy with black hair and flashing dark eyes; in other words, exactly the kind of person the security guard, given his prejudices, probably would have assumed was one of the "bad guys." I could see the future unfolding before my eyes: the security guard pulling his weapon and shooting the client because he lacked rules of engagement and assumed that any person of dark complexion on the property must be a criminal. I recommended to the client that we fire the security man immediately and replace him with an experienced team from a local company that had been well-trained and provided with proper rules of engagement if they were going to be armed.

The members of the security force should always be polite to the client and his or her family and associates and conduct themselves with professionalism. Everything that happens inside the client's family should stay there and the client's personal life should not be an issue of gossip or discussion, except as it relates to the movements and protection of the client.

As with the Secret Service when it protects the President of the U.S. and other top dignitaries, the goal of an executive security detail should be first, and foremost, to avoid any type of threat or incident. In the event, however, that an attack occurs, the best strategy is almost always to escape with the protectee and get him or her to safety as quickly as possible. It is never a good idea to try and shoot it out with the bad guys, although some foreign protective services recommend such foolish practices. We were training a Turkish executive protection team that had previously received some Israeli training. The Israelis had, unbelievably, taught them that when under attack they should stop the car, open the doors, and take cover behind the doors while returning fire. Needless to say, our approach was just the contrary.[21]

---

21 There are literally hundreds, if not thousands, of Israeli security firms. While many are excellent, some are operated by wannabes and fantasists and lack the specialized military or intelligence training they often purport to have.

SECURITY DIRECTORS

Security directors were once retired cops and government agents who wore thick-soled shoes, bad suits, and pocket-protectors, whose seemingly sole function was to walk around and ensure that safes and doors were locked. Probably the only time they were called upon to do anything out of the ordinary was when the CFO got locked up on a DUI charge and the security director was sent downtown to schmooze with his former colleagues at the local police department in an effort have the charges dropped before a court appearance was entered.

Locked in dead-end jobs and viewed as hopelessly ignorant of corporate issues, security directors were almost never promoted to management positions beyond the security function. But no more. Today an increasing number of universities are offering security management degrees, and even MBAs from top business schools and Ivy League attorneys are choosing to go into the security field. Nevertheless, many corporations still hire retired cops or FBI and CIA officers as their security directors, despite the fact that few know much about security. Security is an art today, often with highly technical demands, and just because an individual was a good law enforcement officer who caught crooks for a living doesn't mean that he or she can cope effectively and creatively with the demands of securing the assets, reputation, and officers of a major corporation doing business on a global basis. Moreover, few law enforcement officers have international training, experience, and language skills. Arguably the worst security director I ever met came from law enforcement and claimed to have been all over the globe. In reality he had only seen the inside of the airports in most of the countries he had visited as part of a security detail and had so little knowledge of the world that he had to ask what a hotel concierge was. He had managed to make security a career because he was a former professional athlete and looked the part, even if he had a room temperature IQ and knew next to nothing about real security. Even worse he had a powerful ego and he felt he didn't need to do any research on his assignments or extra work to prepare for the tasks he was assigned. As one of his colleagues observed, "He was so stupid he couldn't find his pockets with both hands."

Similarly, most spooks are not operational; the great majority are intelligence analysts or support personnel. But even those from the Directorate of Operations (DO) at the CIA generally know little about the security of large organizations unless they were part of the security division. This doesn't diminish the service they rendered their country, but it is to say that the role of collecting intelligence and running agents is not the best preparation for protecting inventories and supply chains, planning for business continuity in the aftermath of a disaster, handling the company's executive protection requirements, and managing the security aspects of the corporate IT function. Finally, I have a bias against most government employees looking for second careers in the private sector; too many are tired and just want a secure sinecure from nine to five in order to draw a second income and, hopefully, another retirement check in the future. Today corporate security not only requires training and expertise, but a great deal of energy. Of course, there are always exceptions to every rule, and the old boy and old girl networks, especially in law enforcement, can often be invaluable if problems arise.

One oil company had an former local cop as its security director, who didn't even have a passport until he was named to the job. Unfortunately, as the company grew and the world changed, he was asked to perform tasks for which he had little or no training, and even less aptitude. Ultimately he was called upon to provide country risk assessments to the corporate brass and employees traveling abroad. Unable to perform any kind of cogent analysis, he delegated the function to his secretary, a bright but uneducated illegal alien who knew enough to check out State Department warnings on the web and subscribe to a few newsletters. As noted earlier in this chapter, four company contractors were sent to one of the most dangerous countries in the world where they, along with their driver, were gunned down by terrorists. They were provided with no security and had been assured that everything was fine in the country in question.

A final word of caution, there are loads of bogus security specialists around, claiming to be former SEALs, spooks, or other exotic men of action, who tell would-be employers that they were "deep cover" and therefore can't provide references and will not be acknowledged by their former agencies and units. This is absolutely, unequivocally nonsense, and anyone who suggests such a thing should be avoided like the plague. Even the CIA, in nearly all cases, will confirm its relationship with a former employee even if it won't describe the person's actual position or work history. Any veteran of the intelligence, law enforcement, or special operations community can be checked out to some degree.

PUTTING SECURITY ON THE CEO'S AGENDA

Prior to 9/11, the security function at most corporations was a delegated function and rarely, if ever, crossed the CEO's or Chairman's desk. "Corporate security has never been a mainstream management function," wrote Richard S. Post in 1987. "Senior management seldom thinks about it, except during a crisis, when losses rise to an unacceptable level or a serious incident needs resolving (i.e., an executive kidnapping, product contamination, major employee theft, etc.)."[22] Security, moreover, was viewed as a "non-productive" sector that added nothing to the corporation's bottom line. This began to change, at least temporarily, after 9/11 and the anthrax attacks in the Fall of 2001. According to a Booz Allen Hamilton survey conducted in the last two months of 2001, CEOs were paying far more attention to security matters than before 9/11 and nine out of ten CEOs of companies with revenues in excess of $1 billion indicated they had recently reviewed their company's disaster planning. According to a 2002 article by Paul Adams, "In a growing number of boardrooms nationwide, corporations are making room at the table for a once-obscure executive: the corporate security officer."[23]

Many firms subsequently required visitors to show an ID when visiting corporate headquarters and have their bags screened for weapons and explosives, hired companies to reconfigure mail rooms and institutionalize new procedures for handling mail, set up off-site facilities for data storage and business continuity, and paid more attention to issues such as the interruption of supply chains (U.S. corporations lost billions of dollars as a result of supply chain disruptions following the grounding of all aircraft in the aftermath of 9/11), the safety of traveling executives, and the integrity of the company's information systems.[24] The Great Recession added to such

---

22 Richard S. Post, "No Company Can Take Off Without a Security Belt," *The Wall Street Journal*, January 19, 1987.

23 Paul Adams, "Security Gets a Seat in the Boardroom," *The Baltimore Sun*, February 24, 2002.

24 Prior to 9/11, U.S. corporations were so committed to holding down inventory costs that they had few, if any, spare parts for their machinery or components

worries and in the wake of widespread job cuts and the collapse of major banks and investment houses executives beefed up their personal protection details and even "hardened" their boardrooms and podiums, fearful of angry investors and laid-off employees. One New York boardroom sports reinforced walls and doors, CCTV, and a closet with gas masks, flak jackets, first aid kits, cell phones, and even oxygen tanks.

Rather than harden the boardroom, CEOs need to address the issue of porous security at their headquarters and other offices. Perhaps the greatest vulnerability we see over and over again is the fact that cleaning crews are rarely screened or properly supervised, and yet often have unrestricted access to every office in the company. They are viewed simply as part of the furniture and few executives know their names or even the identity of the vendors for whom they work. Most cleaning crews are made up of recent immigrants to the U.S., often here illegally and hired by office cleaning companies at minimum wage. Many use false names and addresses and don't even speak English since it is not necessary in order to perform the work they do.

Given their poverty and lack of connection to the companies where they work, it is fairly easy to compromise a member of a cleaning crew for a little cash. They are often willing to take the contents of waste baskets, photograph letters and contracts left unsecured on desktops, copy down passwords, and steal thumb drives and floppy discs. All of these are relatively low risk activities and even if caught, the employee is usually just discharged since the legal penalties are light and it is often difficult to prosecute someone successfully. From the employee's point-of-view, he or she can easily find work at another cleaning firm, so the risk is virtually negligible.

Some cleaning companies have been set up solely for the purpose of stealing corporate secrets and have employed trained sleuths to rifle files, ferret out documents and information, and steal personal data on top executives so they can be blackmailed. All companies should have robust programs in place to secure computers and hard files, to enforce clean desk policies, and to shred or otherwise destroy all paper trash or

---

for their products. They have had to rethink this strategy in the aftermath of 9/11 when some production lines had to shut down because companies failed to receive the daily air shipments of parts they need to keep manufacturing their products.

confidential documents. Cleaning crews should be supervised by the company's security department, especially when working in the offices and meeting rooms of top officials and their secretaries and assistants. CCTV cameras can also be installed to watch cleaning crews, but generally are more valuable in the aftermath of a security breech than before because they require constant monitoring and often have low resolution.

A large scam operation was uncovered in the City of London involved West African gangs placing their operatives in cleaning crews, or "subverting" regular members of the crews, with instructions to steal company stationary and letterheads, mail, and signed documents relating to the transfer of money. Once in possession of such items, the criminals utilized the information to instruct banks to make unauthorized withdrawals and transfers to bank accounts they controlled, where the money quickly disappeared, often forwarded to offshore accounts. Various banks and financial institutions reportedly lost millions of pounds to such scams.

While hardened boardrooms and ID checks are of questionable value, beefing up a company's supply chain (by stockpiling parts and having contingency plans for various disruption scenarios) and taking steps to ensure business continuity in the event of a major disaster or power failure are sensible measures and should be adopted by all companies. Moreover, every senior executive at a company should be cognizant of security issues and engaged in crisis management planning and, at least once a year, participate in exercises related to that plan. Any executive who believes that such issues are below his or her pay grade should be shown the door immediately by the board of directors. And directors, too, should be briefed on a regular basis about threats to the company, its personnel, reputation, and share value, and the actions being taken by management to address these issues.

There was no excuse for BP's failure to anticipate the Deepwater Horizon oil spill in 2010 and its fumbling efforts to cap the gushing well. The company's CEO, Tony Hayward, should have been terminated immediately and stripped of his fat annual pension because of his demonstrable lack of focus on potential threats to the well-being of the company and its employees. Litigation against BP is likely to go on for decades and not only is the company's brand forever going to be linked to the disaster but it is likely to suffer on-going financial damage as well. The board of directors should be held accountable as well.

NEW SECURITY DEMANDS

For years, prior to 9/11, U.S. airlines protested that they were in the business of flying passengers, carrying cargo, and doing their best to ensure that baggage arrived on time at the right location. They were not, many airline executives protested, in the security business nor should they be, but the federal government nonetheless mandated that the airlines were responsible for basic security screening at airports and had to pay for it. In virtually every other nation in the world, aviation security was regarded as a government responsibility and too important to be left to the airlines.

In an industry already saddled with low margins and frequent losses, U.S. airlines sought to meet this requirement with what can only be described as a lack of enthusiasm, hiring subcontractors that were the lowest bidders for the job and standing up the cheapest security available that would meet federal requirements. Security screeners were paid minimum wage or slightly higher, had few benefits, and little training. Often aviation security subcontractors competed with Burger King and McDonald's for personnel, and this was evident in the poor performance and high turnover of airport security screeners and was a major contributing factor to the disaster on 9/11.

Following the 9/11 attacks on New York City and Washington, the federal government has attempted to mandate new and more stringent security requirements and regulations for numerous industries, which have often been resisted by the companies impacted, generally because of cost and inconvenience. To cite but a few examples, new regulations have been imposed on the banking and financial communities designed to prevent money laundering, the chemical and energy sectors have been ordered to upgrade their physical security at all levels, new operating rules have been applied to the maritime industry, and nearly all large companies have been affected by "new restrictions on border crossings and international shipments of goods."[25] While many companies are struggling with the poor economy and argue that they cannot afford all of the new government mandates, CEOs and Boards of Directors must be cognizant of the need to provide a secure workplace for employees and customers, and

---

25 Eric Planin and Bill Miller, "Businesses Draw Line on Security," *The Washington Post*, September 5, 2002.

must also recognize the consequences of not properly securing the company's assets, employees, and supply chain. Not only can a major security breech or disaster cost a company millions of dollars, damage its brand, and erode share value, but we live in a very litigious society and in recent years there has been an avalanche of lawsuits in the United States charging that corporations, landlords, and businesses failed in their duty to adequately protect those who relied on them for security. Shopping malls, hotels, and amusement parks have regularly been accused in lawsuits of security lapses, as have major corporations and universities. Scores of lawsuits also have resulted from failures to adequately screen the backgrounds of employees, especially in cases involving bogus doctors and sexual predators. A number of lawsuits will surely arise from 2011 Penn State sex abuse scandal, charging that the university failed to follow up on reports that assistant coach Jerry Sandusky had sexually assaulted or had inappropriate contact with at least eight boys. Landlords, both business and residential, are being sued for criminal attacks on tenants, in lawsuits which contend that tenants have a reasonable expectation of a safe environment. In one case even the manufacturer of the apartment door lock was sued after the rape of a tenant.

A good example of the kinds of lawsuits being filed today was a 2008 action by the family of a temporary worker hired by Wal-Mart in Valley Stream, New York, who was trampled to death by "Black Friday" bargain hunters who broke down the doors to the store. Also named in the lawsuit were the mall where the store was located, a realty company that managed the property, and the security firm charged with crowd control on the day of the incident. The lawsuit charged that Wal-Mart "engaged in specific marketing and advertising techniques to specifically attract a large crowd and create an environment of frenzy and mayhem and was otherwise careless, reckless, and negligent." Wal-Mart settled the lawsuit before it was adjudicated. Indeed, most lawsuits related to security lapses are settled out-of-court, as are the great majority of all tort claims, but there is even more incentive to quietly settle lawsuits charging security problems since a large award to a victim will generally produce extensive media coverage and frighten away customers, especially if the defendant is in the hospitality, entertainment, or related industries.

We were once requested to do a security assessment of one of America's premiere tourist attractions, which was known for its family values and supposedly secure environment. We soon learned that there had been numerous rapes and sexual assaults on the location along with robberies and pickpockets, and even shootouts between rival street gangs and Colombian mobsters. The place was far from being as secure as the public believed, and the company that owned the attraction regularly settled lawsuits brought by crime victims quietly and out-of-court, so as not to generate negative publicity that would damage its brand and share value. Instead of improving security, and disregarding the physical and psychological trauma inflicted on crime victims at the company's main attraction, management viewed lawsuits simply as a normal cost of doing business. As in so many contemporary corporations, there were too many attorneys in the senior management ranks of the company who viewed security issues not as management problems that needed to be corrected, but as legal issues that could be disposed of with a confidential agreement and a check.

A number of companies, confronted with lawsuits alleging poor security, have gone so far as to adopt a "blame the victim" defense in an effort to force out-of-court settlements and reduce payouts. One of the most widely publicized cases was a lawsuit against the Marriott Hotel and Spa in Stamford, Connecticut. In 2006, a young woman was raped in the hotel's parking garage at gunpoint in front of her two young children. The hotel's attorneys claimed that she had "failed to exercise due care for her own safety and the safety of her children and proper use of her senses and faculties." After public outrage and widespread criticism of Marriott, the company withdrew its effort to implicate the victim as having contributed to the crime and ultimately reached an out-of-court settlement with her.

One of the fastest growing areas of litigation involves lawsuits over the failure to adequately protect data and insulate computer networks from hackers and other threats. Because it is often difficult to find the guilty parties in such situations and bring them to justice, victims are increasingly seeking legal redress from the companies that lost a laptop containing proprietary data or had insufficient security in place to prevent the data from being hacked or stolen from the company's main computers.

A few years ago we had a case where an employee, against the written rules of the company, had taken a laptop, containing a great deal of confidential loan information, home with him to work on it at night. The laptop was subsequently stolen and probably sold on a street corner for a few bucks. Fearing the misuse of the data on the laptop, including identity theft, the company immediately recognized that it was facing millions of dollars of potential litigation payouts and attorney's fees and spent months trying to recover the stolen computer. In the meantime, it was forced to contact everyone whose data was contained on the laptop and acknowledge that there was a problem. According to FBI figures, during a twenty-three month period in 2008 and 2009, 221,009 computers were reported stolen, and according to another survey the average corporate laptop theft reportedly cost the company $89,000, although some in some cases losses can run into the tens of millions of dollars.[26] Indeed, the average data breech at a major company costs $6.7 million, according to one researcher.[27]

In the latter category was the loss by BlueCross of 57 hard drives containing more than one million customer support calls at the company's training facility in Chattanooga, Tennessee. In at least 300,000 instances, the computer screens of the BlueCross customer service representative handling the call were visible, along with customer data, including Social Security numbers. According to published reports, the data theft created a "notification nightmare" for the health insurance company. Following the security breech, the company and its security contractor "employed 500 full-time workers and 300 part-time employees, working in two shifts, six days a week, to piece together what happened."[28] To date, the security breech has cost BlueCross more than $7 million just to ascertain which customers needed to be contacted and informed of the problem, and this does not include the cost of any litigation that may flow from the case in the future.

Kidnap victims have also sued their employers for failing to protect them or because of the amount of time it took to secure their release.

---

26 The actual number of stolen computers is probably far higher since the FBI study only addressed thefts actually reported to the authorities. Some have estimated that more than million computers, mostly laptops, are stolen every year in the U.S., including some 600,000 in airports alone.

27 Robert McMillan, "Data Theft Creates Notification Nightmare for BlueCross," *PC World*, March 1, 2010.

28 *Ibid.*

A number of kidnap victims have won handsome out-of-court settlements after charging that their employers negotiated for too long a time in an effort to lower ransom demands, and that those delays unnecessarily aggravated the suffering of the kidnap victims. U.S. jurisprudence has traditionally maintained that one is not obligated to impoverish himself to save another unless some kind of special duty is in force, and corporations historically were not regarded as having such a special duty toward their employees. Today, however, that interpretation of the law is under substantial challenge, although the case law is still spotty because most cases have been settled before adjudication.

Despite 9/11 and its aftermath, many companies are now cutting back on security and emergency management spending since there has not been another major terrorist event in the U.S. A classic example of this kind of short-sightedness involved an attack on a U.S. company in the energy sector in Saudi Arabia that resulted in seven dead, two of whom were Americans, and a number injured. In order to keep costs down at the firm's Saudi facility, located in a petrochemical complex, there was no trained security officer but rather the title of security officer was rotated weekly among the various petroleum engineers that worked for the company. None of the engineers, of course, was an experienced security professional and consequently few steps had been taken to secure the company's facility at the compound or to plan for its evacuation in the event of a terrorist attack. The front door of the facility was often left unlocked as was the back door, used mostly by smokers. No security assessment had ever been conducted and the threat level was so high at the time of the attack that the Department of State had ordered the departure from the country of all non-essential personnel and family members from the U.S. embassy and consulate. When employees raised concerns they were told to keep quiet. "Complain and you are sent home," said one employee.

There were clear security lapses at the site which any security specialist would have recognized, including the fact that the non-English speaking guards at the complex regularly admitted cars inside the perimeter without conducting security checks. When Al Qaeda terrorists attacked the facility, they knew exactly where to go and entered the building without problem from both the front and rear with guns blazing. In the aftermath of the attack, it was clear that the security at the facility was completely inadequate, given the threat, and that the failure to introduce good security systems and procedures virtually invited attack.

NEW SECURITY CHALLENGES

Security problems at major corporations are far more numerous and complex than in years past. Obvious issues include kidnappings, malicious hacking, disgruntled employees, theft, extortion, mail containing deadly substances, terrorist attacks, natural disasters, sabotage, industrial espionage, failing national infrastructure, and various risks involved in doing business in emerging markets. But there are many new security threats about which CEOs need to be aware.

There are, for example, a number of animal rights, environmental and one issue extremist groups that have targeted various companies in the U.S. abroad and their executives. And it's not all raiding mink and chicken farms, opening salmon cages, and spraying paint on fur coats. Animal rights activists have burned down medical research labs, meat plants, slaughterhouses, sports pavilions, and McDonald's restaurants; desecrated graves; threatened shareholders; torched vehicles; beaten executives with pickaxe handles; bombed bio-tech companies; poisoned researchers; mailed letter bombs to people working with animals (injuring, among others, a six-year-old girl whose father worked for a pest control company); and even attacked investment banks supporting firms in their cross hairs, in what one group refers to as secondary and tertiary targeting. The venerable Arkansas-based investment bank Stephens, Inc., was threatened by animal rights activists after providing Huntingdon Life Sciences, a British contract animal testing company, with a $15 million loan. The company was warned by the Acting Director of the FBI that they were a potential target and the company immediately took steps to upgrade their overall security. The Bank of New York was also attacked by animal rights and environmental terrorists for its support of Huntingdon Life Sciences. In a tertiary incident, 45 windows at a Bed Bath & Beyond were smashed in Salt Lake City because of the company's relationship with Stephens, Inc.

In another case, the CEO of a large corporation discovered that animal rights terrorists were attempting to sabotage his private aircraft and even move marker beacons and disrupt air operations at the private airfield where he landed the aircraft close to his vacation home.

To demonstrate the impact single issue extremist groups can have, after animal rights activists began an increasingly violent campaign against Huntingdon in the late 1990s, its share value collapsed, from a high of over 300 British pounds per share to less than two pounds in March, 2001. The company reportedly has weathered the storm and is profitable today, in large measure because of a concerted law enforcement crackdown on SHAC (Stop Huntingdon Animal Cruelty) and other animal rights terrorist groups in Great Britain and the U.S. Nevertheless, the company was forced to take extraordinary measures to protect the names of its customers and shareholders, and even moved its financial base to the United States.

Similarly, environmental extremists, or eco-terrorists, have also carried out deadly attacks here and abroad, torching ski resorts and housing developments, attempting to bomb nano-technology facilities and pipelines, sabotaging logging operations, and vandalizing SUVs and construction equipment.

TOO MUCH SECURITY

Although generally problems arise when there is inadequate or too little security there is also such a thing as too much security. I've encountered executives packing guns who are itching to shoot it out with the bad guys or the ex-military man who wouldn't leave home without two guns (one in a shoulder holster and an ankle gun), a knife in the small of his back, and wire wrapped around his wrist to use as a garrote. There was a former Marine who, when his company was threatened by a single-issue group with a history of violence, proudly showed us how he had created interlocking fields of fire around his house and was ready for those "sons-a-bitches" to show up. He dared 'em to do so. Another of my favorites was the executive from a company targeted by extremists who had a gun rack squeezed into the narrow back window of his Ferrari; it remains to this day the only Ferrari I've ever seen with a gun rack.

While I have the greatest respect for SEALs and Delta operators, occasionally one of the veterans of those organizations has spent so much time in the black world that it's difficult to integrate them back into ordinary society without some difficulty. One such individual-- we'll call him Carlos--had what was described by one of our security executives as having an acute case of the "for realies." He walked around with "eyes big as saucers," observed the security man, "as if he'd driven all the way from New York to Miami and hit nothing but green lights." Carlos was a veteran of the Phoenix program in Vietnam and dozens of operations against the Castro regime in Cuba.

Carlos once took two prospective clients from an insurance company out to dinner. He had a white Cadillac convertible with a sub-machine gun mounted in the front grill. On the way to the restaurant on the freeway, a carload of young hooligans tried to merge from an on-ramp and force the Cadillac into the next lane. Carlos refused to budge and the hooligans flipped him off and then took the next exit ramp, cut over the top to the on-ramp, and tried to cut in front of him. Once again Carlos held his ground and drove the hooligans into the ditch abutting the freeway, where they rolled over. The two insurance executives were thoroughly shaken by the incident which was as far removed from their normal world as anything they'd ever experienced. But the best was yet to come.

When they reached the restaurant, which featured Chinese cuisine, they were greeted by a Chinese man who was the parking valet.

"I park your car," he announced.

"No," replied Carlos. "I'll park it myself."

"I park your car," insisted the valet. "It rule."

Carlos pulled a 9mm pistol from its holster beneath his left armpit, chambered a round, and shoved the barrel into the valet's mouth.

"I'll park the car myself," he informed the valet, who had thrown up his hands and was looking at Carlos with a terrified look on his face.

"Yes, yes," he gasped, trying to speak with the gun barrel in his mouth. "You park your own car."

As the totally speechless insurance executives looked on, Carlos drew back his pistol, set it on the seat, and proceeded to pull into a parking place near the front entrance to the restaurant. After locking the car, Carlos led the way toward the restaurant door. Just before they entered, he remembered that he still had a round chambered in the pistol, so he shot out the light over the door, causing one of the insurance executives to lose it completely, flee the scene and hail a cab for the airport. Carlos' behavior illustrates the potential problems with some, albeit a small number of special operations veterans, who have had problems adjusting to the civilian world after years in the military or CIA.

The death of Edmond Safra is also a cautionary tale. The Jewish billionaire and philanthropist, who lived in Monaco, New York,

Geneva, and on the French Riviera, was deeply paranoid and had turned his homes into fortresses protected allegedly by Mossad-trained guards. He was, according to author Dominick Dunne in <u>Vanity Fair</u>, "obsessed with security. It was widely reported that he felt menaced, and considered himself a hunted man...At each of his many residences he lived virtually surrounded by a private army."[29]

Many of the facts surrounding Safra's mysterious death are still a matter of dispute. What is known is that he died in a predawn fire in his two-story penthouse apartment in Monte Carlo, supposedly after he had barricaded himself in a safe room to escape two masked intruders who stabbed his male nurse. His death, and that of a nurse, Vivian Torrente, were due to smoke and fume inhalation. Ultimately, the chief prosecutor in Monaco concluded that there were no intruders and that a male nurse, Ted Maher, a U.S. Army special operations veteran, had fabricated the whole incident, stabbed himself, and set fire to a wastebasket that quickly spread out of control, in an attempt to ingratiate himself to Safra and look like a hero.

Another disastrous incident involving overkill on the security front was the Hewlett-Packard (HP) spying scandal. In an effort to identify the source or sources of leaks to the media regarding proprietary information concerning the company's business strategy, HP Chairwoman Patricia Dunn hired security specialists to obtain phone logs of calls, and other information, made by certain board members and journalists, which might definitively show a connection between one or more board members and one or more of the reporters. To obtain the records, the investigators used a common tool known as "pretexting," where they assumed the identity of the board members and journalists in order to make requests for records from the phone company. Dunn repeatedly defended her actions by stating that she didn't know that pretexting was a crime if it involved identity misrepresentation. After investigations by the California Attorney General, Congress, and the Justice Department, Dunn resigned, along with HP's general counsel Ann Baskins. Another HP employee and two investigators pled no contest to wire fraud charges and another investigator entered a guilty plea to federal charges.

Companies must take care to ensure that their security employees don't employ too much force in situations like keeping paparazzi away

---

29 Dominick Dunne, "Death in Monaco," *Vanity Fair*, December, 2000.

or in detaining shoplifting suspects, to name but two examples. There has been a great deal of litigation against firms, especially in the retail sector, accusing them of employing overzealous security guards who used either excessive force or racial profiling in addressing inventory control issues.

In the final analysis, the best security is often low key or even invisible security, although in some instances highly visible security can serve as a deterrent. This was the case when we were hired by the Navajo Nation, using funds from the Justice Department, to pacify the situation following a riot in which two Native American police officers were slain at Window Rock. The riot had been fomented by the American Indian Movement (AIM), which allegedly had been paid off by the Chairman of the Navajo Nation, Peter McDonald, who was fighting to keep his position in the wake of being indicted by the federal government on corruption charges. Our team, mostly made up of ex-Delta Force operators, arrived in Window Rock in what we called their Darth Vadar costumes: black utilities, jump boots, reflector visors on their helmets, long batons, and side arms. They looked so formidable that the AIM trouble-makers were totally intimidated and quickly melted away and there was no further serious trouble.

All security should be highly professional, even the security guards at the door, and properly supervised. Security should never be an afterthought but rather an integral part of any business, fully integrated into the management structure, with appropriate access to the CEO and the board of directors when needed.

- 4 -

BOGUS RESUMES AND INVENTED IDENTITIES

"Lying is the first step to the gallows."

German proverb

English nannies used to tell children that blisters would grow on their tongues every time they told a lie. If only it were so. Today the restraints on lying and dissembling have grown weak and inconsequential. From Bill Clinton's "I didn't have sex with that woman" to Enron's bogus profits and Jason Blair's faked stories at the *New York Times*, lying has pervaded all aspects of contemporary society. Others have described lying as spin, or the intentional manipulation of the truth. In the inscription to this author of his book *Spin This!*, Bill Press wrote, "Spin is just a fancy word for bullshit."

Nowhere has lying become more of a problem than in connection with background information. What once was regarded as mere "padding" has blossomed into outright fraud and gross distortion of resumes. By some accounts, more than 38 percent of all resumes contain some misstatement of fact and it is estimated that 17 percent of all employees probably hold some kind of phony credential.[30] The

---

30 ChoicePoint Asset Company indicates that 67% of the resumes they examine have some kind of inaccurate information. See: Mike Aamodt, "How Common is Resume Fraud," *Assessment Council News*, Feb. 2003, p. 7. See also: Michael Kinsman, "Resume Fraud Rampant in the Work Force," *Employment Crossing*, no date. Kinsman states that "Estimates range between 30 and 50% of American workers have lies on their resume." According to *The Wall Street Journal*, "The percentage of executive candidates misrepresenting their education credentials was 16.7% in 1999, says Jude M. Werra & Associates. That's higher than the 14.6% fibbing average over the previous three years,

situation is so serious that some business schools, like the University of California at Berkeley and the Wharton School at the University of Pennsylvania, are now conducting background checks on applicants for admission. A spokesman for Berkeley indicated that five percent of the initial hundred students admitted into its fall 2003 class were subsequently rejected when misstatements of fact were discovered on their resumes. In 2010, 23-year old Adam Wheeler withdrew from Harvard University just before he was to graduate. It turned out that Wheeler had reinvented himself after being suspended from Bowdoin College for academic dishonesty. He subsequently applied to Harvard, claiming a perfect 1600 SAT score. He also said he was a published author and spoke four languages: Old English, French, Armenian, and Old Persian. Of course, he had done none of those things and Harvard apparently didn't look very deeply into his background, even though he was given substantial financial assistance. He was exposed as a fraud only when he applied for a Rhodes scholarship and forged letters of recommendation. Prosecutors charged him with defrauding Harvard and he was ordered held on $5000 bond.

A few years ago, I received a call from a prominent venture capitalist (VC) in New York. He said that he had attended a reception for the new CEO of a company in which his firm had an investment. The man was supposedly a highly-successful "turn around" artist, who had taken the helm of a number of troubled companies and returned them to profitability. The problem, however, said the VC, was something the man had said to him at the reception. "Don't you ever want to do more than just turn a company around?" the VC had asked him. "You know, stay with it, see it grow and prosper?"

The new CEO, he said, sidled up to him and, in a hushed voice, replied, "Of course I would. But I can't. You see, I used to be in the Teams and the Agency won't let me stay anywhere for very long. I have to keep moving."

The VC wanted to know if this sounded legitimate. My immediate response was that it did not; in fact, it sounded like a complete crock. I asked if they had done any due diligence on the individual, and was informed that it had been cursory at best. Thus, upon my

---

says the Milwaukee-area executive-search firm." See *The Wall Street Journal*, February 1, 2002.

recommendation we launched a thorough background investigation of the new CEO. What we found was shocking.

On his half-page resume, he claimed to have been affiliated with nearly two-dozen companies, including a stint as CFO at DHL. Since DHL's former COO was an old friend and former Air America pilot, whose tenure overlapped that of the individual in question, I gave him a call. He didn't remember the man. "You would have thought I'd remember him if he'd been my CFO," he told me with a laugh.

Once it was established that he had lied about his DHL affiliation, we began examining every fact on his resume. What eventually emerged was that the man was a total and complete fraud, a loser who had reinvented himself in the late eighties as a successful businessman and turn-around specialist. For the next decade or so, he had parlayed his bogus resume into a number of real positions, without anyone ever apparently taking the time to check out even the most rudimentary details.

Instead of an MBA, he had a few undergraduate credits at a third-rate university. Contrary to what he had alleged on his resume, he had never been a midshipman in the U.S. Navy (in fact, he had spelled it "Mid-Shipman," with a hyphen) or a member of the "Teams," implying that he had been a Navy SEAL. He misidentified the U.S. military's post-graduate language school in Monterrey, claiming that it was operated by the U.S. Navy when, in fact, it is run by the U.S. Army.

Most egregious of all, he had actually invented the existence of some of the high-tech companies that he had supposedly turned around, and lied about his affiliation with others. In the few cases where it could be verified that he actually worked for a real company, his role was other than he had portrayed it. Finally, we discovered that he had millions of dollars of tax liens against him. The one relatively smart move he had made was to live in a ski resort community, where people tend to be rather transient and a person's background is whatever they want it to be.

In short, the would-be turn-around artist was, in reality, a con artist, with qualifications closer to a mail room employee than a CEO. But perhaps the most unbelievable part of the story was that the largest backer of the company that had hired the bogus CEO wanted to keep him, despite the damning report and contrary to the wishes of the VC. It wouldn't be until more than a year later that we received a message from the company backers that they wished they had listened to us, since the bogus CEO had mismanaged the company into bankruptcy.

Fox Television's "Who Wants to Marry a Multi-Millionaire?" is another cautionary tale for every senior corporate officer in America. Fifty wannabe brides lined up to marry a supposed multi-millionaire they had never seen before. The would-be groom, a 42-year old "real estate investor and motivational speaker" named Rick Rockwell was supposed to choose the woman of his dreams and then marry her on camera; and presumably the handsome couple would live happily ever after. But it was not to be.

While the show drew an enormous audience and was a financial homerun for Fox, there was only one problem: the groom had, at the very least, some questionable things in his background. At the very worst, he was a total fraud.

While several million dollars doesn't buy as much as it once did, Rockwell either was not a millionaire, in any real sense of the word, or was extremely frugal. He lived in a 1,200 square foot house in Encinitas, California, with--in the best Dogpatch tradition--two broken toilets in the back yard. His millions were supposedly tied up in real estate in Vancouver, Canada, but he never produced any evidence that the real estate existed or had the value he alleged. More seriously, it turned out that in 1991 an ex-fiancée, Debbie Goyne, had been able to get a restraining order against Rockwell prohibiting him from coming within 100 yards of her. She told the court that Rockwell had struck her and also made threats against her.

Fox had planned to air "Who Wants to Marry a Multi-Millionaire?" a second time and make it a regular part of their evening lineup, but when the revelations about Rockwell came out they were forced to pull the show. The network lost millions of dollars in potential revenue and saw their franchise tarnished.

This all happened because no real background checks were performed on Rockwell or, if they were, they were incompetent. It should have been clear from the outset to the producers of the show and the Fox executives who gave it a green light that the one thing that could sink "Who Wants to Marry a Multi-Millionaire?" was for the bride or the groom to turn out to be flawed or a fraud. This would destroy the Cinderella-like character of the show, especially to the huge female viewing audience that tuned in.

Proving that Fox executives have an endless capacity for being surprised, four of the thirty-two finalists for the first season of Fox's immensely popular "American Idol" program turned out to have had serious personal issues, including problems with the law. One contestant was kicked off the program after it discovered that he had been in a barroom brawl where a patron had been killed. Another had been arrested on a felony theft charge and a third had appeared on a kiddie porn website. But the most embarrassing incident involved a contestant named Corey Clark who, it turned out, had been arrested on battery charges for assaulting four police officers and his 15-year old sister. According to the network, Clark's criminal charges and pending trial had not been discovered during his background check because the police had misspelled his name when he was booked. Apparently Clark had also been sued by Wal-Mart for passing bad checks. Producers of "Joe Millionaire" were similarly surprised to learn that one of their contestants had starred in a series of bondage movies.

But while the entire Fox debacle was entirely preventable, it is not surprising. Few companies or organizations adequately screen the backgrounds of employees, executives, business associates, and others with whom they come into contact or on whom they often bet the house. As a consequence, they regularly pay a steep price for their failure to do so.

Take the case of Martin Frankel. Frankel scammed a number of insurance companies for more than $200 million before he was unmasked in 1999. He had begun as a stock trader in the mid-1980s in Toledo, Ohio. Although he described himself as a "genius," with an I.Q. of 194, who had made millions for his clients, there is no evidence to support either assertion. Yet, based on his totally fraudulent claims as a brilliant investor, insurance companies in at least three southern states gave him millions to invest on their behalf. Apparently none of the companies did any real due diligence on Frankel. Instead of investing the money, he stole it, diverting much of it into off-shore bank accounts and using the rest to sustain a lavish and very kinky lifestyle.

What is so remarkable about Frankel is the large number of prominent people he managed to hoodwink. The first prominent individual taken in by Frankel was Thomas Corbally, a business consultant with close ties to what was then known as Kroll-O'Gara, one of the country's leading detective agencies. Not only did Corbally apparently fail to conduct a proper investigation of Frankel, but according to the *New York Times*, he "opened his Rolodex to Frankel."[31]

At Corbally's suggestion, Frankel retained Akin, Gump as one of his law firms and used the prestige of Washington insider, Robert Strauss, a member of the firm, to further his nefarious activities. Although a Denver-based law firm had earlier dropped Frankel as a client because he didn't check out, Akin, Gump had no such qualms, presumably because they only performed a superficial background check on Frankel and his companies, if any at all. It was also suggested in the media that Akin, Gump might have been more interested in the large fees that could be generated from Frankel than in his pedigree.

In addition to Strauss, Frankel developed relationships with Thomas Bolan, partner of the late Roy Cohn, and Father Christopher Zielinski, a prominent Catholic priest. Although Jewish, Frankel offered Zielinski a $50 million donation to his charity in return for his assistance in purchasing insurance companies he intended to loot. To his credit, Zielinski turned him down flat. Others Frankel sought unsuccessfully to cultivate included former CBS anchor Walter Cronkite and former Chrysler CEO Lee Iacocca. Iacocca, however, accepted a ride from Frankel, a man he barely knew, on a leased Gulfstream jet, from Los Angeles to Milan, Italy. This raises the issue, of course, of the apparently low threshold of knowledge the former auto executive required before accepting the hospitality of a stranger.

Once again, the Frankel case illustrates just how willing ostensibly smart people can be to accept others at face value, often to their detriment.

Washington, D.C.'s city government probably holds the record for placing people with bogus credentials in senior positions of trust. Fire Chief, Ronnie Few, resigned after it was revealed that he had listed a degree on his resume that he hadn't earned and had been named "Fire Chief of the Year" by the International Association of Fire Fighters, which does not have any such award. Few had tried to blame the errors on an unidentified staff member at his previous job, but his explanation didn't hold up. The mayor of Augusta, Georgia, where Few had worked prior to being selected for the District job said that he had written Few a sterling letter of recommendation because he had

---

31 "Well-Connected Consultant Linked Suspected Con Man to the Powerful," *New York Times*, June 29, 1999.

wanted to get rid of him. A grand jury investigating Few's tenure as fire chief of the Augusta-Richmond County fire department accused him of "financial misconduct," "out of control spending," "gyping the county," and forging receipts for his moving expenses, among other charges.[32]

Sam Kaiser, general counsel to the District's Chief Financial Officer, resigned and was subsequently charged with embezzlement when it was learned that he neither possessed a law license or even a law degree. His resume, by contrast, indicated he had received a law degree from Cambridge University and was a member of the bar in both New York and Washington. Kaiser was sentenced to four-and-a-half years in prison and ordered to pay $514,000 in restitution. The city's manager of its Parks and Recreation Department also inflated his resume with bogus credentials and phony job titles.

St. Martin's Press was embarrassed in 1999 when it published a controversial book by J.H. Hatfield alleging that then-Governor George W. Bush had been arrested for cocaine possession in 1972. Far from being a respected journalist, the way he was portrayed by St. Martin's, Hatfield was an ex-con who had spent nearly five years in prison for trying to hire someone to murder his boss. He had provided no proof of his allegation about Bush and once his credibility was impeached, St. Martin's was forced to recall the book, a costly and embarrassing business decision. Sally Richardson, the president and publisher of St. Martin's trade division, said, "We didn't suspect for a minute. We had no idea."[33] In reviewing Richardson's remarks, one would have thought any due diligence about Hatfield would have been an invasion of his privacy, irrespective of how outrageous his allegations about a then-presidential candidate. Hatfield died of a drug overdose in an Arkansas motel room in July, 2001.

The list goes on and on. In 1998, Octagon Inc., a Reston, Virginia, company was bilked out of $1.3 million by a con man, James Khan (no pun intended, I'm sure), whose real name was Jamshid Hashemi Naini, who purportedly offered to broker a deal to sell Iran $72.6 million

---

32 "Few Called 'Problem Employee' in Georgia," *The Washington Post*, July 11, 2002, p. B3.

33 Sally Richardson, quoted in "The Ex-Con and the Bush Book," *Newsweek*, Nov. 1, 1999.

worth of satellite phones. Octagon reluctantly hired a private investigator to look into Khan's background, but only after it had already put up a deposit of $1,265,000, which Khan had diverted to another bank account. In a feeble attempt to justify his incompetence, Octagon's chief executive, John Thomas Royall, said, "If you think Octagon was stupid for doing the deal, there were a lot of other companies just as stupid."[34]

Equally fatuous was the statement made by William R. Hazard, a founding partner of the recruiting firm of Hazard, Young, Attea & Associates, after his company failed to properly check out the background of one of its candidates for the Montgomery County, Maryland, superintendent of schools. "We try very hard to avoid this kind of surprising revelation...but it's incredibly difficult," said Hazard, after it was revealed that Elfreda W. Massie had not disclosed a history of financial problems, including personal bankruptcies.[35] By contrast to Hazard's assertion, a basic background check that would have revealed Massie's financial history would have cost a few hundred dollars or less and is not difficult at all. The Hazard firm, according to the *Washington Post*, has a history of failing to properly scrutinize its candidates, despite the fact that its searches can cost as much as $60,000.[36] The Episcopal Bishop of Atlanta, Rev. Robert G. Trache, who had been elected bishop six months before, was dismissed in March, 2000, when it was discovered that he had filed for Chapter 7 personal bankruptcy after running up debts of $122,000. A standing committee of the Episcopal diocese, charged with overseeing the election of a new bishop, claimed that a 15-year background check and psychiatric evaluation had been performed on Trache, but apparently did not identify his financial problems.

If you are not convinced already of the need to perform some kind of due diligence on everyone who works for your company, then consider the following examples as well:

---

34 John Thomas Royall, quoted in "Encounter With Global Con Artist Left Reston Firm Reeling," *The Washington Post*, Jan. 23, 1999.

35 "School Chief Searches Not Perfect, Firm Says," *The Washington Post*, May 5, 1999.

36 *Ibid.*

⅄ A 27-year old man enrolled at a Catholic high school in the Washington, D.C., area and claimed to be Director Steven Spielberg's nephew. His impersonation succeeded for a year and a half, during which time he made a one-hour vanity film in which he played a transvestite trying to pass as a woman in a lesbian bar. I'm serious. He was arrested for possession of child pornography, misrepresenting his age to school officials, sexually assaulting a teenage boy, and contributing to the delinquency of a minor girl.

⅄ A Boston lawyer named Stephen Fagan abducted his two daughters during a custody dispute and fled to Florida. Adopting the name, Dr. William Martin, he claimed to be a Harvard-trained psychiatrist and married first one, then another, well-to-do woman who apparently supported him. Far from being a Harvard graduate, Fagan had graduated from Suffolk University and failed the bar exam five times before finally passing. A fixture of the Palm Beach social scene, his ruse lasted for two decades before his real identity was discovered.

⅄ Christopher Rocancourt, who masqueraded for years as "Christopher Rockefeller," was arrested and charged with impersonating a member of their Rockefeller family in order to bilk gullible acquaintances out more than $1.5 million. Far from being a scion of the well-known family, Rocancourt was the uneducated son of a French prostitute, but he was able to scam enough people to live like an international playboy "in New York and Los Angeles, where he kept the keys to the Wilshire apartment in his pocket, a Ferrari in the garage and a genuine Penthouse pet for a wife."[37]

⅄ Pat Buchanan was surprised to learn that his hand-picked Reform Party running mate in the 2000 presidential race, Ezola Poster, was a member of the ultra-right John Birch Society.

⅄ Dr. Michael Swango may have been the most deadly serial killer of all time, facilitated at every step by an indifferent medical establishment and the failure of virtually every institution he worked for to check his past. Not only did he regularly

---

37 "Playboy Lifestyle Sputters to a Halt For Fake Rockefeller," *The Age* (Melbourne), April 18, 2003.

misrepresent his background, but he routinely failed to note such things as his criminal conviction for the non-fatal poisoning of co-workers on an ambulance crew in Quincy, Illinois, and the fact that his medical license had been suspended. After he was released from prison, he was certified as a paramedic in Virginia. Ultimately, the University of South Dakota named him to a residency in internal medicine solely on the basis of his less-than-candid resume. His residency there only ended when "The Justice Files" featured him on one of its shows. Despite a trail of dead bodies, he subsequently was hired by a VA hospital, the State University of New York at Stony Brook and, finally, a mission hospital in Zimbabwe. When he came under suspicion of killing patients at the mission hospital, he landed a job as a physician in Saudi Arabia, but was arrested when he returned to the U.S. to obtain his visa.[38]

A so-called expert in the epidemiology of burns and executive director of the National Burn Victim Foundation, who purported to have a variety of university degrees and often worked as a plaintiff's witness in court cases, plead guilty to misrepresenting his background in Prince William County, Virginia. Under oath Gary S. Stocco repeatedly testified that he had investigated hundreds of child-abuse cases and attended surgical procedures for burn victims.[39] In reality, Stocco was a former state police officer and parking lot security guard who "hadn't been involved in any criminal investigations or surgeries." In fact, he didn't even have a college degree.

---

38 Dr. Harold Shipman, a "well-loved family doctor" in Hyde, England, is believed to have murdered more than 300 patients with lethal injections. His crimes came to light only when another physician became suspicious due to all of the death certificates Shipman needed cosigned. A computerized tracking system might have called attention to Shipman years earlier. See: "Could Better Monitoring Have Stopped a Homicidal Doctor?", *U.S. News & World Report*, January 22, 2001.

39 "Roving Burn 'Expert' Was False Witness," *The Washington Post*, November 3, 2000.

⅄ The *Louisville Courier-Journal* reported that a local attorney had become an English barrister and had been recruited to assist in the prosecution of Serbian war criminals at the World Court. The story, however, was fictitious.

⅄ In 2008, a phony aircraft engineer employed by Qantas Airways was sent to prison for nearly three-and-a-half years for endangering the lives of passengers by performing highly sensitive safety checks.

⅄ The United Nations confirmed that it had not checked the background of a weapons inspector who lacked a four-year college degree and headed a number of sadomasochistic sex societies. He had been a founding officer of the Leather Leadership Conference, a former chairman of the National Coalition for Sexual Freedom, and a co-founder and past president of the Black Rose, described as a "pan-sexual S&M group." While Jack McGeorge, a former Marine and EOD specialist, may have been able to contribute to the inspection process in a number of ways, his presence as an inspector was a embarrassment to both the U.N. and the U.S. State Department at a time when the Bush Administration was deeply committed to ensuring that the inspections process in Iraq was as credible as possible. The U.N. subsequently acknowledged that it had not conducted back-ground checks on any of the inspectors.

⅄ Shareholders of vitamin maker PDK Labs learned that their former chairman had plead guilty to securities fraud only after federal prosecutors unsealed guilty pleas from an earlier stock manipulation case. The ex-chairman, Michael Krasnoff, not only was still on PDK Labs' payroll as a consultant, but he had also admitted to defrauding the company of $2 million through a series of kickbacks.

A major target of one of our investigations into corporate mismanagement, when asked about apparent discrepancies in his background, angrily retorted, "You don't investigate people at my level." We knew we had him at that moment, and it turned out that he had, indeed, invented much of his personal history.

Even Iran's president, the Holocaust denying Mahmoud Ahmadinejad, has been tripped up by a resume padding scandal. In

2008, it was revealed that his close ally and choice for Interior Minister, Ali Kordan, didn't really possess a law degree from Oxford University, despite the fact that Kordan had apparently circulated forged copies of the degree to members of parliament and the media. Kordan was eventually impeached by the parliament, but not before an aide to Ahmadinejad was fired for trying to bribe lawmakers to withdraw their opposition to Kordan.[40]

THE "I'LL HAVE TO KILL YOU IF I TELL YOU" PLOY

The creation of false identities has long been a staple of the intelligence world and spy novels and movies. In the past two decades, Soviet/Russian agents were arrested in New Zealand and Finland trying to obtain passports in the names of citizens of those two countries. Several Israeli agents, who were weak on trade-craft, also were detained in New Zealand for attempting to acquire birth certificates and other documentation needed to obtain passports.

The opening paragraphs of this chapter described a bogus CEO who tried to deflect questions about his background by inferring that he had worked for the U.S. special operations and intelligence communities. This is a ruse that people fall for over and over again. Perhaps one of the most amazing tales involved Ronald Carl von Neumann, a shadowy Washington-area figure, who claimed to have been a former intelligence agent, U.S. Marine, and Ivy-League educated attorney. None of it was true. Von Neumann defrauded dozens of people in a variety of scams ranging from practicing law without a license to hustling immigration cases and selling his supposed "influence" with powerful Washington figures. After von Neumann was arrested and his fingerprints sent to the FBI, it turned out that he was, in reality, Reufus Leinson Cail, a habitual criminal with a history of more than twenty arrests for forgery, embezzlement, and fraud. He had even lied about his race; instead of being a Caucasian, he was, in reality, a light-skinned African American.

He had reinvented himself sometime in the mid-1980s, adopting a new name, a new history, a new racial identity, and acquiring a D.C. Bar card by exploiting a loophole in the law that automatically granted membership in the bar to lawyers who practiced in the city prior to

---

40 Ali Larijani, "Iran Minister Impeached Over False Degree," *CNN World*, Nov. 4, 2008.

1972, when the D.C. Bar was created. Whenever he was questioned too intensely about his background, he would lower his voice and claim he'd been an intelligence operative and could say no more. Even after his arrest and conviction, he continued to maintain that he had "worked in the intelligence field."[41]

In addition to phony degrees and other paraphernalia, von Neumann created a "vanity wall" of photos of himself with powerful figures like George Bush Sr., Jimmy Carter, Gen. Norman Schwarzkopf, and others by buying tickets to Washington fund raisers and inaugural balls.

Another bogus CIA con man was Oswald LeWinter, who claimed to have been a former intelligence agent in order to pull off numerous swindles. One of the key sources for the now discredited "October Surprise," LeWinter was later repudiated by Gary Sick and others who had originally maintained that the release of American hostages in Iran had been delayed to ensure the election of Ronald Reagan as president. LeWinter apparently attempted to con Harrods owner, Mohammed Fayed, into believing that his son Dodi had been killed, along with Princess Diana, by British intelligence agents, using the Israeli Mossad as their instrument. According to LeWinter, who wanted $15 million for documents that would "irrefutably" prove the so-called conspiracy, the Royal family was behind the plot and had tasked MI6 to kill the young couple because they were outraged by the Princess' relationship with the Egyptian playboy. LeWinter surfaces over and over during the past quarter century selling one whacked-out conspiracy theory after another to the gullible, from attempts to divert the finger of suspicion away from Libya in the Pan Am 103 bombing case to his claim to have been the CIA's former deputy director of counterespionage with intimate knowledge of the assassination of President Kennedy.[42] During his career as a con artist, he posed as

---

41 Ronald Carl von Neumann, Dateline NBC transcript, "The Imposter?; A Man Who Posed As An Influential Washington, D.C. Lawyer is Revealed as a Con Man," January 10, 1999, p. 9.

42 There are many articles about LeWinter, but one of the best and most entertaining is, "Tinker, Tailor, Poet, Spy?," *The Washington Post*, Feb. 15, 2001. Regarding conspiracy theories, he many have been correct that Libya was not the major perpetrator of the Pan Am 103 bombing, but his theory of why they weren't is totally without merit.

everything from a Marine to a New York police detective and a fully accredited ambassador of the Sovereign Order of the Knights of Malta.

Finally, there's the strange case of the late John Patrick Savage. Savage maintained he was the CIA's deputy director of European Affairs and purported to be running a number of covert projects overseas. Taking a page from dozens of Nigerian scams, he told would-be marks that he had access to billions of dollars in secret funds deposited in foreign banks by Philippine dictator Ferdinand Marcos and other tyrants that was needed for vital CIA operations. In order to keep the transactions completely confidential, he said he required money from private sources to facilitate the unfreezing of the hidden assets. Anyone who put up a modest amount of money for a short time would be guaranteed a sizable return on their investment.

When I met him, at the behest of a client who was interested in doing business with Savage, he used a variation on the same theme, describing himself as an investment banker and CIA operative who had made millions using a brilliant scheme he had devised. With a straight face, Savage described how tens of millions of dollars were left behind every day in banking accounts around the globe because of rounding errors. He had developed a methodology to collect all of those bits and pieces, he alleged, and it had made him an enormously rich man. I asked him, as a purported English banker, a question about LIBOR, the London investment bankers overnight rate, but he only stared back in bewilderment. So much for his knowledge of banking. I advised my client that Savage was probably a con man and that he should stay away from him.

And the problem is not confined to the U.S. At any one time there are any number of Israeli con men crisscrossing the globe, all posing as former members of the Mossad or Israeli special operations units. One of the most brazen is Ari Ben-Menashe, who has on various occasions claimed to have led the bold Israeli raid on Entebbe to rescue the passengers of a hijacked French jetliner in 1976 and to have been the inside man in the destruction of the Iraqi nuclear reactor at Osirak in 1981. In reality, he is a swindler who has conned Third World countries out of millions during the past two decades, including the government of Zambia which allegedly paid him $7 million for grain that was never received. His most recent scam involved Zimbabwe's strongman Robert Mugabe. According to published sources, he was behind the treason charge filed against Mugabe's foe in the last election, Morgan Tsvangirai. Ben-Menashe's Canadian-based PR company was reportedly retained by Mugabe for a fee of $1 million to set up Tsvangirai by luring him to a videotaped meeting under false pretenses. Although Tsvangirai stormed out of the meeting after Ben-Menashe began discussing Mugabe's elimination, the videotape was cited as evidence of a treasonous conspiracy and Tsvangirai was arrested.[43]

There is an old saying around Washington that former intelligence agents, especially CIA veterans, get the best and most lavish obituaries when they die. This is a tradition that has evolved over the years in recognition of the fact that intelligence officers are generally forced to live anonymously while alive, and therefore it's only fair they receive proper acknowledgment and recognition in death. By the same token, once an intelligence officer has retired, it is--with a handful of exceptions--possible to verify that they once worked in an intelligence capacity. No details will be forthcoming from the Agency, other than the were employed there, but most retired officers, even from the Directorate of Operations (DO), will provide basic information about their careers on their resume. In addition, the intelligence community is very tight and it is generally possible to authenticate a person's bona fides by speaking to others with verifiable intelligence backgrounds.

With respect to active duty members of intelligence agencies, most will not acknowledge their profession, especially if they are involved in operations. To do so could jeopardize them, or their colleagues, if they are working undercover. The public should also beware of anyone purporting to be acting on behalf of a spy agency in a business capacity. Most are con men. Intelligence officers rarely, if ever, need to tell those on the outside of their affiliation to the secret world.

Along the same lines, dozens of Americans are exposed every year for falsely claiming to have served in the military or exaggerating their service records. After a mortician from Maryland was murdered by his gay lover, it was discovered that he passed himself off for years as a retired Army general. He even marched in local parades in full uniform with ribbons on his chest and was active in civic associations and local Democratic party politics. In reality he had joined the Army as an

---

43 For more on Ari Ben-Menashe, see "Of Liars and Lives," *The Review* (Australia), April, 2003, p. 22.

enlisted man and served three years as a cook, never rising above the rank of Specialist.

Connecticut Attorney General, Richard Blumenthal, was exposed for falsely claiming to be a Vietnam veteran during his race for the U.S. Senate in 2010. He repeatedly spoke of his service in Vietnam to veterans and other groups, telling one audience that, "We have learned something important since the days I served in Vietnam."[44] In reality, the popular Democrat had received five deferments and joined the Marine Corps Reserve in 1970. Blumenthal reportedly lied about being Captain of his college swim team as well.

Pulitzer Price winner and Mount Holyoke professor, Joe Ellis, suffered public humiliation for having maintained, for many years, that he had served in Vietnam, including a stint on the staff of American commander Gen. William C. Westmoreland. While he had served in the U.S. Army, Ellis had taught at West Point and never been deployed outside the country. Toronto Blue Jays' manager, Tim Johnson, also falsely claimed he had served in Vietnam.

A Washington, D.C., man pleaded guilty in 2001 to impersonating a U.S. Air Force Major.[45] So convincing was his act that Jeffrey A. Klotz was even able to check out M-16 rifles, pistols, and vehicles from an Army Reserve depot. He also reportedly rode around Andrews Air Force Base in fire trucks assigned to protect Air Force One. In the late 1990s, another phony Air Force officer, who generally called himself Lt. Col. Lamar Reed, swindled more than $50 million from European companies that thought they were supplying equipment to the U.S. military for a top secret project. With little more than a phony letterhead, military uniform, mail drop, and hired black limo with NATO flags, Reed first conned Electronic Data Systems (EDS), and subsequently a string of other firms, by holding out the prospect of billions of dollars of potential business if they cooperated with him. The fictitious Reed was successful despite the fact that he sported a blonde ponytail beneath his military cap, a very unmilitary touch. Reed turned out to be Anthony Errol Marsden, a man with more than fifty aliases, who had been born in California in 1953 and prepared for his scam with bit parts in movies.

---

44 "More Blumenthal Claims on Vietnam Emerge," New York Times, May 22, 2010.

45 The actual charge was making a false official statement.

In their landmark book, *Stolen Valor*, B.G. Burkett and Glenna Whitley document hundreds of cases of bogus Vietnam vets, Medal of Honor winners, and Navy SEALs, including the story of the supposedly sixteen year old Navy SEAL assassin from Vietnam who conned Dan Rather and CBS. "At age sixteen," Rather told the viewing audience of a highly-promoted one-hour documentary special, "Steve was a Navy SEAL, trained to assassinate. For almost two years, he operated behind enemy lines then he broke. He came home in a straitjacket, addicted to alcohol and drugs."[46] As Burkett and Whitley point out, Steve was a SEAL and an assassin only in his imagination. In reality, he had joined the U.S. Navy at the age of seventeen and "was an 'internal communications repairman' assigned to rear area bases." It was the height of irresponsibility that CBS had gone forward with Steve's tale without conclusively verifying his background.

There are so many phony SEALs that the SEAL alumni organization, VeriSEAL, has posted a "Wall of Shame" on its web site dedicated to publicizing bogus SEALs. In 1999, a former SEAL, Bob Wiegand, was operating an internet store from his home selling SEAL memorabilia, when he was approached by a man named Rob Kane. Kane claimed to have been a member of SEAL Team 6, the organization's first dedicated anti-terrorism unit which carried out the mission that killed Osama bin Laden. Kane alleged that during his time on active duty he had won the Navy Cross, the Silver Star, the Bronze Star, and a Purple Heart.[47] He purchased a number of items from Wiegand, including SEAL tee-shirts, hats, and a flight jacket.[48]

Kane, it turned out, was a con man. When Wiegand later visited Kane's office in Anchorage, he discovered that his office was a shrine to Navy SEALs, decorated with all of the items he had earlier purchased from him. Wiegand said that Kane had "invented" a whole

---

46 B.G.Burkett and Glenna Whitley, *Stolen Valor*, (Dallas, Texas: Verity Press, 1998), p. 88.

47 Since the end of the Vietnam War, at last check only two Navy Crosses, the second highest award for valor after the Congressional Medal of Honor, had been awarded to Navy SEALs, and one was posthumous.

48 "Mystery Man," *Anchorage Daily News*, June 25, 2006.

persona based on his phony career as a SEAL. "That was his pitch to everyone," said Wiegand, "that he was a Navy SEAL."[49]

Ultimately Kane lured Wiegand into a crazy expedition, allegedly funded by George W. Bush, to find the so-called Yamashita gold in the Philippines, a common scam described in more detail in Chapter Five. Wiegand was hired, along with a number of other U.S. military veterans, to provide security for the mission but he returned to the U.S. after only two weeks in the Philippines because of his skepticism about the whole operation. Wiegand remains bitter about Kane's deception. "The nicest thing I can say is that he is a big phony and I'd be happy to interview him with you [the reporter] in any alley."[50]

According to Burkett and Whitley's research, even some of the most poignant photographic images of weeping vets at the "Wall" [the Vietnam Memorial in Washington] are actually of imposters. This has, say the authors, robbed a generation of both its history and its heroes. Indeed, every phony serviceman and woman is a disgrace to the country, but even more is an embarrassment to those who put their trust and faith in them in the civilian world.[51]

PHONY DEGREES & CREDENTIALS

Phony college degrees are a national plague. Sandra Baldwin resigned in 2002 as president of the U.S. Olympic Committee after it was learned, contrary to her resume, that she had not graduated from the University of Colorado nor did she hold a Ph.D. from Arizona State. Less than twenty-four hours after being named Vanderbilt's women's basketball coach, Tom Collen resigned after reports surfaced that he had not earned the two masters degrees listed on his resume. Collen fatuously defended himself by stating that he always believed he had received the two degrees. "There was never any intention to

---

49 *Ibid.*

50 *Ibid.*

51 Another veteran who did yeoman's work exposing bogus medal winners was the late Marine Corps Colonel, Mitchell Page. Colonel Page, who was awarded the Medal of Honor at Guadalcanal during World War Two headed a national crusade to expose those who falsely claimed to have won the Medal of Honor. In 1994, at Colonel Page's urging, Congress passed legislation increasing the penalty for selling a Medal of Honor.

deceive anybody," he said. "It was just a mistake that was never caught."[52] Yeah, right. Five months earlier, George O'Leary, had been booted as coach of Notre Dame for falsely claiming he had a master's degree and had received three football letters at the University of New Hampshire. The real story was that he had dropped out of the university after only two years and had never actually played in a game. Notre Dame's president, in an embarrassing and wholly gratuitous statement, defended the search process, saying, "This was a vigorous process. We can tell you everything about [the candidates'] background."[53]

California's first poet laureate, Quincy Troupe, also resigned because of a doctored resume. He claimed to have been a college graduate, but wasn't. Ditto Mike Freeman, a long-time sportswriter for the *New York Times* who claimed to have graduated from the University of Delaware when he left to join the *Indianapolis Star*. He hadn't. What's more embarrassing was that the *Indianapolis Star* apparently conducted better research on Mr. Freeman's background than the *New York Times*.

Employers must also beware of job applicants and employees with mail order degrees. Everything from a Ph.D. to law and medical degrees can be purchased, often for under one hundred dollars, from unaccredited mail order "universities," most of which are just mail drops or seedy offices. In one survey, *Government Computer News* found more than fifty government contractors, mostly in technology disciplines, with suspect credentials. When confronted with their deceit, some recipients of mail order degrees try to dissemble or simply bluff their way out of their dilemma. Take, for example, the case of Massachusetts infectious disease lab chief, Ralph Timperi, who bought a Ph.D. from a diploma mill for $499.00. "I briefly used the Ph.D. designation," Timperi told colleagues in an email, "not to mislead, but because I thought I had earned it."[54] If that's the case, Timperi is either too dishonest or too dumb to be running an infectious disease lab.

---

52 "Collen Quits at Vanderbilt Because of Resume Errors," *USA Today*, March 5, 2002.

53 "O'Leary Resigns as Coach at Notre Dame"; *The Washington Post*; December 15, 2001; p. D1.

54 *Newsweek*, November 24, 2003, p. 29.

Because teachers and other government employees often receive raises and preferential promotion treatment if they can increase their educational attainments, diploma mills are doing a brisk business trafficking phony degrees to dishonest civil servants. And in some cases, the taxpayer has even paid for the bogus degrees, under a federal provision that allowed agency chiefs to authorize such payments in order to recruit or retain an employee.[55] The General Accounting Office, in a report to Congress, found that 463 "students" at just three unaccredited institutions of supposedly "higher learning" identified themselves as employees of the U.S. federal government.[56]

GAO investigators typically found that diploma mills "frequently use names similar to those used by accredited schools, which often allows the diploma mills to be mistaken for accredited schools. For example, Hamilton University of Evanston, Wyoming, has a name similar to Hamilton College, a fully accredited school in Clinton, New York."[57] On their resumes the devious government employee, and his private sector counterpart, will often just list the degree and the university as "Hamilton," not differentiating between the accredited school and its suspect imitator.

The GAO investigation covered only a very small sample population of unaccredited schools, but their findings were disturbing. They found that most diploma mills--such as Barrington University (Mobile, Alabama), Lacrosse University (Bay St. Louis, Mississippi), and Pacific Western University (Los Angeles, California)--awared degrees based on life experiences and required no classroom instruction. Others required only a few research projects or papers. One federal government employee described his Master's degree from a diploma mill as "joke," saying he had received it after paying the school $5000.00.[58]

---

55 The Homeland Security Act amended Section 4107 of title 5, U.S. Code, by restricting such reimbursements to degrees from accredited institutions.

56 Robert J. Cramer of the U.S. General Accounting Office, testimony before the Committee on Governmental Affairs of the U.S. Senate, "Diploma Mills: Federal Employees Have Obtained Degrees from Diploma Mills and Other Unaccredited Schools, Some at Government Expense," May 11, 2004, p. 2.

57 *Ibid.,* p. 7.

58 *Ibid.,* p. 7-8.

The notorious internet serial killer, John Robinson, created numerous on-line identities and manufactured phony degrees and credentials whenever he needed them. According to John Douglas and Stephen Singular, "...he'd covered the walls of his office with official-looking documents detailing his credentials (nobody at the facility realized that all of them had been forged from a boxful of blank certificates; whenever he needed a new degree or qualification, he simply pulled one from the box and wrote on it whatever he wanted to)."[59] Today, given color copiers and digital photography, virtually any certificate or identification card can easily be forged. And for those who want a shortcut, a number of mail-order catalogs offer official-looking, but bogus, ID cards of every possible variety. "For a small fee, or often for free, Internet users can download programs or buy software that will print driver's licenses, birth certificates, immigration cards, job certificates, and school transcripts," writes Carolyn E. Mayer.[60] Some of the sites even offer IDs with holograms, bar codes, high-definition printing and magnetic strip encoding, and other security features.

Last time this author checked, there were more than 21 million results on Google under the heading "Counterfeit IDs." One site advertises, "We sell state ID cards of every US state." Another site offers, "only high-quality fake passports, driver's licenses, ID cards, stamps and other products for a number of countries like Australia, Austria, Belgium, Brazil, Canada, Israel, Italia (sic.), Finland, France, Germany, Malaysia, Mexico, Netherlands, New Zealand, South Africa, Spain, Switzerland, UK, USA and others." In 2010, the Government of Bosnia-Herzegovina reported that it had broken up a criminal ring selling fake IDs, including passports, birth certificates, and identity papers for prices up to 2000 Euros.

Even with the templates and technology readily available on the Internet some criminals are just too stupid to get it right. A fake Mississippi driver's license seized during a routine traffic stop from an

---

59 John Douglas and Stephen Singular, *Anyone You Want Me to Be*, (New York: Scribner, 2003), p. 9.

60 Carolyn E. Mayer, "Web Also Revolutionizing ID Fakery; Panel Eyes 'Tremendous Problem' of Counterfeiting Services," *The Washington Post*, May 19, 2000.

illegal alien had a photo of Jose Pacheco and his girlfriend instead of a single head shot.

Some catalogs also sell how-to books on creating phony ID's, awards, and certificates. *Who Are You? The Encyclopedia of Personal Identification*, claims to be, "The first book to reveal the tricks and truths of the identity game from all sides of the Game! Learn how to steal or protect any identity..." Other titles include, *New I.D. in America, The I.D. Forger: Homemade Birth Certificates & Other Documents Explained, Acquiring New I.D., Reborn in the USA, Counterfeit I.D. Made Easy*, and *The Criminal Use of False Identification.*

In years past, someone intent on mischief had to be fairly resourceful to secure a photo of himself with a prominent person. Either they would purchase a ticket to a major fundraiser or, in the case of Lyndon H. LaRouche's cult-like U.S. Labor Party, members would run up to a politician or celebrity in a restaurant or on the street and throw their arm around the shocked target of the scam while a confederate snapped a photo. Now, with the help of computers and digital cameras it's relatively easy to substitute your face for someone else's in a photograph or even insert your image in a photo of a major historic or political event. Thus, just because someone has a wall full of photographs of himself with prominent personages doesn't mean that the photos are genuine.

Catalogs like NIC Law Enforcement Supply will sell you everything from badges to ID cards. The ID card list includes "Certified Appraiser," "Intelligence Officer," "Company President," "Special Weapons Permit," "Firearms Dealer," "Special Investigator," "Bail Enforcement Agent," "Organized Crime Bureau," "Ordained Minister," "Pilot," "Travel Agent," and even "Archaeologist." One can also order a "federal style credential and badge case" for your laminated photo ID's and matching badge. If your goal is to impersonate a CIA officer there is virtually an unlimited array of CIA-branded merchandise available through the mail. Among the special touches for your office are a 8x10 glossy photo of CIA headquarters in Langley, Virginia; a poster with the CIA seal and the legend "America is at Peace Because the CIA is at War!"; a "CIA crest commendation wall plaque"; and a "CIA credo collectors' print"; not to mention a CIA crest mug, a CIA key ring, and CIA folders embossed with "Top Secret," "Classified," and "Special Activities Division," for your desk. There's even a matching wardrobe, whether you want to sport a "classic polo" with a CIA crest, a CIA baseball cap, black sweat shirts, or CIA tee-shirts emblazoned with "Instructor Camp Peary," "Weapons Instructor," or "Staff Langley." So many firms were selling CIA branded material that the Agency, purely out of self-defense, opened its own gift shop at headquarters offering literally hundreds of branded products.

Similar branded products are available with the insignia and logos of the FBI, DEA, the Army's Delta Force, and the U.S. Navy's SEALs. We actually had a phony SEAL come to our headquarters in Washington wearing a gold "Budweiser" around his neck, the distinctive eagle and trident emblem of the U.S. Navy SEALs, which he had bought, presumably, through the mail or in a second-hand shop. He had hatched a scheme to supposedly recover hundreds of millions of dollars in World War Two Philippine bonds allegedly guaranteed by the U.S. government. The bonds could be obtained, of course, for pennies on the dollar, yielding enormous profits to anyone willing to bankroll the scheme. The phony SEAL had contacted a possible investor who, in turn, wanted us to check him out.

As with most con men, the guy had amazing chutzpah. Sporting the gold Budweiser and not batting an eye, he sat across from one of our senior executives, former commander of SEAL Team Three, Gary Stubblefield, and brazenly talked about his career in the Teams. I could see Gary growing more and more tense by the moment as the phony SEAL's lies rolled off his tongue. Finally, Gary asked him the number of his BUD/S Class, the twenty-five week Basic Underwater Demolition/SEAL training course taught at the Naval Amphibious School in Coronado, California. No one ever forgets the number of his BUD/S class and every man forms lifelong bonds with others in his class. "That's classified," replied the imposter. Gary almost came up out of his seat. His answer confirmed, beyond the shadow of a doubt, that he was not the real thing. We quickly showed the man the door.

Among the phonies was the infamous Shawn Eckardt, who was hired by figure skater Tanya Harding to attack her chief rival, Nancy Kerrigan, before Olympic tryouts for a spot on the 1994 U.S. Olympic team. Eckardt clubbed Kerrigan on the knee, and was later arrested and sentenced to 18 months in prison. On his fictitious resume, Eckardt claimed to be CEO of NZUS-Group, a mysterious international security organization that "operates worldwide serving only selected clientele."[61]   He alleged that he had "150 employees...engaged world-wide (sic.) in Executive Protection."[62] According to the biographical material he invented, Eckardt had an engineering degree and worked with the Blackstone Corporation of Switzerland in the early 1980s, whereupon he set up a company called Executive Management International. "Shawn Eckardt," continued his resume, "is today a noted expert on Terrorist Trends and Profiles, Counter-Espionage, and Close Protection Techniques."[63]   None of it, of course, was true, and in reality Eckardt was an overweight loser, fantasist, and wannabe of no verifiable skills or training who even botched an attack with a metal rod on a defenseless female figure skater.   According to authorities, he was attempting to sell his bogus skills to various companies in the Portland, Oregon, area.   He died in 2007 at the age of 40 after changing his name to Brian Sean Griffith in an effort to escape his past.

In the post-9/11 period, the government has finally begun to target so-called "document mills" that sell phony ID cards to anyone with the appropriate amount of cash, often in open air markets around the country.   According to authorities, a phony U.S. residency permit, or green card, can be purchased for as little as eighty dollars.

Many of the purchasers are illegal immigrants eager to acquire fake driver's licenses and Social Security cards.   Others are teenagers and college students desirous of securing ID's that will help them pass as 21 years of age so they can drink in bars and clubs.   But some of the 9/11 terrorists acquired phony identification cards from document rings, and the FBI and other federal agencies want to foreclose that possibility in the future.   In 2002, the U.S. Immigration and Customs Enforcement (ICE) agency launched Operation Card Shark and in the following two years closed down three document mills in the Washington area alone and seized documents valued at $450,000.   Despite such efforts, however, a local D.C. Council member was quoted by *The Washington*

---

61 "A Brief on the NZUS-Group," (date unknown), accompanying a letter to Mr. L.K. Jabang, Minister of the Interior of the Gambia, offering to "train, organize and equip a Head of State Security group for the Gambian government."

62 Appendix 2, Confidential N.Z.U.S. 14, sent to Minister of Interior Jabang of the Gambia.

63 *Ibid.*

Post as saying he drove by one document mill every day. "It's totally blatant," said Council member Jim Graham. "In this age of terrorism, it's a national embarrassment, as well as a national threat. They're selling illegal documents two miles from the White House."[64]

There are more than a half dozen locations in the District of Columbia, according to a knowledgeable source, where illegal immigrants, fugitives, and anyone else can acquire a phony driving license, birth certificate, or green card, and this is true of virtually every major metropolitan area. But even more alarming is the ease with which a real driver's license can be obtained under a false name or alias in some jurisdictions. In 2009, the *Washington Post* ran a front page article regarding how easy it was for undocumented aliens to acquire Maryland driver's licenses. The article described a Parcels Plus store in a suburban shopping center that served as a mail drop for "at least forty-two undocumented immigrants living in states along the Eastern Seaboard to fake a Maryland residence so they could get a driver's license."[65] According to the article, "Along with New Mexico, Hawaii and Washington state, Maryland does not check the immigration status of drivers when they apply for a license. The policy has made the state vulnerable to widespread fraud by illegal immigrants living outside Maryland--as well as to criminals seeking to create false identities..."[66]

In 2008, I was offered real passports for sale from a number of countries, including one in the European community. The price varied, but averaged around $25,000. Similarly, a variety of other authentic IDs are available if you know where to look. In addition to driver's licenses, these include birth certificates, green cards, library cards, and other forms of identification with which to build what is known in the intelligence world as a "legend" or new identity. Unlike the shortcuts and bogus IDs described above, these are infinitely more difficult to ferret out because they are, by contrast, real. And, with the advent of websites like Facebook and MySpace it has become easier than ever to steal another person's identity.

---

64 "Fake IDs Targeted in Raids by U.S. Agents," *The Washington Post*, November 11, 2004, p. B1.

65 Lisa Rein and N.C. Aizenman, "Easy-to-Get Licenses Expose Md. to Fraud," *The Washington Post*, March 28, 2009.

66 *Ibid.*

LIARS EVERYWHERE

Despite the number of new tools, like the Internet, for rapidly accessing information about individuals, the number of people with fictitious backgrounds or identities is growing every day. Some are posting wholly fictitious lives and resumes on their Facebook and My Space sites where they take on a life of their own. Jeffrey Rothfeder, a former national editor of *Bloomberg News*, was about to become CNBC's managing editor when it was discovered he had doctored his academic credentials. Bausch & Lomb confirmed that its CEO, Ronald Zarrella, did not have an M.B.A., as he had claimed. Apparently the company had performed no due diligence on Mr. Zarrella when he was hired. Veritas' CFO, Kenneth Lonchar, resigned in 2002 after it was discovered that he didn't really have an MBA from Stanford Unversity. The company's name, ironically, means "truth" in Latin. Jeff Papows, former CEO of IBM's Lotus Software unit, resigned after reports surfaced that he had falsified his resume with respect to his educational and military background. CEO of MCG Capital, Bryan Mitchell, falsely claimed a degree from Syracuse. RadioShack's CEO, David Edmondson, stepped down after it was revealed, according to <u>Forbes</u>, that his resume was "a-cock-and-bull story." Among other things he claimed to have two degrees he had not earned.[67]

Resume distortion is a national epidemic. As noted at the beginning of the chapter, someplace between 17 percent and nearly 50 percent of all executive candidates distort their resumes in some fashion, and the number is rising. The most common distortion, says David Granger, "is to expand the dates of employment. Al Dunlap did it in the bio he submitted to the 1998 *Who's Who* -- with dates well beyond those that the companies would have reported."[68] He also conveniently forgot to mention on his resume two jobs from which he had been fired.

Top executives are much more likely to cheat on their resumes than other employees, largely because they have longer, more complex, CVs. And the higher one goes, the more likely there are to be errors of fact on a person's resume. The guy who works at an entry level position

---

67 Chris Noon, "RadioShack Names Acting CEO as Edmondson Steps Down," Forbes.com, Feb. 21, 2006.

68 Granger, David; "You Just Hired Him"; *Fortune*, October 29, 2001; p. 205.

generally has a short, succinct resume, affording little room for distortion or misrepresentation.

Prominence and celebrity do not guarantee that a person is telling the truth about his or her background. Former Associate Justice of the Supreme Court, William O. Douglas, lied about many things in his background. He regularly misstated his class rank in law school and the date of his first marriage (so that it wouldn't be apparent that his wife had put him through law school). In addition, he lied about being in the military so that he could be buried in Arlington Cemetery.[69] Vice President Joe Biden also lied about his class standing in law school.[70]

Far more than the embarrassment factor, employers have a real financial stake in making certain that the resumes of those hired have not been exaggerated or distorted. Settlements and court cases have awarded millions of dollars to the victims of people with phony qualifications and those who were victims of crimes carried out by employees who had not been subjected to background checks. Sometimes it's not what people put on their resumes, but what they don't, that's important. In 1998, medical device company Becton Dickinson hired Seymour Schlager. Although he had an impressive resume, it had failed to mention that he had spent 1991 to 1997 in prison for attempted murder.

Despite the abundance of reasons for subjecting all employees to background checks, a majority of American companies and organizations still resist the idea, often for financial reasons. Business firms will spend hundreds of millions of dollars on executive compensation and perks, and yet refuse to allocate a few thousand dollars to screen employee backgrounds, even though the failure to do so will leave the company potentially open to millions of dollars of liabilities. Although it had suffered from years of complaints and problems, it was not until 2002 that the Boy Scouts of America announced that it would finally begin conducting background checks, for sex crimes and drug convictions, of its adult volunteers. But only for new volunteers; the 1.2 million current volunteers were given a

---

69 For more about Douglas's misstatements, see "Bruce Allen Murphy, *Wild Bill: The Legend and Life of William O. Douglas*, (New York: Random House, 2003).

70 Mike Aamodt, "How Common is Resume Fraud?," *Assessment Council News*, February, 2003.

pass, an incredibly short-sighted decision since the organization was publicly acknowledging that background checks were prudent.

Particular attention should be paid to checking out foreign nationals and companies with whom you are doing business. In far too many cases, U.S. companies find the task daunting or too expensive and simply decide, often at their peril, to take the individual at face value.

Job applicants with any discrepancies on their resumes, especially degrees from unaccredited schools, should be rejected out-of-hand. Similarly, if you discover employees with degrees from unaccredited diploma mills, they should be summarily fired. Anyone with such a degree is an inherently dishonest person and represents a serious potential liability.

- 5 -

FRAUD

"Police in Uzbekistan arrested a group
of suspected swindlers who tried to
sell what they said was [a] $1 million
U.S. bill offering it at half price."

ABC News, Tashkent, Uzbekistan
April 17, 2006

George H.W. Bush, George W. Bush, Mitt Romney, Alan Greenspan, Timothy Geithner, Dick Cheney, Bill Clinton, Ben Bernanke, assorted top officials of the CIA, senior compliance officers of the New York Federal Reserve, and now Barack Obama: what do they all have in common? Well, if you are a conspiratorialist, they are all involved in a series of major frauds, stealing billions upon billions, perhaps even trillions, of dollars from ordinary citizens in the U.S. Who says so? Well, Leo Wanta, for one.

Self-proclaimed "Ambassador" Leo Wanta is at the heart of one of the looniest conspiracy crazes of all time, but one that has managed to acquire adherents both in the U.S. and abroad. Wanta asserts that he was the ambassador from Somalia to Canada and Switzerland at a time when Somalia had no recognized government. Claiming to be Ronald Reagan's "most-trusted intelligence agent," according to Greg Syzmanski in an article in the *Idaho Observer*, Wanta maintains that he parlayed $150 billion borrowed from the U.S. Treasury into $27.5 trillion by means of shrewd currency trading, mostly in rubles.[71]

---

71 Greg Syzmanski, "Following the Money Backwards Leads to President Reagan, Russian Rubles and Ambassador Leo Wanta," *The Idaho Observer*, January, 2007.

Tasked by Reagan with safeguarding the money for the American people, Wanta ultimately found himself the target of forces more powerful than anything he had ever imagined, all of whom wanted to get their hands on the trillions he controlled. A sinister cabal led by President George H.W. Bush and Bill Clinton, Wanta claims, has been locked in an unrelenting struggle with him for control of the money ever since.

In the 1990s, Wanta was charged with income tax evasion by the federal government. His own attorney, as part of Wanta's defense, described him as "delusional." Not surprisingly, Wanta was convicted and served six and a half years in federal prison. But once he was released he immediately returned to his old theme, enlarging on the supposed conspiracy and using the web to spread his gospel.

Now, you ask, what does this have to do with anything? Surely, you assert, no one with a triple digit I.Q. could believe this nonsense? Unfortunately, the Wanta hallucinations have spawned a cottage industry of conspiratorialists who ardently believe the absurdities he and his close followers regularly post on the internet, and elements of his story are finding their way into criminal frauds and scams around the globe.

One of the most bizarre cases involves an extremely successful American businessman, who we'll call Bob Miller. A person of unquestionable skill and intelligence in his own industry, Bob wasn't sophisticated when it came to high-level international banking and politics. It all began with a con artist who drew him into a web of lies and false promises that lured him on a wide goose chase across the globe, exhausted him emotionally and physically, and cost him tens of millions of dollars.

He was told by the scammers, who alleged that they were former CIA and FBI agents, or individuals with deep contacts within the intelligence community and at the highest levels of the U.S. and various foreign governments, that they had a foolproof plan for investing his money in a secret market that traded so-called medium term notes. In reality, medium term notes exist and generally paid someplace between seven and nine percent return per annum prior to the onset of the 2008 recession. Similar scams have reportedly traded in short term notes, prime bank guarantees, and other financial instruments. The scammers, by contrast, told Miller that they could make him an astronomical amount of money, in the billions of dollars in a matter of months, if he would put up a guarantee for several hundred million dollars to fund their trades.

He took the bait and provided the scammers ultimately with a guarantee of $350 million. Soon he was informed that his account was worth more than $7 billion, but when he tried to take his money out of the scheme the excuses began. He subsequently withdrew his guarantee, without losing any money, but then gave the scammers $50 million in cash to invest. Now he believed that he was owed both $7 billion plus the return on his $50 million investment.

When he tried to get his money, he was told that an amazing conspiracy of powerful forces was arrayed against him and they wanted his money for their own purposes. According to the scammers, who took a page from the Leo Wanta fabrications, the conspirators included George H.W. Bush, then-president George W. Bush, Federal Reserve Chairman Ben Bernanke, former Fed Chairman Alan Greenspan, and a host of other government officials and prominent individuals, including the Chairman and CEO of Deutsche Bank Josef Ackermann. Some of the funds, it was alleged, were going to be used to fund covert off-the-books CIA operations, with the remainder going toward the personal enrichment of the conspirators. In some related scams it is claimed that part of the money will go to finance humanitarian projects around the globe.

The scammers promised on a number of occasions that the monies would be transferred to Miller's account, but each time nothing happened and Miller was given excuses that could only be described as absolute fantasies. He was fed stories that appeared on the various Leo Wanta websites and blogs, including that Robert Armenta, the chief enforcement officer of the New York Federal Reserve, had been arrested for being involved in the plot to steal his funds, that Treasury Secretary Tim Geithner was arrested for being complicit in the conspiracy but had cut a "secret" deal with the administration, and that Miller was not the only target of the Bushes' grand plot and that among the other victims was Queen Elizabeth, who lost $50 million. President Obama, he was further told, had been "working hard behind the scenes to procure the payments for both the Refunding Programme and the relevant Settlements," but ultimately the Bush conspirators got to him and he, too, succumbed to their blandishments. According to one breathless web posting, "Obama condones brazen theft and the exploitation of other people's money for private gain." Even the CIA was brought into the story when the scammers sent Miller a bogus message, allegedly from a leading U.S. Senator, saying that the Agency would quietly see that he got his funds. But, of course, nothing happened. The Senator, the scammers maintained, had been compromised along with the CIA. In an effort to convince Miller that he was being scammed, an overture was made to the Senator in question, who said he had no knowledge either of Miller or the matters in question. Miller, ever in denial, responded: "What did you expect him to say. Naturally he denied it."

Now there are certainly those who might believe that Miller deserved to lose his money because he fell for such a preposterous story. However, he is not alone. Among the various dupes have been churches, housing authority benefit plans, banks, and otherwise prudent investors. Indeed, hundreds of well-to-do Americans fall prey every year to schemes and scams that offer to provide them access to the secret inner workings of the financial system in ways that will provide them with fantastic returns. Among the leading characteristics of such scams are the following:

- There is a parallel financial world that only the scam artist knows about. Often it is alleged that this world was set up by the Rothschilds, the Rockefellers, certain Arabs, the U.S. Government in the wake of World War II, the CIA and even the Illuminati, and this is how they became fabulously rich;

- Secrecy is all important or everyone would be involved (hence your banker or financial adviser will be unaware of this opportunity). Banks don't acknowledge such programs because if it was generally known that such high rates of return could be achieved people wouldn't put their money into savings accounts and CDs paying a low interest rate. In some cases, the scam artists require that the "investor" sign a non-disclosure or non-circumvention agreement, thereby adding to the sense that they are protecting some kind of extraordinary secret;

- The returns are always unrealistically high. If the returns sound too good to be true, most likely they aren't real;

⅄ "[H]igh rates of return are generated by repeatedly trading (or buying and selling) financial instruments";[72]

⅄ "Transactions are overly complex and nonsensical," utilizing terminology inappropriate and inaccurate in normal banking transactions. A few examples, according to the Federal Reserve are: "conditional SWIFT," "master commitment," "key tested telex," and funds of good, clean, clear and non-criminal origin"[73];

⅄ Ultimately the victim cannot get paid because of a conspiracy of leading figures in the political and banking worlds (especially the Federal Reserve), the interference of the CIA and Mossad, or some *deus ex machina* excuse.

The Federal Reserve Bank of New York regularly puts out advisories regarding various scams "involving the Federal Reserve Name."[74] Among the scams specifically noted by the Fed are "'Prime Bank' and Other Financial Instrument Fraud Schemes," "Federal Trading Program" scams (in which "a target is told that the Federal Reserve uses a 'Federal Trading Program' to enhance the U.S. economy," "Private Placement Programs/High Yield Investment Programs," and "Discovered 1930s Notes and Bonds" (more on this later). Nevertheless, despite the best efforts of the Fed and other government agencies to alert the public to scams there seems to be a endless list of suckers so greedy or gullible that they fall for these absurd schemes over and over again.

Once they are defrauded, many of the victims are characterized by a complete state of denial, as in the case of Bob Miller. Sometimes it is because they enticed relatives, friends, or business associates to invest with them. Others simply can't deal with the fact that they've lost their money and that they did something so foolish. Miller, for example, kept calling well-placed friends and associates, requesting they get in

---

72 Board of Governors of the Federal Reserve System, Division of Banking Supervision and Regulation, "'Prime Bank' and Other Financial Instrument Fraud Schemes," May 20, 2002.

73 *Ibid.*

74 "Scams Involving the Federal Reserve Name," Federal Reserve Bank of New York website, February 13, 2009.

touch with the CIA Director and inquire when he was going to get paid. He even hired a law firm, of dubious credentials, and had them prepare a lawsuit against the Bush family, Greenspan, Mitt Romney, and others whom he felt were involved in the conspiracy to steal his profits from the phantom trading programs. However, to date the lawsuit has never been filed.

PHONY CERTIFICATES AND FRAUDULENT 1930S NOTES AND BONDS

A variation on this scam was brought to my attention in 2003 by a prominent former military officer working for a leading construction company. He had been approached by some Filipino businessmen who wanted his company to undertake a series of projects in the Philippines and presented a series of certificates as collateral for the projects. The certificates purportedly controlled a trust set up by the late Filipino dictator, Ferdinand Marcos, which possessed vast amounts of gold, presumably from the famous Yamashita hoard. Named for the Japanese General Tomoyuki Yamashita, the gold was thought to be part of the loot stolen by the Japanese during their march through Asia in the early part of World War Two. Some proponents of the story even claim that the British crown jewels had been set to Singapore early in the war when it appeared that a German invasion was imminent and were part of the Yamashita treasure which was supposedly hidden in the Philippines as Japanese fortunes in the war began to wane.

Most of the stories suggest that the treasure, if it really existed, was buried in an underground chamber in the Philippines dug by prisoners of war. According to the legend, the prisoners were then shot, bayoneted, or buried alive, along with some of the soldiers, so that the location of the treasure would remain a secret until could be shipped to Japan.

The so-called trust agreement was stamped with the dubious admonition "Cloak With Secrecy," and in it the alleged "grantor," Ferdinand Marcos, "hereby offers his services, faith and solemn belief in God Almighty who sent His only Begotten Son, Jesus Christ to save mankind from its sinfulness." Beneficiaries of the trust are listed as "the Poorest of the Poor families, Farmers, Fisherman, the Aged, Street Children, through development projects such as free education, hospitalization, housing, job opportunities, etc. anywhere in the Philippines and other parts of the world as determined by the Trustee."

Executed in 1983 in front of a notary in Quezon City, the Trustee is listed as Malbert A. Marcos, of whom there is no identifiable record.

Obviously bogus, the document was part of a scam to get the construction company to advance funds to the Filipino businessmen to begin the so-called projects. One can only presume that they intended to steal the funds once they received them.

The Yamashita gold has been the inspiration for countless scams and a number of expeditions by treasure hunters convinced that it really exists. One such expedition was headed by a young Californian, Ned Burris (not his real name), and dubbed "Project Solomon." He approached me in 1996 and asked to retain me as chief of security and logistics for what he believed was going to be the recovery of the gold and other treasure from a site in a remote region of Quezon Province. He had established a partnership to fund the search for the gold and had spent hundreds of thousands of dollars on the effort. He supposedly learned of the site from "an elderly Filipino, known to have been a WW II Japanese collaborator. He described how the treasure site was first developed as an underground munitions depots (sic.) and then converted to store vast treasures."[75] Using ground penetrating radars, bore holes, and other geophysical reconnaissance techniques, as well as by studying the vegetation patterns on the surface, Burris was absolutely convinced he'd found a void beneath the surface of the site. He was also certain that word of his discovery would leak out and that he'd soon be in a fight for his life as corrupt Philippine officials, especially in the military, sought to confiscate his treasure on one pretext or another. There was also the issue of how to move what Burris estimated to be one hundred metric tons of gold.

NIGERIAN 419 SCAMS AND OTHER CONS

The world is fully of con artists and fraudsters, and their victims include some remarkably intelligent individuals and corporations. Over the years I've handled a continuous stream of fraud cases, many employing the same techniques and scams year after year.

Most people, of course, know about the infamous Nigerian scams, known as Section 419 scams after the section in the Nigerian legal code that governs such infractions, where people are contacted by email and

---

75 "American-Philippine Development, Ltd., Business Plan," Number 008, dated February 15, 1996, p. 21.

offered fabulous rewards for facilitating the transfer of funds to another beneficiary. The most common victims of such scams are doctors. The dead person who left money in a foreign account is a common ploy. One communication is from a Johnson Dube, who said his father was murdered in Zimbabwe after he deposited fifteen and a half million dollars in a South African bank account. According to Dube, who claims he got the name of the email recipient from a non-existent organization call the "International Exchange Network On Line," he needs someone credible to set up a foreign bank account where the South African funds can be transferred before they are frozen at the request of the Zimbabwean government. For this service, he will pay 25 percent of the total funds, plus another 5 percent for expenses. Once the email recipient bites, he is asked to wire a small amount of money (compared to the promised return), often ten or twenty thousand dollars, to an overseas account to cover some extraneous costs associated with the transaction. Mr. Dube, of course, would have been happy to cover those costs but all of his funds are frozen and he is being watched by the government.

Things are bad in Robert Mugabe's Zimbabwe, where the government recently printed a hundred trillion dollar note, so it's plausible, isn't it, that Maria Stevens, whose late husband was murdered by Mugabe's henchmen, has selected you to help her move $28,750,000 from a secret account in Europe to an "offshore account."

Another email sender, Wumi Kone, says that he needs help because his father, "a highly reputable busnness (sic.) magnet (sic.)" died mysteriously in France. He had $12.5 million secreted in the Ivory Coast which Kone needs help recovering. Another Ivorian, Dennis Dumas, maintains that his father was poisoned by his business associates and left $5.5 million in an account which he needs a foreign associate to recover. According to Dr. Richmond Hubert, General Robert Guei of the Ivory Coast was murdered, along with his family, leaving no next of kin and a $28 million bank account, which he wants you to claim.[76] An Iraqi oil consultant by the name of Khalil Al Nasser was allegedly tortured to death by Saddam Hussein and his banker, Khalifa Abuhail wants your help in grabbing his $17.5 million bank account since his entire family died in the Gulf War and he left no will.

---

76 Interestingly, General Guei was a real person and the military ruler of the Cote d'Ivoire for about ten months. He died mysteriously, along with his family, in 2002.

Mr. A. Hernandez of the Ivory Coast was killed in a car crash, along with his wife and three children, and his attorney, Barrister Kenneth William, wants your help in "repatriating the money and properties left behind by my client before they get confiscated or declared unserviceable by the Bank where these huge deposits were lodged." Another barrister, Paul Maxwell, wants you to pretend to be next of kin to another victim of a car crash, James Bendon. The roads are apparently more deadly than anyone imagined, for Dr. Victor Weil, "a Manager with American Express Bank here in Buckingham Palace" (who knew there was a bank in the Queen's residence), desires your assistance "to stand in as the next-of-kin" to the late Mr. Eric Frostell, who died, along with his entire family, in a terrible auto crash on July 14, 2004.

Sheikh Khalifa Algosaibi, the chairman of Khalifa A. Algosaibi Holding Company in Saudi Arabia, also has passed away and his attorney, Mark Dencer Esq., desires your assistance to claim a bequest administered by his law firm, but to do this he needs "the help of a foreign (sic.) and that is why I am contacting you." Mrs. Marie Kular, a "born again Christian," is dying of cancer and wants your help in utilizing the money left to her by her late husband to fund "orphanages, widows." Mrs. Anita Cole Norman of Nigeria is also dying, but of lung cancer, and wants to see that her late husband's $8 million is safely "distributed among charity organization (sic.)." Don't try to call her, however, because "I have since lost my ability to talk properly as a result of impairment in the speech center in the hippocampus area."[77] A Kuwaiti woman, Mrs. Sarah Ghassan, is also dying of cancer and wants your help in collecting $25 million her late husband, Hassan Ghassan, the former owner of Petroleum and Gas Company,[78] placed on deposit in Europe. Zedina Traore is a born again Christian dying of cancer and soliciting your help in recovering her late husband's $9 million bank account in order to fund churches and orphanages. She has selected you, she says, because you are apparently a "Christian individual."

---

77 The hippocampus is more related to long-term memory and spatial navigation than to speech. The speech center lies in the parietal lobe of the left hemisphere of the brain for most people, and language recognition center in the right hemisphere.

78 There is no record of a company by that name.

Plane crashes also are taking their toll. Take for example the email from a Dr. Jan de Vos, who claims to be in charge of African Merchant Bank in South Africa.[79] De Vos wants your help in claiming a $20 million account left by a man who was killed in a plane crash. The account, he tells you, has been dormant without any claims on it, and he wants to transfer this money to a foreign bank account, which he is asking you to set up, because he cannot have foreign accounts as a banking official. According to Brian Capon, a "gas consultant" named Michael Gambone died aboard a Swiss Air flight that crashed into the Atlantic without any heirs, leaving $55 million in a bank account in the U.K. Mr. Capon doesn't want to see it go to the British treasury so he's willing to offer you 30 percent of the funds for posing as the next of kin. Christian Eich also died, along with his wife and two children, in the crash of an Air France Concorde, leaving no other relatives, and lo and behold he left "huge" funds that the unsavory management of a bank in South Africa intends to use to "purchase of war (sic.) arms." If you are willing to provide "your trust, unconditional cooperation and assistance," Joseph Kabeki would like to recruit you to stand in as Mr. Eich's next of kin.

Then there's Steve E. Daggash, who says he is chairman of the contract award committee in the Nigerian Federal Ministry of Aviation. The government "over awarded" a contract to upgrade radar and landing facilities at the Kano airport, he claims, and now there's $21.5 million left over in the account. He wants your assistance, once again, in setting up a foreign bank account where this money can be transferred and he'll pay you 20 percent of the amount for your time and trouble. Another apparently corrupt official, Abdukadir Mohammad, "chairman special committee for budget and planning of the ministry of petroleum here in Nigeria," is seeking a partner "in our bid to transfer some amount of money into a foreign account."

Mr. Idris Umar has esophageal cancer and doesn't care for his family and friends so he selected your name at random and is offering to make you heir to his estate, with includes a cash deposit of $19 million. The late Martins Wilzek also left his fortune to you because "he must have been in contact with you in the past or simply you were

---

79 There is an African Merchant Bank in South Africa but it is not headed by Dr. Jan de Vos. Perhaps the best known Dr. de Vos is a historian who lives in Mexico City. There is also an orthopedic surgeon by that name in the U.S.

nominated to him by one of his numerous friends abroad who wished you good." Professor Charles Soludo, the alleged governor of the Central Bank of Nigeria, would like your assistance in acquiring "a building in your country for me to buy." Similarly, Dr. Yaw Ansu, who claims to be a "Regional Director (West Africa)" of the World Bank, wants your help to "secure my personal fund (sic.) and necessary documents to enable me invest (sic.) successfully in your country." Ismail Hamid of the Ivory Coast wishes that you would help him establish "a safe account in your country" so that he can make investments with his late father's $8.5 million. His father, according to Hamid, was assassinated in a "political uprising."

All of the scams described above have certain things in common. They begin with a mass set of faxes or emails sent to names, generally in the U.S. and Europe, gleaned by the scam artists from newspapers, web sites, business directories, and other sources. Generally it is purported that someone has died, leaving behind a large dollar-denominated account which requires the help of a foreign confederate to acquire, often by posing as the next-of-kin. In virtually all of the scams, the deceased person's relatives are also conveniently dead.

Often there is a sense of urgency involved in the transaction: the dead person's account is on the verge of being confiscated by some government or the person making the contact is also dying of a terminal disease. Although most of the emails assure the receiver that "there is absolutely no risk to you" and "no cost involved," this ultimately changes once a victim is hooked. At that point, it suddenly becomes necessary to bribe a foreign official to release the funds or fees must be unexpectedly paid to facilitate the transaction. In every case, the victim is asked to wire money, usually a modest amount in relationship to the purported payoff, or told that someone will stop by to pick it up. The victim is assured that it is just a temporary setback and that once the money is paid that everything will be all right.

Other scams send emails indicating that you won the South-West Australia Lottery, despite the fact that you've never heard of it or bought a ticket. You have received one million Euros and for a slight handling and processing fee the money will be yours. Or maybe it was the Easter Celebration Lottery Draw where you won a cash prize of a half million dollars.

AFRICAN GOLD SCAMS

One of the most recent scams coming out of Africa relates to phony gold sales. Our firm received a number of calls from otherwise sensible and reputable U.S. companies that had become ensnared in African gold scams, generally involving, but not limited to, Guinea, Mali, Uganda, and Nigeria. In every case the mark was told that large amounts of gold could be purchased at a discount, as much as fifty percent below market price, because the local producers didn't have the wherewithal or sophistication to transport it out of the country to a major depository or gold refinery. Of course, this is nonsense. There is a twenty-four hour a day global gold market and no legitimate producer of gold needs to sell at a steep discount.

Generally, once the mark is on the line, he is told that the gold is waiting for him and all he needs to do is make arrangements for a private plane to pick it up and to pay the local taxes, often 6.5 percent of the total value. The mark pays the taxes but the gold is never shipped; either the sellers disappear or they use various excuses to explain why the gold shipment is delayed and delayed and delayed. The Eskimos allegedly have twenty-three future tenses, including the future that never comes. This is like the future that never comes. As one blogger wrote, "they tell you the gold is ready to be shipped...then there will be some kind of problem...so you need to send more money...then there is another problem...and you need to send more money!"

If the mark is in the country and makes too much of a fuss he is sometimes arrested on bogus charges and then his problems begin to multiply. Virtually all of the scammers have a pet minister or two on the payroll who can run interference for them by alleging that the gold was being exported illegally, or that the taxes were not paid to the right authority, or that money laundering was involved.

Some marks who have visited the country to conduct due diligence have been feted at meetings and dinners with top government officials and the so-called owners of the gold mines, only to find out later than the people they met with were not the real ministers or owners of the gold mines, but rather imposters who later disappear. And what often is purported to be a sample of the gold is generally the only gold in the client will ever see.

DUE DILIGENCE

While cons, scams, and swindles go on all the time, it is during economic declines, especially recessionary periods, that many scams are revealed, especially Ponzi schemes. Named after Charles Ponzi, an Italian career criminal who migrated to Boston and ultimately set up an investment company that promised to double investors' money in 90 days, Ponzi schemes pay off early investors with money received from later investors, often attracted by stories of the riches being earned by those before them. The cycle keeps going until investors lose confidence and demand their money all at once. Scam artists like Ponzi have often spent a substantial portion of the monies invested with them on luxurious lifestyles, not to mention paying off early investors, and therefore are unable to return investors' money and the whole scheme collapses. This is what happened with Bernard Madoff, architect of the largest Ponzi scheme of all time. Investors are estimated to have lost $18 billion with Madoff, many of them fellow Jews that he met in connection with various Jewish charities and philanthropic organizations that also placed their money with him.[80]

Madoff maintained an air of exclusivity about his company, Bernard L. Madoff Investment Securities LLC, and most of his clients found him via word of mouth, clamoring for Madoff to let them invest with him. Most did little or no due diligence, but had they done so all of the warning signs were there for anyone to see. One would assume that a company with $55 billion under management would use a major national auditing firm, but Madoff used a sole proprietor named David Friehling. Friehling was the only member of a firm called Friehling and Horowitz because Jerome Horowitz retired in 1997 and died in 2009. Friehling subsequently pled guilty to securities fraud charges in March, 2009. "Many of the people who invested with Madoff didn't know they were relying on a rinky-dink accounting firm to watch over their investments," writes Stephen Gandol.[81]

On the other hand, a number of the big firms, including KPMG, BDO Seideman, PriceWaterhouseCoopers, and McGladrey & Pallon failed to raise any warning flags and gave "clean bills of health to the numerous firms that invested with Bernard Madoff."[82] Defrauded

---

80 Some sources suggest that the real number is in the range of $50 to $64 billion.

81 Stephen Gandol, "The Madoff Fraud: How Culpable Were the Auditors?", *Time*, December 17, 2008.

82 *Ibid.*

investors are now suing these firms because they did very little due diligence on behalf of the feeder firms they represented to ensure that Madoff was legitimate and actually had the funds invested as he represented. According to Gandol, "Observers say it's likely that all the accounting firms did was check the statements that Madoff himself produced."[83]

The SEC (Securities and Exchange Commission) received a number of tips indicating it was impossible to obtain the consistent level of returns that Madoff claimed but there was no investigation or follow-up. And Madoff provided his clients with only very rudimentary information about their accounts, with no trading records or explanations relating to the growth of their investments.

What is amazing is how few firms do any serious due diligence before going into business deals with people they barely know. For many companies, a quick Google search by a secretary or low-level staffer is considered sufficient to substantiate the bona fides of a person or firm despite the fact that the web can easily be manipulated and loaded with false information. I've had extraordinarily wealthy clients who won't spend a few thousand dollars to do a substantive background check on someone

Even prominent executive recruiting firms rarely do more than a cursory check of the backgrounds of many of the executives they are trying to place in key positions, relying instead on recommendations of previous employers. But this can be very problematic. Many companies, fearing lawsuits, do not pass along derogatory information about former employees, no matter how bad their performance or behavior. For example, a large pharmaceutical company hired a research scientist for a top job based, in large part, on the recommendations of his former employers. The scientist had outstanding qualifications on paper and was one of the few people in the country with his particular specialty. What the new employer didn't know was that the scientist was exceptionally obese (Jabba the Hutt is a close comparison), unstable mentally and too lazy to do the work he was hired to perform, and had fallen far below the expectations of all of his previous employers. Each of those companies, however, was happy to have him move along and, to that end, gave him, if not

---

83 *Ibid.*

glowing reviews, than certainly passing marks without any suggestion of his negative work performance and personal issues.

The new pharmaceutical company, unhappy with his performance, decided to fire him after he received a bomb-making manual which he had ordered in the mail at his office. He allegedly also made threats against his superiors and claimed he would sue the company for anti-Semitism if they followed through. Our investigation clearly found that there was no anti-Semitism involved in the company's decision to fire him, especially considering that most of his co-workers did not know he was Jewish. Indeed, he was married to a non-Jewish woman and, while under surveillance, did not attend religious observances on Yom Kippur, but rather played card games on his computer. Ultimately, he was fired from the company but soon found a new position at another pharmaceutical firm since the terms of his separation were, by agreement, kept confidential. Thus, any new senior-level employee at a company should receive a thorough background check, including, if possible, off-the-record interviews with former coworkers and superiors.

By the same token, many of the "Know Your Client" reports commissioned by banks and financial institutions and performed by reputable investigative firms are sloppy and haphazard, full of errors, and consist of little more than research, much of it hearsay and unsubstantiated, acquired through data-basing. This is particularly true of efforts to address the credibility and trustworthiness of businessmen and women in the CIS countries, the Middle East, and Africa. In Russia and most other CIS countries, there are countless publications that will print anything for a price, and many prominent business figures have been victims of character assassination and misinformation which was commissioned by business rivals and other enemies. In one case, a leading business figure who headed a multi-billion company with more than 25,000 employees was described as the "illegitimate son of the president" of the country, thus minimizing his role as an entrepreneur and innovator, even though his father and siblings were still alive and readily identifiable. Dubious blogs and minor publications in Moscow also levied a host of other charges against him including the accusation that his company was a front for gangsters (unlikely if he was the president's illegitimate son), that he paid enormous kickbacks to government officials (no evidence cited), and that the company was owned by relatives of the president (no evidence cited and contrary to public filings in Europe). The bogus information was accepted unquestioningly by several investigative firms, despite its dubious authenticity and lack of supporting evidence, and created a host of problems for the company as it tried to do business in the U.S. and Western Europe. Even people who should know better like Cherie Blair, an attorney by training and wife of the former British prime minister, should have known better than to enter into a business arrangement with an Australian named Peter Foster without first doing a background check. If she had she would have learned that he had a criminal record and was a boyhood friend of a former topless model who was one of Mrs. Blair's so-called lifestyle coaches.[84] As a result of her apparent carelessness, the *Times of London* ran a front-page headline inquiring, "Should We Care If Mrs. Blair Is Bonkers?"[85] She was subsequently forced to make a public apology for embarrassing her husband and the government.

Another embarrassing example of the failure to perform due diligence was the signing of a supposedly twenty year old Dominican baseball player by the Washington Nationals. The player, who used the name Esmailyn Gonzalez, was given a $1.4 million signing bonus, which was double what he had been offered by other teams. It subsequently was revealed, however, that Gonzalez was in reality a 16-year old boy whose real name was Carlos Alvarez Daniel Lugo. The failure to properly check out the young man's identity and background cost Nationals' manager Jim Bowden, and a number of his assistants, their jobs. What is so unbelievably shortsighted about this case is that the team was willing to spend $1.4 million on the player, and probably several hundred thousand dollars additionally on lawyers, travel and bonuses to various Dominican scouts and facilitators, but wouldn't allocate five to ten thousand dollars on an investigation to check out the player's identity and bona fides. According to Bowden, he relied on Major League baseball's office on investigations, which is more focused on steroid use, gambling, and bad behavior. In reality, when the stakes are this high there is no substitute for conducting your own investigation, especially if your job depends on it.

---

84 Marc Champion and James R. Hagerty, "Britain's First Lady, Always a Bit Flaky, is in Hot Water Now," *The Wall Street Journal*, December 11, 2002.

85 *Ibid.*

Failure to do due diligence can even get you murdered. I was contacted by a long-time client who was doing business in Russia at the time. One of his colleagues, a man in his sixties from the state of Georgia, had met a "wonderful young woman" in Moscow and was absolutely smitten with her. He wanted to marry her and bring her back to the U.S., but the American embassy, for some strange reason, he suggested, wouldn't give her a visa. She was not only beautiful, he went on, but brilliant, and had a Master's degree in one of the hard sciences. He asked me if I would look into the situation and I agreed to do so.

I spoke first of all with the man at the U.S. embassy's visa office in Moscow who had denied her a visa. He said that during the young woman's interview it was clear that far from having a Master's degree, she had very little education and that the only thing she could talk about in complete sentences was the Moscow club scene. He distrusted the young woman's motive for marrying a man four decades older than she was, and felt strongly that she just wanted a ticket to the U.S.

Our man in Moscow, a former GRU (Military Intelligence) officer, then picked up the investigation and soon learned that the young woman was a former hooker and not from Russia, but rather from the Ukraine. She belonged to a mafia gang, it was determined, that engineered marriages between very attractive young women and older businessmen from the United States and Western Europe. Each woman would return to her new husband's country of origin and within months he would die mysteriously and the wife would inherit all or part of his estate, which she would promptly turn over to her mafia colleagues. She would then be permitted to stay in the husband's country or, if she so desired, return to Russia where she'd be given a new identity and set up to meet another lonely and unsuspecting man with money.

When we presented our report to our client, he was extremely grateful and immediately persuaded his friend to drop the girl and get out of the country before something happened to him. Had we not investigated the girl it is likely that he would have married her and shortly thereafter been murdered.

BASIC RESEARCH OFTEN LACKING

Even though the web provides a world of information at the touch of a keyboard, many companies are guilty of doing little, if any, meaningful research about overseas markets and suppliers, potential threats, cultural norms, and geopolitical issues. The media also has often failed to do basic research, especially when the target is a member of their industry.

Robert Maxwell's whole life was a fraud. Indeed, we were engaged by one of the insurance companies involved to conduct an independent investigation of Robert Maxwell's mysterious death aboard his yacht in November, 1991. From an insurance point-of-view it made a great deal of difference whether his death was accidental, a suicide, or even murder.

Maxwell was a legendary British media baron and former member of Parliament who had a gift for languages. Born of desperately poor Jewish parents in Czechoslovakia, he immigrated to Great Britain in 1940 and a short time after that changed his name from Jan Ludvik Hoch to Ian Robert Maxwell. He served with distinction in the war and afterward purchased a minor publisher and changed its name to Pergamon Press. There is some debate today as to where he got the money but in the years that followed he parlayed Pergamon Press into a media empire that owned newspapers, publishing houses, and television networks. During this period of time he had unusual links to Communist Eastern Europe and the USSR, going so far as to publish a number of hagiographies of the drab and uninspiring leaders of various Soviet satellite states.

By the late 1980s, Maxwell was in deep financial trouble as a result of bad investments and high interest rates. In November, 1991, he flew to the Canary Islands and boarded his super yacht, the Lady Ghislaine. Late on the night of November 5, while cruising along the coast, he fell overboard and drowned. There are many conspiracy theories that suggest that Maxwell was murdered by the Israeli Mossad because he was trying to shake the organization down for funds to save his faltering empire. Another unidentified vessel was supposedly in the same vicinity when he fell overboard, and according to one theory it was under the control of Israeli agents who dispatched frogmen into the water. The frogmen allegedly boarded Lady Ghislaine and injected Maxwell with a powerful sedative, some say a nerve agent, and then pushed him into the water.

Many press reports and books later asserted that Maxwell was a Mossad agent and had been throughout his adult life. By contrast, what is known from files made available immediately after the collapse of the Soviet Union is that Maxwell was Soviet agent of influence and that he had been bankrolled by the Soviets. There were instructions that Pergamon Press should be the second outstanding invoice paid each month in Great Britain after the subsidy for the official communist party newspaper, *The Red Flag*. Pergamon, under the guise of being a scholarly publisher, was an ideal way of collecting intelligence about British and NATO weapons systems, strategies, and intentions. This was about to come out when Maxwell, who had always striven for British respectability, left for the Canary Islands.

We could find no evidence that he had been murdered although there were plenty of rumors. It was well known that Maxwell was an insomniac and roamed the deck of his yacht late at night. There was opening in the railing on each side of the vessel where a man could stand and urinate over the side if he was so inclined. Maxwell, who was a large man and overweight, often relieved himself in this fashion, and had the boat lurched at that moment or had he had a heart attack or a spell of dizziness he could have tumbled in the sea. Although a strong swimmer, he had been drinking and could have been stunned by the fall and drowned. The Spanish autopsy, which has been criticized as inadequate and unprofessional, concluded that he died of a heart attack.

There were several other peculiarities, however. In normal times he generally took one of his mistresses with him on the vessel, but this night he was alone. Moreover, when he arrived in the Canaries he had gone to his favorite restaurant and ordered his favorite meal. Afterward, instead of using his usual car and driver, he took a cab to the yacht.

We concluded that his death was more likely a suicide than either an accident or murder. His creditors and detractors were closing in on him and his whole empire, and for that matter his life, was on the verge of imploding, and the result was likely to be public disgrace and possibly even criminal charges, not only for his work with the Soviets but because he had looted the pension funds of some of the companies he owned. He was buried with state honors on the Mount of Olives in Jerusalem, therefore it is hard to believe that the Israelis killed him and then gave him an elaborate public funeral.

In the end, the insurance companies concurred with our assessment and refused to pay on his policies, maintaining that the most likely explanation for his death was suicide.

- 6 -

NAKED INTELLIGENCE

"The availability of technology
has democratized the gathering of intelligence."

Our client, a Russian oligarch, described how he and his fellow oligarchs were invited to the Kremlin for a meeting hosted by then-President Vladimir Putin. He was shown into a large conference room where there were name cards at each place. Russia's wealthiest businessman,[86] Mikhail Khodorkovsky, was there, as were Roman Abramovic, Viktor Vekselberg, and more than a dozen others. After all of the oligarchs were seated, Putin entered the room and took his place at the head of the table. Following perfunctory greetings, Putin announced, "Before each one of you is your FSB [Federal Security Service] file. There is enough in each file to send every one of you to prison."

Putin smiled coldly at the little assemblage. "But I'm not a vindictive man. You all made your money quickly and easily, and you are welcome to enjoy it. But I would appreciate it if you would use some of it to help our nation."

There were nods and murmurs of approval around the table. But then the other shoe fell.

"The only thing I absolutely cannot tolerate is for you to use your fortunes to influence the political system. Stay out of politics," he said firmly, "and everything will be alright. But defy me and you will become my implacable enemy."

As we know, Mikhail Khordorkovsky failed to heed Putin and he was soon arrested and remains in prison, his oil empire broken up and

---

86 Mark Hollingsworth and Stewart Lansley; *Londongrad*; (London: Fourth Estate, 2009), p. 5.

sold off in pieces. Abramovic and others spend most of their time in London and aboard their yachts, putting as much distance as possible between themselves and Putin.

The key to Putin's triumph over the oligarchs was, of course, that he had so much well-documented information on each of them. The oligarchs, in turn, knew they were guilty of a multitude of crimes or, at the very least, questionable activities, and with the exception of Khodorkovsky all chose not to challenge Putin.

There's no such thing as real privacy anymore. If you believe otherwise, you're destined for trouble. We live in a largely transparent world, or what some have called "a see through world." This is a result, in large measure, of our increasing dependence on new and ever improving technologies for communications, commerce, travel and data storage and processing. Technologies, moreover, that were once the exclusive, or nearly exclusive, domain of governments are now available to corporations, the media, and even ordinary citizens. Not only are great stores of information at our fingertips but we can acquire high-definition cameras, parabolic listening devices and recorders, night vision equipment, digital enhancement equipment, infra-red detection devices, and even drones and other robotic tools that intelligence agencies would have fought and died for only a few years ago. Indeed, I was recently at a home where the owner had purchased a very expensive telescope that was so powerful he could read the street numbers on houses twenty miles away.

All of the tools used by intelligence agencies are now employed by private firms in one form or another as they collect competitive intelligence for companies locked in fierce competition around the globe for scarce resources, new markets, and new products and technologies. In addition to the use of new spy technologies, this includes such standard, and relatively mundane, elements of intelligence collection as surveillance and counter surveillance, going through dumpsters and garbage (known in the trade as "trash pulls"), and compromising and recruiting members of the opposition.

We resorted to good old-fashioned surveillance and a little added ingenuity when we were asked by a Russian client to try and ascertain who was on board a 151-foot yacht out of St. Tropez, that was already at sea. With the assistance of a detective I had worked with before from Paris and aided by two former French Navy commandos, I leased a deep-V-hull swift boat and we trolled the French coast looking for the yacht. Our plan, once we found the yacht, was to hire a hooker with the biggest rack we could find and take her out near where the subjects were anchored. Then we would have her strip off her shirt and we'd pretend to take photos of her, nude from the waist up, as she posed near the bow of the boat. We hoped that her performance would draw an admiring crowd to the rail of the yacht and we'd get their photos by ostentatiously taking pictures of the girl when, in reality, we'd be shooting over her shoulder with a telephoto lens. We ultimately located the target vessel in Sardinia but the guests had already departed.

In another case we simply resorted to financial inducements to discover information critical to U.S. national interests. After the collapse of the former Soviet Union, we were hired to build a case against a government official in one of the CIS (Commonwealth of Independent States) countries who was going to seek the presidency. He was personally attractive and married to one of the leading newscasters in his country. The problem was that he was not a strong supporter of democracy nor considered friendly to the United States and Western Europe. Instead, he was believed to be a thug and thief, and on Moscow's payroll. He claimed to have no secret bank accounts nor any other income except his salary when he worked as chief-of-staff to the former president. In addition to a thorough background investigation, we initiated a global search for assets in his name, and eventually hit pay dirt in the British Virgin Islands, where we located a firm that managed his money with two nominees acting on his behalf. We were even able to obtain the front page of his nominee documents. It turned out he had stolen nearly $800 million while in the government, and when that was made public, along with some other derogatory information, his candidacy was over before it started. Instead, after a series of tumultuous events the pro-Western candidate assumed the office of president, despite electoral fraud, extensive voter intimidation, and massive corruption. It was, as we liked to say, a good day at the office.

Some national airlines "bug" the seats in the first class cabin, on the premise that business executives possessing trade or industrial secrets are far more likely to fly in the front of the plane than back in tourist. Depending on the country and the airline, if your laptop is in your checked luggage the hard drive may be copied by agents in the baggage hold or "lost" once it gets to its destination so that the laptop can be accessed by agents on the ground.

The same logic that concerns first class seats applies to suites in major hotels, since the high tariff generally restricts occupancy to "people of interest." Many of the priciest hotel suites in France, China, and Russia, to cite only a few examples, have audio (and sometimes video) surveillance systems than can be turned on and off at will, depending on who is staying in the room.

A long-time acquaintance, with a penchant for attractive women, has been videotaped in "flagrante delicto" so many times by hostile intelligence services that he has developed a standard response when someone shows up trying to blackmail him. "How do I get copies?" he asks, as he thumbs through the incriminating photographs. "My wife thinks I'm a lousy lover and these will prove I'm not."

The would-be blackmailers always give up in disgust.

It's not just rooms and telephones that are bugged. One old trick used by cops or federal agents who wanted to learn what was going to be discussed by a couple of suspects at a restaurant table, but didn't know which table they'd sit at, was to ask the proprietor to leave the salt and pepper off all the tables. Inevitably the suspects would ask for salt and pepper. When they did, the waiter would bring over two shakers with microphones inside. Since the suspects themselves had requested the shakers, it would not arouse their suspicions.

The listening device used to bring down Mafia chieftain Paul Castellano in the early 1980s was hidden by the FBI in a lamp in the kitchen of his Staten Island residence.[87] By technological standards, the bug used against the so-called "boss of bosses" was antediluvian, both in terms of size and the quality of its transmissions. The conversations themselves were saved on a reel-to-reel recorder. Today everything is digital; technology has made eavesdropping far easier, but at the same time more difficult than ever to detect. Tiny television cameras with pinhole lenses are virtually impossible to find with the naked eye and some microphones are even smaller. You can purchase Electromagnetic Field Detectors (EMF meters) to search for hidden eavesdropping devices but you need a good deal of practice to be able to distinguish a "bug" from normal wiring in the walls or other electrical devices.

---

87 Joseph F. O'Brien and Andris Kurins, *Boss of Bosses*, (New York: Simon & Schuster, 1991), p. 182.

One of my previous companies was involved in the largest civil RICO case in U.S. history on behalf of one of our Russian clients. The other side requested a meeting in Europe to discuss a possible settlement offer. The negotiator for the other side turned out not to be an attorney but a hitman, code name McIntosh, with twenty-three confirmed kills. When he greeted our team, he gave the lead member a warm embrace and surreptitiously attached a tiny transmitter to the back of his tie, which was only discovered after the meeting. Of course, we had already bugged the room where the negotiation was held.

Any telephone hooked to a land-line can be turned into a transmitter and lasers can be aimed at windows to eavesdrop on the conversations inside rooms miles away. Your cellphone also emits a signal, even if it is not switched on. The only way of preventing this is to take the battery out, but it can still be used to pick up your conversations.

Heat and other sensors can unlock the darkness and let authorities or hostile competitors know what's going on in your home or hotel room, even if you have the curtains pulled. Contemporary cameras have such high resolution that items smaller than a cigarette pack can be photographed from satellites overhead. New lenses, night vision devices, and digital enhancement techniques mean that photographs can be taken almost anywhere under virtually any conditions.

The Global Positioning System (GPS) in your car can provide an exact location to the manufacturer if you've had a breakdown, accident, or someone has stolen it (which is why it is often referred to as a vehicle recovery system), but the GPS can also be used to track the movements of your vehicle. Rental car companies are now using GPS to monitor usage of their vehicles to ensure that customers comply with the terms of their contracts. Even your tires can give you away. Goodyear, Michelin, and various other tire companies have embedded Radio Frequency Identification (RFID) chips in their tires, allegedly as a low air pressure warning system. RFID readers along the highway read the chips and can pinpoint the location of your vehicle. Wal-Mart and other high volume stores put RFID tags in some of their products as a form of inventory control and management, and these chips can also be scanned by roadside readers. Some airlines are even tagging your luggage with RFID chips, purportedly to help keep track of bags and to aid in the recovery of lost luggage.

Only the very rich and powerful can enjoy even a modicum of real privacy today, and it comes at a steep price. By the same token, he very rich are often the chief violators of others' privacy, especially the privacy of their spouses and girlfriends.

Over the years we have represented the wives of some of the most prominent men in the country during messy divorces. One of the most unforgettable cases involved, arguably, the most glamorous and recognizable woman in America at the time thanks to her husband's high profile and fortune. Walking with her on Fifth Avenue was an experience guaranteed to stroke any man's ego, as every head, men and women alike, whipped around to take in her beauty. After several years of marriage, she and her prominent husband were getting a divorce and her financial manager retained us because he was suspicious that her husband was eavesdropping on her.

It was worse than he had imagined. She was still living in the spectacular apartment she had shared with her husband, and we quickly discovered that the whole place was wired with both audio and video. Not even the bathrooms were completely private. Her husband kept close tabs on her and even knew the content of her conversations with her attorney. She was also being shadowed by private detectives every time she left the apartment. There apparently was no part of her life that hadn't been compromised in some fashion.

In another illustrative incident, a major American entertainment company was attempting to close a deal in France, but every time the firm's president and his advisers believed they had reached an agreement, the French would come up with yet another demand. It was infuriating and no matter how hard the Americans tried to anticipate each new French demand, the French always seemed to be one step ahead of them. Finally, the Americans were convinced they had met all of the French requirements and that the deal was as good as done. To their shock and dismay, however, the French made yet another demand. The Americans were totally exasperated and, although they wanted the deal very badly, didn't know what to do.

One of the company's executives, an IT specialist, was in Paris to advise the negotiating team and it didn't take him long to realize there was only one explanation for what was going on. The negotiating team was quartered in a suite in one of Paris' leading hotels, and he invited the president to take a walk with him outside. "They're eavesdropping on us," the IT specialist blurted out. "Just like in the movies."

The president was incredulous and dismissed the notion out-of-hand. But the IT specialist persisted. "I'll prove it," he told his boss. "But you'll have to play along with me."

The IT specialist quickly outlined a plan to test his theory. They were to return to the hotel suite and the president was to express out loud his frustration with the French. Then he was to announce to his team of negotiators that he was giving up on the deal and leaving Paris as soon as the company's jet could be readied.

They went through the charade and moments later, the telephone in the suite rang. It was the chief French negotiator. Upon reconsideration, he explained, his side had decided not to press the last issue and would concede it to the Americans. In other words, they had a deal.

The president of the American company was suddenly a believer. The French had clearly listened in on every deliberation in the hotel suite and knew exactly what the American position was before it was even communicated to them. In a similar incident, every word uttered by U.S. negotiators aboard a French charter flight concerning a major aerospace competition was recorded by French intelligence agents, to the detriment of the American negotiating position.

The French are engaged in a massive global espionage effort targeted less against the nation's adversaries than its friends and allies around the globe. The French government operates break-and-enter teams that burglarize companies of interest, and French agents have been discovered in garbage dumpsters in Houston searching for computer passwords. They also have operated cleaning crews, whose real job is espionage, engaged by leading U.S. companies that compete with French firms. In one case, they compromised the translators at a firm contracted by a top U.S. defense contractor and stole thousands of pages of documents about proprietary technologies that were being sold to a Middle Eastern country.

In addition to spying, the French are notorious for bribing foreign officials involved in the selection of competing firms and technologies. Bribery was formerly so common that bribes were considered legitimate, and therefore deductible, business expenses by some European countries. In recent years the French government has tightened up its laws on bribery and prosecutes around a hundred cases a year, but almost all relate to public corruption, i.e. bribery of French government officials. Bribery of foreign officials is still generally viewed as unsavory, but necessary.

ECONOMIC WARFARE

Spying has been called the second oldest professional in the world. The industrialization of spying, however, is a phenomenon of the twentieth century. For most of the past one hundred years, massive amounts of information have been collected and interpreted by the world's various intelligence organizations. While initially performed mostly by humans, given the huge volume of information available today, most spying is done by technological means. Intelligence agencies listen into telephone calls, monitor faxes and e-mails, collect credit card and travel records, and closely watch financial flows around the world. Much of this information is sifted through by computers looking for key words and suggestive word patterns, names, and phone numbers and locations of interest. While U.S. intelligence agencies were clearly dysfunctional in the months and weeks leading up to the September 11 terrorist attacks, since that time enormous resources and energy have been devoted to better analyzing information and discerning patterns of activity and connections that are not readily apparent.

With the collapse of the former Soviet Union, ideological rivalries were largely supplanted by economic competition, with some nations recasting their intelligence establishments and refocusing them on the acquisition of competitive intelligence and industrial secrets. As a former chairman of the House Intelligence Committee observed, one hundred of the world's 173 countries, more than half, are involved in economic espionage. Of those hundred, approximately sixty nations, more than half, are engaged in economic spying against the United States. During the 1990's, in the midst of the dot com boom, there was so much espionage going on in Silicon Valley that it was nicknamed "the valley of the spies." Eavesdropping was widespread and pervasive, including panel trucks trolling the streets scanning telephone calls (analog in those days) and computers for some snippet of information that might yield inside information on a forthcoming IPO or new product. Executives of hi-tech companies were often blackmailed in connection with lifestyle issues and nations like China regularly preyed on Americans of Chinese heritage, especially those with relatives still in China, often threatening to harm those relatives in some way if the U.S. relative didn't cooperate.

Former FBI Director Louis Freeh told Congress in 1999 that economic spying cost the United States $2 billion a month, although most observers believed the figure is far higher.[88] Freeh also described espionage aimed at stealing U.S. intellectual property and trade secrets as the greatest threat to the nation's security since the end of the Cold War. Of course, this was before 9/11 and the conflicts with Islamic terrorism and Iraq, but a case can still be made that Freeh's analysis of the threat is still valid and that efforts to undermine U.S. economic supremacy represent a far greater threat to this nation in the long run than those emanating from Islam and the Middle East.

The lengths to which some companies will go to collect competitive intelligence was evidenced when corporate spies hired by Oracle were found going through the garbage of arch-rival Microsoft during its antitrust trial. Incidentally, in most U.S. jurisdictions this is perfectly legal. Garbage, so long as it is in public view on the curb, in a trash can, or a dumpster is generally regarded as discarded property which can be taken by anyone passing by.

Not all corporate sleuthing is conducted against aerospace, defense and other high-tech targets. When measured in economic terms the stakes may be equally high with respect to some very low-tech targets. For example, some years ago I was approached by the CEO of a company in the chicken processing business. Their headquarters was a beautiful round Palladian-style structure with classical columns, more typical of something one would find on a university campus than connected with a business that made its money processing and packaging chickens. At the top of the columns, the names of the firm's chicken products, such as "Wing Dings," were carved in the masonry as if they were Roman inscriptions.

According to the CEO, a few days earlier an employee who worked on the loading dock at one of their major plants told his supervisor that two men had approached him and tried to buy information concerning the number and size of the shipments coming in and out of the plant. Since the company was private, the CEO was convinced that the two men worked for their primary competitor and were attempting to learn their sales and production volumes by basing their estimates on the

---

88 "FBI: Spies Cost U.S. Firms $2B a Month," *USA Today*, February 20, 1999.

loading dock figures. The competitor had already been caught trying to steal the company's proprietary chicken processing technology and the company, in turn, had won a large damage award against the competitor.

Our initial skepticism about the case quickly evaporated after we recorded a second meeting between the loading dock worker and the two men in a local restaurant where they repeated their offer and even sweetened it. The case continues to be a reminder that while the targets of some corporate espionage may seem mundane, the consequences, in terms of lost revenue, market share, proprietary technology, and lost jobs may be no less serious than the theft of high-tech intellectual property and national defense technology.

Just as someone on the loading dock was targeted in the case just cited, almost anyone in a company can be the target of corporate espionage, even a secretary or someone on a cleaning crew, as noted in Chapter Three. Actually, secretaries, file clerks, and other low-level workers, especially technicians, may have access to more sensitive data than high-level executives who often concentrate on big-picture issues and whose computer literacy extends only to using their email accounts. Ronald Pelton, Aldrich Ames, members of Walker spy ring, and so many other spies who inflicted so much damage on the security of the United States were all relatively low-level employees of their organizations. The former Soviet Union specifically targeted lonely women working on Capitol Hill or the U.S. government with specially-trained Casanovas who would draw them into a relationship and then induce them to steal secrets.

SECRECY

Secrecy, or at least discretion, is often appropriate, but sometimes it can be carried to an extreme and become absurd. A good example was a meeting I had in a motel near Miami International. The motel had a fourteen-piece Latin band in the bar and more "floaters" in the pool than any other hospitality establishment in the U.S. They had recently failed to discover a dead body under a bed for three days, and the room was occupied during that time by new guests every night.

The client I was scheduled to meet with called me at my office in Washington on several occasions and swore me to secrecy, saying that no one should know of my rendezvous with him and that I should be very low key. I asked at one point if one of my colleagues could accompany me, and he quickly rejected the idea out-of-hand. Finally, the day of the meeting arrived and I made my way to the motel. The lobby looked like something out of the Star Wars bar scene, full of suspicious-looking characters and guys listing from the heat they were packing in their armpits.

Taking my client at his word, I was dressed in an open-collar shirt, a dark sport coat, and a pair of slacks, nothing fancy that called attention to me. I had asked the client how I would recognize him and he said I should sit on one of the couches in the lobby and he would find me.

My long-time friend and business associate, Larry Ursich, had accompanied me and I had described the client's paranoia, so he was sitting a short distance away so as not to spook him. The hour of the meeting came and went, and I was growing impatient when a tall figure appeared in the doorway. I blinked my eyes is disbelief. The guy was at least six-six and rail thin. But the real attention getter was that he was an albino, with pink eyes and white hair, and dressed from head to toe in white, including white shoes and a white belt. Every conversation in the lobby stopped dead in its tracks and every set of eyes was firmly fixed on the albino, who walked directly over to me, shook hands and sat down.

"Did anyone follow you?" he asked.

"No," I responded, not believing that he thought I might be the one that attracted unwarranted attention.

We completed our business within fifteen minutes and during that time there wasn't a soul in the joint that was unaware of the albino's presence or that we were having a meeting in the lobby.

NO PLACE TO RUN

Scores of Americans go missing every year in the U.S. and overseas. In some cases the missing person has simply decided to drop out, in other cases they are running from the law, creditors, or unhappy marriages. We've managed to locate a number of criminals wanted in connection with crimes in the United States who have fled the law, changed their names and appearances, and hunkered down in foreign countries hoping to avoid capture. One such individual was a West Coast swindler who had left his partners holding the bag after stealing a large amount of money from the firm's clients. A member of the LDS Church, he was ultimately discovered hiding out in Samoa, where there is a large Mormon community. We had pieced together a great deal of information regarding his flights from the U.S., surreptitious communications with his family, and even where his pets were shipped (to another location in the South Pacific).

We were prepared to snatch him and transport him by boat to nearby American Samoa where he could be handed over to the U.S. attorney, but at the last minute, using information we generated, the government of Samoa decided to cooperate with U.S. authorities and had him arrested and extradited back to California. The lesson is that it is harder than ever before to disappear without a trace. Computer data banks made it relatively easy to trace phone and computer communications, travel records, banking information, and identity cards, including passports and driver's licenses.

It is virtually impossible to avoid video surveillance systems in many Western countries. Most stores and fast-food restaurants employ CCTV (closed circuit television) cameras to enhance their security, and governments are now installing cameras in public places to monitor terrorist or criminal activities. It's estimated that there are four million CCTV cameras in the United Kingdom alone, and that every Londoner is photographed an average of 30 times a day.[89] Officials in New York City recently announced they were going to step up video surveillance in public places and in the subway system, and police cameras have been upgraded and boast excellent resolution.

You can even be viewed from overhead platforms, such as spy satellites and UAVs (unmanned aerial vehicles). U.S. government tracking systems are so sophisticated that, prior to Osama bin Laden's death at the hands of SEAL Team Six, they constantly monitored the lawless region along the Afghan-Pakistani border for anyone 6'4" to 6'6" tall, which was thought to have been bin Laden's height, by measuring the shadows they cast, even if mounted on a mule.

A half century ago, a clever bank robber or dropout could acquire a new identity with relative ease, providing that he or she had sufficient funds, and melt into the populace of some out-of-the-way or end-of-the-earth place. Today only if one is not connected to the modern world in any way can he or she hope to truly live below the radar, that is to say if they don't have a job, credit cards, a passport, a driver's license, a phone or computer, or any real property. Indeed, the less time one spends interfacing with technology the better. However, if it

---

89 There are an estimated 500,000 surveillance cameras in London.

is absolutely necessary to have some connectivity, one can buy a prepaid wireless phone and dispose of it after making a few calls. And if you must have a computer, there is software that reroutes your IP address to remote servers so that it cannot be easily traced. But if you really want to drop out, the best advice is to completely erase your digital footprint.

This is supported by the case of the Unabomber, Ted Kaczynski, who was finally found living in a remote cabin in Montana, after years of being pursued by the FBI, and then it was only because of a tip-off received from Kaczynski's brother, who thought he recognized his estranged brother's Luddite rants in a published manifesto from the Unabomber. Few criminals on the lam, however, want to live a subsistence life in the northern Rockies as a way of hiding from authorities.

Some who go missing in remote places are the genuine victims of foul play or accidents, as in the case of two young men who disappeared in Nicaragua. I was contacted on a Sunday in November by the family of one of the missing men and we immediately went into action. While we were initially concerned that the men may have been kidnapped, it soon became apparent that they had been hiking on a volcano located on a 107 square mile island named Ometepe in Lake Nicaragua. Neither man had much climbing experience and it appeared that they had decided to climb the volcano at the last minute, and had not taken adequate clothing or supplies of food and water with them. Search teams spent days looking for them with little success, but we were convinced that they were someplace on the volcanic mountain. Finally, a search team saw vultures circling over a site and discovered the bodies of both men. It appeared that they had reached the summit late in the day and hadn't realized how cold it could get at altitude despite their proximity to the Equator. Our best guess was that they were cold and hungry, saw the lights of a coastal village and tried to make their way down the treacherous slope in the dark in the direction of the lights. Probably one of the men slipped on the loose rock and the other tried to grab him, and they both tumbled down the slopes and over the edge of a precipice, where they landed on a ledge amidst dense foliage. One was probably killed outright and the other succumbed soon afterward.

CONCLUSION

In business, as in war, all combat is mortal. To think otherwise is to recall the brainless Carter Administration ambassador to a troubled Latin American nation who told his security detail to just try and "wound" any assailants because killing them would be immoral, especially since they were, in his opinion, justified in becoming revolutionaries. The loss of trade secrets and other critical information can lead to the collapse of a company or even a whole industry. One need only remember the disappearance of the machine tool industry in the United States and its shift to Japan, after the Japanese stole blueprints, patents, and designs, and reverse engineered as much equipment as they could get their hands on.

Whether we like it or not, we live in a world where it's possible to get just about anything on anyone. This reality has transformed both business and statecraft, and the person or country with the best and most up-to-date information is likely to win, whether it's a competition for new markets and products or for global political and military supremacy. In an attempt to better protect trade secrets, the U.S. has adopted the Uniform Trade Secrets Act and the Economic Espionage Act of 1996, which criminalizes the theft or misappropriation of trade secrets either to benefit a foreign power or purely for economic purposes. Such laws, however, are poorly enforced and have penalties that are too weak to be a deterrent to many industrial spies.

CELEBRITY CRISES

"How fast will your sneakers/jackets/sports
drinks fly off the shelves when your poster boy
is photographed slam dancing nude with a porn
star or gets busted outside a nightclub at 3 a.m.
with enough crack rocks to pave a driveway?"

Eric Dexheimer[90]

More than ten years ago, I was asked to meet with one of the Hollywood studio chiefs and explain the kind of services we provided. When I finished, he sighed deeply and said, "Jeez, I wish I had met you guys a few months ago."

"Why?" I inquired.

"Well," he began, sighing heavily again, "There was this ingénue." He spit the word out like it was something sour. "We were filming [in an Asian country] and she walked off the set one day, claiming that the local toilet paper chaffed her precious little bottom and she wasn't going to go back to work again until we got her a case of Charmin. It cost us more than $300,000 a day for every day she didn't work."

"So what did you do?"

"Well, none of our guys knew what to do so we sent one of our vice presidents over there, first class, with a case of Charmin. It took three days before she was back to work and it cost us more than $1 million dollars. What would you have done?"

I told him there were two large U.S. military bases in the country at that time and we would have just found one of the PXs (post exchanges) and paid fifty bucks to the first serviceman or family

---

90 Erick Dexheimer, "Jocks on the Rocks," *Denver Westword*, October 22, 2006.

member that would go inside an buy us a case of Charmin. The studio chief shook his head and repeated, "I sure wish I'd known of you guys a few months ago. Would have saved us some real money."

Then there was the veteran actress and Hollywood liberal who found one of her rings missing (valued at $60,000) and decided to polygraph (use a lie detector) her entire staff, all of whom were black or Hispanic, to learn if any of them had taken it. So much for her liberal ideals. We met with her agent and told him that it is generally prohibited for private sector employers, with a few exceptions, to require a polygraph examination as a condition of employment and referred him to the Employee Polygraph Protection Act of 1988. And should her use of the polygraph become public, we continued, it would likely be a public relations disaster, given the race and ethnicity of her employees. The actress took our advice and canceled the polygraph tests. The following day the ring was discovered in the pool house where it had been left by her daughter.

The case of former NBA player Jayson Williams illustrates the darker side of celebrity crises. In 2002 he was giving a tour of his 30,000 square foot New Jersey mansion and handling a shotgun when it allegedly discharged, killing a 55-year old limo driver, Costas "Gus" Christofi. On January 11, 2010, he was sentenced to five years in prison after pleading guilty to aggravated assault. He had earlier paid $2.75 million to Christofi's family to settle a wrongful death suit.

Celebrities, by their very nature, have more than their share of crises, some large, some small. From accusations that the late Michael Jackson sexually abused children and Hugh Grant dallied with a he-she on Sunset Boulevard to celebrities accused of murder (O.J. Simpson, Phil Spectre, Ray Lewis and Robert Blake, to name only a few), trouble just seems to follow many actors, sports stars, and other people in the limelight.

Such crises are fodder for the tabloids and grist for celebrity-obsessed television programs, and it would end there if it were not for the fact that so many major corporations have sizable investments in celebrities as spokespersons and endorsers of their products. According to Bill Kinlay, CEO of Mindshare, "Personality endorsements always come with baggage attached. Individuals can screw you--and more importantly, your brand, up, that's the problem."

For example, a celebrity charged with sexual misconduct, especially involving children or under-age women, generally is damaged goods and not the kind of representative most companies want hawking their products or even appearing on programs they sponsor. CBS canceled a Michael Jackson television special after he was charged with molesting a young boy, representing a major financial loss to the network. Jonathan Holiff, president of the Hollywood-Madison Group, which specializes in celebrity endorsements, subsequently asserted that, "Jackson is beyond any image resuscitation." Only in death has the pop star been somewhat rehabilitated.

Sports Illustrated estimates that golfer Tiger Woods lost $22 million in endorsements after revelations of his sordid marital infidelities became public.[91] Among the companies that dropped him were Gillette, AT&T, TAG Heuer, Accenture, and Gatorade. The *New York Post* said that a year away from golf and all of the negative publicity associated with Woods could cost him $180 million in lost endorsements, tournament prizes, and appearances.[92] In addition, it was estimated that Woods' problems could cost $591 million in losses to the PGA and various companies that had hired him to promote their products.[93]

Among the sports and entertainment celebrities who have lost corporate endorsements in recent years are: Madonna, who was dumped by Pepsi after her "Like a Prayer" video showing burning crosses; Olympic sprinter Ben Johnson, who tested positive for steroids (Diadora); basketball star Kobe Bryant, who was charged with sexual assault (McDonald's, Nike, and Nutella); Atlanta Falcon's star quarterback Michael Vick, who was sent to prison after a dog fighting conviction (Coca Cola, Kraft Foods, Nike, Upper Deck, Rawlings, Donruss, and AirTran); Bill Maher, who called Americans "cowards" for lobbing cruise missiles at distant targets on his television show "Politically Incorrect" (Sears and Federal Express); golfer Fuzzy Zoeller because of racial slurs; O.J. Simpson, who was tried for a double homicide (Hertz); supermodel Kate Moss, after she was photographed allegedly using cocaine (Chanel, Burberry, and H&M); Eric Clapton, who revealed he was alcoholic (Anheuser-Busch); golfer John Daly as a

---

91 "Report: Woods Lost $22 Million," *ESPN Golf*, quoting an AP story, July 21, 2010.

92 Todd Venezia, James Fannelli, and Holly Sanders, "Tiger To Suffer a '180M' Slice," *New York Post*, Dec. 13, 2009.

93 *Ibid.*

result of his drinking problems (Callaway and Wilson sporting goods), and Olympic swimmer Michael Phelps, after he was photographed smoking marijuana (Kellogg's). Dennis Rodman was dropped by Converse shoes simply because of his erratic behavior and bizarre apparel. After pleading guilty to felony cocaine possession, former Dallas Cowboy football star, Michael Irvin, not only lost more than a million dollars a year in endorsements but was sued by one of the company's that hired him for $1.2 million in lost sales and another $200,000 for an advertising campaign that was canceled. According to Richard Morin, citing a study of publicly traded companies, "...if the celebrity endorser's publicly revealed behavior is notorious enough, it can cause the company's stock price to drop, decreasing the total value of a firm by as much as 2 percent."[94]

Sometimes organizations just don't do enough research before retaining high-profile celebrity spokespersons as in the case of Cybill Shepherd, who was hired by the Beef Industry Council to promote beef consumption until it was learned that she didn't eat meat. Similarly, James Garner also sold beef until he had a heart attack and a triple bypass. Actress Helena Bonham Carter was fired by Yardley cosmetics after it she admitted that she didn't wear makeup. The Rolling Stones' Voodoo Lounge Tour, which was sponsored by Volkswagen, was progressing without a hitch until drummer Charlie Watts told a questioner, "I wouldn't be seen dead in a Volkswagen. I prefer Mercedes myself." Tennis star Martina Hingis endorsed Italian athletic shoes made by Tacchini until she sued the company alleging that their shoes caused injury to her feet.

Today some stars are just so radioactive that they couldn't give away their product endorsements. A good illustration is actor Mel Gibson, whose tirades against African Americans and Jews, and threats against his estranged wife have probably ended his career, certainly as a celebrity endorser. Figure skater Tanya Harding and NFL great O.J. Simpson also belong in the same category for obvious reasons. Among the problems that generally eliminate sports and entertainment stars from consideration as endorsers or spokespersons are steroid use, HIV affliction, serious substance abuse, anti-Americanism, anti-Semitism, racism, sexual battery, and, of course, felony crimes. Even less serious

---

94 Richard Morin, "When Celebrity Endorsers Go Bad," *The Washington Post*, February 3, 2002, p. B5.

crimes can ruin careers of celebrity endorsers, as in the case of Jennifer Capriati's arrest for shoplifting.

Many sports stars and celebrities suffer from a lack of education and judgment, and are often surrounded by people of questionable motives, who are eager to make themselves "indispensable" by procuring prostitutes and drugs or getting the star into risky investments and pastimes. We were retained by the owner of a well-known sports team to investigate the theft of a vehicle from the home of the team's major franchise player, who was also accused of hosting a series of noisy parties that had produced complaints by neighbors and visits by the police. When we arrived at the player's house, we were shocked to find 311 weapons strewn about the residence, ranging from handguns to assault rifles. The player already had a gun charge pending in another state and was so clueless he didn't even know how to clear a weapon. Since nearly all of the weapons had been purchased for cash out of car trunks and from members of his posse, there was no inventory of what he had and we could only speculate on how many weapons may have been taken by party guests and possibly used in the commission of crimes. We quietly disposed of all of the guns and got counseling for the player, but several years later he acquired more weapons and was suspended by the league after being arrested on a gun charge and other inappropriate behavior. He pled guilty to carrying a weapon without a license and was sentenced to two years of probation. Polls suggested that he was "one of the most disliked people in sports." Once worth tens of millions of dollars a year in endorsements, he is now damaged goods.

STALKING

What do Madonna, the late Princess Diana, tennis greats Martina Hingis and Serena Williams, Sylvester Stallone, Steven Spielberg, Cher, Rod Steward, Elizabeth Taylor, Olivia Newton-John, Michael J. Fox, feminist writer Germaine Greer, and the ten women named in 1982 as Omaha's "most eligible women" have in common? They are just a few of people who have been stalked by obsessed fans and mental cases.

Not only celebrities are victims of stalking. One of the worst stalking cases we ever handled involved a beautiful young woman who was about to be married. She began to receive highly pornographic and explicit mail, as did her husband-to-be and his family. The letters claimed that the young woman was a slut and a whore, and one letter announced that the writer would "see you at the wedding all dressed in white! What a joke." Other letters warned the husband-to-be that the young woman was a gold digger and would give him everything he wanted in bed until his wife-to-be got her hands on his money. In letters to the future parents-in-law, the writer accused the young woman of making various slurs against them and telling them not to let their son marry such a vile and contemptible young woman. "We expect complete confidentiality from you," one letter read, "and expect you to just destroy this letter or save it and give (sic.) to your schmucko son with his divorce papers in about 3 years." In a letter to the future groom, the writer said the only things the bride-to-be excelled at "is a good blow job and opening cans with her nose."

The letter writer, purporting to be the young woman, also canceled various wedding commitments, such as the caterer and the ballroom for the reception, and described in detail how easy it would be to sabotage the wedding. "One of the letters closed with," Remember what goes around comes around and sometimes those ghosts come back to haunt you and possible (sic.) to hurt you." As time went by, the letters became more graphic and threatening, thereby crossing the line and becoming criminal behavior. Typical was a letter that expressed hope that the young woman would be raped, that her left arm would be cut off, that she would get AIDS, that she would crash her new car and be paralyzed, concluding with, "I hate you and you just won't go away you won't get out of my face so i (sic.) can only wish tragedy for you; wish you would just not exist." The letter writer was clearly threatening to harm the young woman and we began to coordinate our investigation with local law enforcement. We also commissioned a profile of the stalker from a firm run by former members of the FBI's Behavioral Sciences Division. They concluded, among other things, that the letter writer was likely a woman trying to write in a man's voice.

The letters and efforts to sabotage the wedding were a nightmare for the bride-to-be and her future husband and in-laws. We collected fingerprints and other evidence and ultimately concluded that the letter writer was someone the bride knew very well because of the vindictive nature of the letters and references to personal information known only to a small circle of the young woman's friends and relatives.

The culprit turned out to be the young woman's stepmother, who was only a few years older than the bride-to-be and insanely jealous because the father was neither as attractive nor as well-off as the future groom. Accordingly, we staked out the wedding and had the step mother under constant surveillance except when she went into the women's bathroom and wrote a profane threat on the mirror with a lipstick. Fortunately, one of the bride's best friends found the message before anyone else saw it and we erased it so that it would not upset other guests. In the end, the wedding and reception went off without a hitch and the issue of the stepmother was handled within the family.

We have also represented several CEOs and other prominent corporate figures who have been stalked by strangers. In one case the victim, who headed a firm which specialized in hi-tech investments, turned down a request for funding from a young man who, to all outward appearances, was a benign and good-humored geek. The geek then underwent a frightening character transformation and angrily confronted the CEO near her car and made threatening remarks. He subsequently entered her office suite and tried to barge into her office before he was stopped by building security. When the CEO contacted the police they said there was little they could do and recommended that she ask the court for a restraining order. Fearing for her life, the CEO wanted more direct action. We subsequently were hired and ultimately met with the geek's parents, who lived in the Midwest and were very worried about their son, whom they described as having "mental issues." With their help, we managed to get the son institutionalized before he did something for which he would have been arrested. He fit the categories of a resentful or rejected stalker, according to a study by Paul E. Mullen and three colleagues in *The American Journal of Psychiatry*, who often believe they are persecuted and exhibit delusional behavior and signs of paranoia and schizophrenia.[95]

Most stalkers, however, appear to be seeking intimacy or sexual contact with the objects of their unwanted affection. Studies suggest that the great majority of stalking victims are women being stalked by men, although Catherine Zeta-Jones testified in court about a jealous woman who threatened to slash her "like O.J. did." In the case of males, by contrast, according to one study 41% of their stalkers are other men. Late Night TV host David Letterman had a stalker named Margaret Mary Ray, a diagnosed schizophrenic. Ray was repeatedly

---

95 Paul E. Mullen, et. al., "Study of Stalkers," *The American Journal of Psychiatry*, August, 1999.

arrested and was sentenced to multiple terms in jail and mental facilities before her suicide in 1998. Although she also reportedly stalked retired astronaut Story Musgrave, she was quoted as saying of Letterman, "I love him and want to spend the rest of my life with him."[96]

In a more typical case, we were contacted by representatives of a leading female sports figure, who was better known for her beauty than her athletic triumphs, after a naked man was found in the swimming pool next door to her home (he had missed the address by one number) with her name tattooed over his entire body, and I mean his *ENTIRE* body. Immediate steps were taken to protect the sports star and to have the man committed to a mental facility.

The most dangerous category of stalker, according to the Mullen study is the predatory stalker, who follows the victim in preparation for an attack on them. Mark David Chapman, who murdered Beatle great John Lennon fits in this category, as does Mike Abram, who broke into George Harrison's home near London and stabbed the former Beatle and his wife. Abram had spent time in a psychiatric ward and had long-term substance abuse problems. According to his mother, "He hates them [the Beatles] and even believes they are witches and takes their lyrics seriously."[97] To illustrate the bizarre thinking of some stalkers, the recording artist Bjork was stalked by a man who built an acid bomb with the intention of disfiguring the star whom he loved so much. He eventually shot himself, but police found over twenty hours of videotape showing the dead man fantasizing about killing Bjork because he could not bear seeing her with anyone else. The acid bomb was intercepted in the mail before it reached Bjork in England.

Perhaps one of the most infamous murders by a stalker was that of Rebecca Schaeffer, a popular television actress. She was stalked for three years by an Arizona resident named Robert John Bardo who eventually showed up at her apartment in Los Angeles and shot her to death when she answered the door. He had secured her address for $250 from Tucson detective agency which obtained it by accessing California Department of Motor Vehicles (DMV) records. After his arrest, Bardo was tried, found guilty, and sentenced to life without the

---

96 "Letterman Stalker Margaret Mary Ray Dies," *The Washington Post*, October 7, 1998.

97 John Leland, "Bloody Attack on a Beatle," *Newsweek*, January 10, 2000, p. 53.

chance of parole. The state of California subsequently enacted legislation prohibiting the release of personal information by the DMV.[98] Her murder also figured prominently in the California state legislature's decision to pass one of the toughest anti-stalking laws in the nation.

Stalking celebrities, nevertheless, continues to be a serious problem. As recently as August, 2010, Academy Award winning actress Sandra Bullock was forced to obtain a three-year restraining order from a judge in Los Angeles against a man obsessed with her, who has been confined to a mental hospital in Wyoming. Even ambush journalist Michael Moore had to get a restraining order on a former employee who was subjecting him the same kind of relentless scrutiny for which he is so famous.

Stalking is a growing problem on university campuses. In one of the best-known cases, in 2009 a man named Stephen P. Morgan killed a 21-year old Wesleyan University student, Johanna Justin-Jinich, whom he first met when they both attended a summer school course at New York University. Ms. Justin-Jinich was Jewish and Morgan had expressed strong anti-Semitic views. It turned out that he had made harassing phone calls to her and sent her at least 38 email messages described as "insulting."

Technology has aided stalkers in a number of ways. In 1997, the Academy of Television, Arts and Sciences, lost the names, addresses, and phone numbers of its 9000 members, many of whom were celebrities, although the list was subsequently returned after a lawsuit was filed by the Academy. Various data banks, containing information about real property ownership, driver's licenses, lawsuits, and other records can be relatively easily obtained. Once a stalker has an address, he or she can generally find an image of the house on Google Earth. Perhaps the most disturbing recent news regarding technology that aids and abets stalkers was the revelation that cellular phone companies like AT&T "had this little deal where you could find your family member through her cellphone" using the phone's GPS.[99] "When cellphone users sign up for a 'family plan' that includes two or more phones, they

---

98 The Driver's Privacy Protection Act of 1994.

99 Justin Scheck, "Stalkers Exploit Cellphone GPS," *The Wall Street Journal*, August 5, 2010.

have the option to contact the carrier and activate a tracking feature intended to allow them to keep tabs on their children."[100] The U.S. Justice Department estimates that 25,000 adults are stalked every year using GPS systems.[101]

CONCLUSION

Gary, Rob, Willie and I arrived in the ski resort late in the afternoon and drove to a sprawling modern house of stone and timber perched on a bluff. We were met by the owner, a forty-ish woman who had been one of the founders of a billion dollar international company, and now divided her time between various homes throughout the U.S. and the Caribbean. She had lustrous dark eyes and hair that cascaded to her waist, but there was something very restless about her and she had two private jets on standby so she could travel anywhere at a moment's notice. She had been married nine times and was going through a messy divorce with her most recent husband, an ex-con whose portrait in the living room displayed him dressed in all black and sneering like Elvis. The client was generous, but needy, and clearly was using drugs to dull the pain she felt in her personal life.

She was convinced that her soon-to-be-ex-husband was stalking her and probably even tapping her telephones, which was why we brought a former White House electronic countermeasures specialist with us. After dinner, she invited me to take a tour of the house. When we reached her bedroom, she led me into a walk-in clothes closet as large as a two-car garage, and pulled me down next to her on the carpet. She opened her safe and asked me to hold up my hand. She languidly licked my third finger and then slid a ring with a diamond the size of a grape onto it. Then she pulled out more rings and repeated the same action until all of my fingers were covered with rings containing priceless gems. She explained that she was missing many pieces from her collection and believed that her most recent husband had taken the items, although she couldn't be sure. I asked her if the items were insured but she didn't think so, nor did she have any kind of inventory of her jewelry or bills of sale. She wanted the house completely secured, she said, so that nothing else could be taken and that she and

---

100 *Ibid.*

101 *Ibid.*

her children would be safe. Given that the resort's cell phone providers were still analog, and not digital, there was a good chance that the husband was eavesdropping on her calls, and a mysterious van had been parked on the residential street on numerous occasions. We provided her with a comprehensive plan on how to reconfigure her life and home to better ensure her privacy.

In the final analysis, stalking is a form of assault, even if the victim is not physically harmed. As in the case cited above, the victim felt a total sense of vulnerability and her anxiety fed her drug dependency.

In recent years stalking has been criminalized in virtually every state and generally courts are willing to shield victims of alleged stalking with restraining orders and harassment charges. Nevertheless, many victims complain of long-term psychological problems as a result of stalking, including clinical depression. That is why stalking must be dealt with quickly and effectively before the experience has a lasting impact on the victim.

- 8 -

CORPORATE GOVERNANCE

*"Every day you pick up the business
section and it reads like a crime page."*

Nancy Smith
Former SEC Official

"I am no bin Laden," pleaded Parmalat executive, Giovanni Bonici, in response to vitriolic news accounts and demands that he return to Italy (from Venezuela) for questioning, following the collapse of the Italian milk products company.[102] Then he switched to the Eichmann defense, trying to distance himself from other top officials accused of looting more than $7 billion from the company, by announcing, "I am only a solider. I obey."

The very fact that Bonici would even have to protest that he was no Osama bin Laden, the most notorious terrorist in the world, suggests how far corporate executives have fallen in public esteem following recent corporate scandals and disclosures of rampant corporate greed. Enron, Tyco, Adelphia, Global Crossing, Conrad Black's Hollinger International, ImClone, Credit Lyonnais, Health South, WorldCom, Arthur Anderson, Fannie Mae, Freddie Mac, AIG--the list of shame goes on and on, and with it a growing number of indictments of corporate officers. In addition, hardly a day goes by when some other example of corporate malfeasance doesn't make news. Allfirst Bank, a subsidiary of Allied Irish Banks, fired its chief executive after one of the bank's currency traders, who was subsequently indicted, lost $750 million in fraudulent currency transactions.

---

102 *The Independent* (London), "Wanted Parmalat Executive Insists He Is 'No bin Laden," January 5, 2004.

In 2002, R.J. Reynolds was accused of knowingly violating the U.N. sanctions on Iraq and helping Russian and Colombian organized crime organizations launder billions of dollars. That same year Broadway National Bank was also convicted of assisting criminals launder millions of dollars in drug proceeds. After more than one hundred separate investigations of wrong-doing, Credit Lyonnais was described by *Forbes* as, "The Dirtiest Bank in the World."[103] The former chairman of Inverworld plead guilty to conspiracy to commit fraud and money-laundering after bilking Mexican investors out of more than $300 million.

Dozens, if not hundreds of companies, have been accused of misstating, if not outright fabricating, their financial statements, from Sunbeam and Waste Management to Enron. In June, 2002, WorldCom owned up to a $3.8 billion "accounting error." The telecom giant had earlier acquired MCI, which had already suffered from an accounting scandal that sent one of its employees to jail for cooking the books.

Insider trading allegations have plagued dozens of brokerage firms and other financial institutions. Former Merrill Lynch star analyst, Jack Grubman, was given a life-time ban from Wall Street. A former FBI agent has been charged with providing stock traders with secret information regarding corporate criminal probes so that they could short-sell stock in the affected companies. Just weeks before the collapse, moreover, some Wall Street analysts were still recommending their clients buy Enron stock. Laura Unger, an SEC commissioner described her concerns regarding "analysts still continuing the strong buy recommendation as recently as the last couple of weeks when it [the stock] was at 90 cents."[104]

CORPORATE BOARDS

In 1962, a man who was only too happy to serve on a number of corporate boards told a reporter, "No effort of any kind is called for.

---

103 "The Dirtiest Bank in the World," *Forbes*, December 13, 1999. The real dirtiest bank in the world was the VEF bank in Riga, Latvia, which was offered to the author for next to nothing. The Treasury Department encouraged me to take it over on the understanding that I would clean it up, but the recession made any consideration of the VEF bank unrealistic.

104 "'Analysts' Take Heat for Enron Buy Recommendations," *Energy on Line*, December 7, 2001.

You go to a meeting once a month in a car supplied by the company, you look grave, and on two occasions say, 'I agree.'...If you have five directorships, it is total heaven, like having a permanent hot bath." One seldom needed financial or accounting expertise to be a director, or even a member of the audit committee. To illustrate the point, O.J. Simpson, who probably has a room temperature I.Q., once served on the audit committee of Infinity Broadcasting.

"In earlier decades," writes Edward Iwata, "corporate honchos ran their businesses free from the scrutiny of shareholders. Executives cut backroom deals with see-no-evil directors, who often were golfing buddies of CEOs--what Vanguard Group founder and shareholder activist John Bogle calls 'the happy conspiracy.' Top Executives pocketed outrageous pay packages, loans and other perquisites even if their companies were tanking."[105] GE's Jack Welch, generally regarded as an effective manager, lived like a pasha at the company's expense with a penthouse apartment in New York City overlooking Central Park, a 737 aircraft and helicopters at his disposal, lifetime membership in three expensive golf clubs in the south, rare wines, extravagant floral displays, high-tech communications equipment, and just about every other perk he desired. Jane Welch's divorce papers even mention a $15,000 "dog umbrella stand." And then there was the birthday party Dennis Kozlowski threw for his wife in Sardinia, paid for by Tyco, which cost more than $1 million, and had a gladiator theme. The centerpiece was an ice sculpture of Michelangelo's David, strategically mounted on a table so that vodka could be poured into guests' glasses through its genitalia.

Similarly, not long ago when a senator or congressman left Capitol Hill, especially a senator or congressman who had important committee assignments, he or she would likely be named to the board of directors of several large corporations. The hours were short, the pay was considerable, and the meetings were usually held in vacation spots. No more. Thanks to the epidemic of corporate failures, shareholder lawsuits, and out-and-out criminality on the part of some executives, service on corporate boards is no longer looked upon as a plum assignment.

---

105 Edward Iwata, "Activist Shareholders Claim Bigger Voice in Running Companies," *USA Today*, March 5, 2004.

"It's very different now than six golf games and a few meetings a year," says Dana R. Hermanson of Kennesaw State University's Corporate Governance Center. "What was once an honorary way to cap off a career is now a real job with real expectations and time commitment of at least a few hundred hours a year...And if you look at what they get paid, you can see many politicians saying, it's just not worth it."[106]

Former House Majority Leader Dick Armey concurs: "I studied [corporate board membership] for a long time. I knew that historically it has been a popular thing for former members to do. But I decided against it for three reasons: It takes a lot of time and hard work, especially in this post-Enron world. It takes a lot of what my wife and I call 'relationship maintenance,' and there is a lot of potential legal exposure. And the pay is just not commensurate with all that."[107]

Post-Enron, potential legal exposure, and inadequate compensation. This just about sums it up. In just a little more than a decade, board membership has gone from a mark of respect to a mark of Cain, from something to be proud of to something to be side-stepped or handled with kid gloves if unavoidable. And if Enron, Tyco, Global Crossing, and WorldCom weren't enough, the second round of corporate failures in the investment banking, mortgage, insurance, and construction sectors that accompanied the Great Recession have totally transformed the roles of corporate officers and board members.

Today there is also tighter oversight over corporate CEOs and other officers. One of the poster boys for bad behavior was Gary Winnick at Global Crossing. He didn't just ruin his company, on the way down he sucked the lifeblood out of it for his own benefit. Never has the term "personal cash cow" been more appropriate.

Born into a middle-class family, Winnick graduated from C.W. Post, a small college near his home on Long Island, and then became a furniture salesman. In 1970, he joined Drexel Burnham as a broker, and moved to Los Angeles, where he went to work on the bond desk next to a young man named Michael Milken. After learning the ropes, Winnick left Drexel to start his own investment firm, which he called

---

106 Ben White; "Declining a Place at the Table"; *The Washington Post*; February 27, 2002; p. E4.

107 *Ibid.,* p. E1.

the Pacific Capital Group (PCG). It was there that he got the idea, actually from someone else, to launch Global Crossing as a player in the hot-and-getting-hotter telecom industry, tapping into the rich market of voice and data traffic from the United States to Europe via an undersea fiber-optic cable. Already a wealthy man by normal standards, he pumped $15 million of his own money into the new firm and it was off and running.

"While he may not have understood anything about fiber-optic loops or building an undersea broadband network--he bought a video that showed how undersea cable was laid--Winnick knew how to do one thing very well: raise money," writes Julie Creswell in *Fortune*.[108] With the help of Salomon Smith Barney and the now-infamous Jack Grubman, Winnick took Global Crossing public. Thanks to inflated projections and a great deal of hype, the company's initial market cap was $38 billion, which was greater than that of Ford Motor Company. Winnick's share of Global Crossing was estimated at a cool $1.4 billion.

In 1999-2000, in addition to selling large blocks of Global Crossing stock, he received almost $3 million in bonuses, plus various fees the company paid to Pacific Capital Group, Winnick's own holding company. Earlier he had entered into a sweetheart deal with PCG Telecom, a subsidiary of Pacific Capital, whose staff consisted of Winnick and three Global Crossing board members, to provide marketing and development advice in exchange for two percent of Global Crossing's gross revenues. When the deal was canceled by Global Crossing on June 30, 1998, in addition to nearly $10 million in fees, Winnick and his team were paid $135 million in stock as compensation for the termination.[109]

Winnick profited in every way he could before the company collapsed, including $3.8 million for the renovation of his office suite. The furniture alone cost $1 million. Global Crossing also paid $400,000 a month in rent to PCG for its office space in Beverly Hills; the building, of course, was owned by PCG. A corporate culture of greed ran rampant at Global Crossing, as an investigation by my company confirmed, involving other top officers running up millions

---

108   Julie Creswell with Naomi Prins, "The Emperor of Greed," *Fortune*, June 24, 2002, p. 110.

109 *Ibid.*, p. 114.

of dollars in expenses and even putting their mistresses on the company payroll at salaries of more than a half million dollars a year. Four of Global Crossing's top executives received at least $23 million in personal loans from the company, as well as extravagant after-tax signing bonuses and stock options. The company also had five corporate jets, including a Boeing 737, to shuttle its senior management around the globe.

Global Crossing also paid more than $1 million to build-out its Washington, D.C., office suite, which was nearly 12,000 square feet and included $18,000 desks and a etched glass wall showing its international reach.[110] In order to curry favor in Washington, Winnick helped Democratic National Committee Chairman Terry McAuliffe turn $100,000 worth of stock into $18 million.

As the company slid toward bankruptcy, with employees losing their jobs and pensions and vendors going unpaid, Winnick continued to pour money into his nine acre Bel Air mansion, which was valued at nearly $100 million.

SARBANES-OXLEY

Given the excesses of Winnick and others, Congress passed the Sarbanes-Oxley Act of 2002, which was signed into law by President George W. Bush on July 30, 2002. The act, which applies only to public companies, requires much more rigorous accounting and auditing standards, stronger financial disclosures, and restricts conflicts of interest. It imposes new criminal penalties for destroying, altering, concealing, and falsifying corporate records. The act mandates that the CEO and CFO must certify in writing the accuracy of the company's financial statements, with criminal penalties for knowingly putting out untrue statements or information or omitting key data. The act also established a five member Public Company Accounting Oversight

---

110 My previous company, GlobalOptions Inc., was offered the space by our landlord since we were located in the same L Street building and needed room to expand. We moved in just days later and enjoyed the lavish surroundings, although I brought my own office furniture rather than use the ultra-modern furnishings purchased by Global Crossing. It was just a coincidence that we had already been engaged to do an investigation of the company by one of its creditors.

Board (PCAOB), overseen by the SEC, to govern the audits of public corporations.

Sarbanes-Oxley spawned a plethora of lawsuits, especially in corporate haven Delaware, contending that the state was doing an inadequate job of protecting shareholders. One of the suits filed was against the management and directors of The Walt Disney Company over the severance package given to Mike Ovitz by Chairman and CEO Michael Eisner. Ovitz had been hired as president but it didn't work out and he left after 15 months on the job with $38 million in cash plus stock options worth $101 million. Ultimately, shareholder anger led to the ouster of Eisner.

Sarbanes-Oxley was widely criticized in some circles for imposing an onerous new regulatory regime on U.S. companies, however studies show that compliance costs averaged less than one-half a percent of revenues for large companies, although the percentage, and its relative financial burden, was far higher for small companies. It has also been asserted that Sarbanes-Oxley compelled some companies to leave the U.S. for foreign domiciles where there is less regulation.

EXECUTIVE LEGAL FEES

Insurance companies covered the cost of the legal defenses of Tyco's Dennis Kozlowski, Adelphia's John L. Riggs, Credit Suisse First Boston's Frank P. Quattrone, and Rite Aid's Frank M. Bergonzi. However, shareholders are increasingly objecting to companies, either directly or in conjunction with rising insurance premiums, paying legal fees for corporate executives charged with wrongdoing. Some boards of directors are imposing new conditions on top executives in their employment contracts requiring that they agree to repay the money if they are found guilty of breaking the law or violating their corporate responsibilities.

Today some executives are conducting their own due diligence before taking a job as CEO or a member of the board. One senior executive hired an investigative firm, which he paid for himself, to do due diligence on a West Coast tech company that wanted him as CEO. When his sleuths questioned certain accounting practices, the company admitted, reluctantly, that the Securities and Exchange Commission was also showing a strong interest in the same subject. On hearing this, the executive said thanks but no thanks. It was not the first time he had declined such an offer. In fact, he'd purportedly had come to the same conclusion on at several occasions before. "You absolutely want to know what you're moving into," he said, "because once you say yes, the gun is at your head."[111]

MEETING THE MOB

The car picked me up at my hotel in Moscow at the arranged time. We then drove around for forty-five minutes to ensure that no one was following us. Finally, we pulled up on a narrow back street at an Uzbek restaurant and I got out of the car. A burly guard was standing near the door and he indicated with the flick of his head that I was to go inside. Once inside I was waved up a set of stairs. Another gunman was standing on the landing and there was a third at the top of the stairs, where I was escorted to a table behind a screen. A few minutes later my host arrived and we had a pleasant lunch, with several of his guards standing with their backs to the screen for the entire lunch to ensure that no one uninvited could approach the table.

Over the years I have met with many of the mob leaders from the Balkans and the CIS countries. It is always an experience to be remembered. The interesting thing is that while I have no illusions about any of them, the crimes they have committed or the people they've killed, I found nearly all of them to be reasonably straight-forward in business dealings. Moreover, I liked most of them personally.

Simion Mogilevich was perhaps the most formidable of all of those with whom I've spent time. He has been described as the most dangerous man in the world, the head of the Russian mob, as the "Brainy Don," and, by the FBI, as "more powerful than a John Gotti."[112] A short, stocky man with a degree in economics who chain smokes and often wears a leather jacket, Mogilevich inspired such fear that even leaders of the U.S. intelligence community said it was "too dangerous even to be in the same room with him." He is on the FBI's Ten Most Wanted list and most everyone gives him wide berth. Waiters in Moscow serve him with trembling hands, fearful that they will spill something or somehow incur his displeasure. Ironically, he's fairly laid-back under most circumstances.

---

111 Joann S. Lublin and Carol Hymowitz, "Fearing Scandals, Executives Spurn CEO Job Offers," *The Wall Street Journal*, June 27, 2002, p. A1.

112 Jeanne Meserve, "FBI: Mobster 'More Powerful Than a John Gotti'," CNN.com/crime, October 21, 2008.

In many parts of the world it's necessary to do business with warlords, gangsters, corrupt officials, and assorted low-lifes, including presidential bagmen and kidnappers. That's because business in many parts of the globe is far from pristine and if you are to survive, much less prosper, you may need to interact with people like this; the key, of course, is not to be corrupted or tainted yourself. In a majority of the world's nations businesses generally have to pay some form of extortion or "protection" money to ensure that government licenses will be issued, inspections will be passed, inventory will not be damaged, and that the company can operate without the threats against management and employees. This is just a cost of doing business so long as the amounts are not exorbitant and may require some contact with underworld figures or corrupt office holders.

In Russia, a nation long known for corruption at every level of society, recent government efforts, supported by President Dmitry Medvedev, to eliminate bribes have not succeeded, in fact things have become worse according to Prosecutor General Yury Chaika. A recent report for Russian law enforcement agencies states that the average bribe has risen from 23,100 rubles ($770) in 2009 to 30,500 rubles ($1,015) in 2010.[113]

FOREIGN CORRUPT PRACTICES ACT (FCPA)

The Foreign Corrupt Practices Act (FCPA) was enacted in 1977, after the Securities and Exchange Commission (SEC) conducted a number of investigations which revealed that more than 400 U.S. corporations admitted paying bribes or questionable fees overseas to foreign governments and politicians to facilitate business opportunities. The Act makes it illegal for U.S. citizens or foreign citizens living in the United States, U.S. corporations or foreign companies governed by the SEC or organized under the laws of the U.S., to pay anything that could be construed as a bribe in exchange for business. Since many U.S. competitors, including those in Europe, have no qualms about paying bribes, this often places U.S. firms competing for business overseas at a great disadvantage. Moreover, many countries, especially in the Middle East, require foreign firms to have a local partner and it can only be presumed that the local partner, irrespective of any

---

113 *USRBC Daily Update*, October 15, 2010, p. 1.

documents he may sign or promises to the contrary, takes care of local officials in exchange for their support.

Although some bribes are transferred in a suitcase in cash or simply wired to an official's overseas bank account, contemporary bribery is much more sophisticated and discreet than in the past. We worked for a major U.S. defense contractor locked in a tight competition with a European competitor for a multi-billion dollar contract in a key Eastern European nation, and it was discovered that the competitor had paid hundreds of thousands of dollars in bribes to various government officials involved in the final decision as to which defense system would be selected. Some of the children of those officials had their private school tuitions paid by third parties, officials received loans and mortgages at highly favorable interest rates, car loans were paid off, luxury vacations were charged to corporate accounts, and they were given expensive gifts. Although the European defense system was far inferior to the American product, the corrupt officials were willing to compromise the security of their country, and for that matter, potentially the European continent, for a few Euros.

In this case, our information was relayed to the U.S. ambassador to the country in question as well as the U.S. Trade Representative and they told the leadership of that country that the U.S. expected the competition to be fair and transparent, and if it was not that the U.S. was prepared to suspend military cooperation take other retaliatory steps. The U.S. company ultimately received the contract.

By the same token, U.S. firms need to monitor their overseas sales staff to ensure that they are not paying illicit bribes in exchange for contracts. According to Mark Brzezinski, "No longer does the Justice Department rely solely on tips from whistle-blowers or business competitors to build cases. Today, officials are turning the tools of organized-crime investigations to anti-bribery. They are setting up sting operations, as took place in a recent investigation in which defendants from the United States, Britain and Israel allegedly tried to bribe a country's defense minister to provide access to outfit the country's presidential guard."[114]

The 1988 Trade Act included revisions to the Foreign Corrupt Practices Act (FCPA) which clarify what management is expected to know, and

---

114 Mark Brzezinski, "Obama Administration Gets Tough on Business Corruption Overseas," May 28, 2010, A23.

when, and thus what could be deemed criminal actions on the part of management. Exempted are certain routine actions such as obtaining licenses and setting up phone and mail service, which may require facilitation fees in some countries, by contrast to government policy decisions that could lead to a contract.[115]

BUSINESS CONTINUITY

Under the heading of corporate governance, the matter of business continuity planning and preparation should also be discussed. In view of power outages, natural disasters, and terrorist attacks, to mention only a few potential difficulties, it is absolutely incumbent on senior management at any company or organization to take steps to address such problems before they occur. During the great power blackout of 2003, which hit parts of eight states and Canada, affecting 50 million people, 2000 Wal-Mart stores were forced to close, more than 50 automobile plants were shut down, 1200 flights were canceled, and even Detroit's water system lost so much pressure it could not continue to operate. Buses and subways were affected and streets became gridlocked when traffic lights went out. Firms in the affected area lost billions of dollars in missed sales and production.

The same thing happened on 9/11, including many companies housed in the World Trade Center Complex that not only lost employees but all of their records and data. Even the Securities and Exchange Commission (SEC) lost irreplaceable records from pending enforcement cases.[116] However, the 9/11 attacks did spur many companies to undertake business continuity planning, although they tended to be larger, more affluent companies. Indeed, according to the *Financial Times* companies with sales of more than £500 million were twice as likely as companies with a turnover of less than £11 million to have a business continuity plan.[117] Not surprisingly, the most likely disruption companies tried to anticipate was IT failure. Businesses also

---

115 Michael R. Czinkota and Ilkka A. Ronkainen, *Global Business*, (New York: Routledge, 2011), p. 31.

116 David Hilzenbth, "SEC Papers Lost in N.Y. Attacks," *The Washington Post*, September 13, 2010.

117 Mark Hubbard, "Lock the Door Before the Horse Has Bolted," *Financial Times*, March 9, 2004.

recognized the need for backup data storage at off-site facilities. Sandler O'Neill was one of the firms hit hardest by the attack on the World Trade Center. Only 66 of its 171 employees survived. Headquartered on the 104th floor, when the company tried to stand up its operations again in the aftermath of the attacks, it was discovered that, "Every phone number of every person Sandler's traders had done business with over the years was vaporized in the Sept. 11 attacks."[118] The company didn't have an evacuation plan nor had it set up proper backup systems to retain data, including phone directories.[119] Trading operations were salvaged only because a back-office assistant who had answered the trading floor phone for years had a remarkable memory and recalled many of the names and numbers.

A number of New York based firms reduced their footprints in the city and began to scatter their operations to other cities. Other companies with multiple locations reconfigured their computer networks and data systems so that one office could assume the workload of another office in the event of a natural disaster or some other crisis that totally shut down operations at a single location. Some companies have adopted decentralization as a way of addressing cataclysmic events.

In summary, among the elements of a comprehensive business contingency/continuity plan are the following: 1) develop an evacuation plan for each company venue (which should be exercised on a regular basis), 2) establish backup offices in secure locations, 3) have a backup data storage site, 4) outfit all offices and facilities with flashlights, smoke hoods, and other emergency supplies, 5) hire or designate a corporate risk manager, 6) implement a backup communications system, 7) consider decentralizing corporate offices and facilities, and 8) establish a layered management structure where each key executive has a designated replacement in the event they are traveling or incapacitated when the crisis occurs.

For some clients we have gone so far as to purchase small, motorized scooters to facilitate travel to backup sites, under the assumption that traffic lights won't be operational and that there will be massive traffic jams. Another client asked us to set up contingency

---

118 Katrina Brooker, "Starting Over," *Fortune*, January 21, 2002, p. 60.

119 *Ibid.*

systems for saving several hundred million dollars of art masterpieces from her lavish apartment in New York City in the event of a crisis. As she explained, the paintings represented he common heritage of all mankind and, in many respects, were even important than her life and those of her loved ones. Accordingly, we devised a system for removing the paintings from their frames, rolling up the canvases and inserting them in airtight waterproof tubes and taking them to one of several rendezvous points where they would be evacuated by boat or helicopter.

Unfortunately, as 9/11 recedes further and further into the past, some companies are reducing their planning for disaster management mitigation and recovery, and it is becoming rare now to see a company that has a comprehensive and well-rehearsed plan, with provision for backup work sites, communications systems, data networks, and alternative forms of transportation.

CONCLUSION

In the final analysis, every board of directors or corporate management team should consider having its own investigative capability, either by hiring an outside firm or by standing-up an internal team. Without an independent means of keeping track of corporate operations, especially overseas, management can suddenly find itself target of a government investigation, shareholder suits, or charges of negligence by the board of directors. Management can no longer plead ignorance regarding foreign bribes, wasteful spending, health and safety issues, discrimination, or lack of preparedness in the wake of a catastrophic event. Management's compensation must be tied not only to economic performance but to how well executives protect shareholder value, corporate reputation, market share, and brand identification. An investigative capability can also be used to watch the competition.

- 9 -

HI-TECH = HI-RISK

"(T)he Internet is now a profit-generating
machine for organized, dedicated and highly
skilled teams of criminals. They operate in
a truly global environment, largely with impunity
and without fear of the law enforcement response
that serves as their only deterrent."

Threat Working Group of the
CSIS Commission on Cybersecurity
for the 44th President

I had been summoned by a leading venture capitalist: they had lost a number of laptop computers and were concerned that proprietary information regarding some of their forthcoming deals and Initial Public Offerings (IPOs) had been lost. All but one of the computers had disappeared from their headquarters in Midtown Manhattan. When I arrived at their offices, I was greeted by the man who had called me along with the head of the firm, who was, to say the least, skeptical of his colleague's concerns.

There was no security, or even a receptionist, at the entrance, and the offices were opulent but extremely laid back. This was important, the CEO told me, in order to stimulate creativity on the part of their executives. Nor did he want to intimidate the firm's clients from the hi-tech world, who were notoriously casual in their dress and lifestyles. Casual was the order of the day: floppy discs and DVDs were lying about on desks and computers, and I spotted several passwords on ink blotters or taped to keyboards, and none of the file cabinets around the office had locks. They were not totally oblivious to security, the CEO informed me, as he pointed to a door across the large open bullpit where he said all of the deal files were kept, inferring that they were kept under lock and key. But as he was speaking, a bicycle messenger walked out of the room with a pack under his arm.

"Who's that?" I asked.

The shocked CEO sputtered that he didn't know, adding that the messenger clearly didn't belong in the file room. We tried to head the messenger off, but he sprinted for the entrance and disappeared down a stairwell. Shaken by what he'd just witnessed, the much subdued and far more respectful CEO invited me into his office to discuss a security audit of the company. Unbelievably, at that very moment we spotted a pizza delivery man wandering around the office carrying a large Domino's pizza warming bag. He appeared to be eying the desktops.

"Did someone order pizza?" one of the firm's employees inquired of no one in particular.

"No," responded the others in the room.

With that, several employees confronted the pizza delivery man, who claimed that he had gotten off the elevator on the wrong floor. He quickly retreated toward the entrance with several executives of the company in tow. While they couldn't prove that the pizza man was up to no good, he was most likely looking for a purse or laptop to slip into his delivery bag, with no one the wiser.

Most missing laptops are sold on the street or fenced through discount outlets, and the contents of their hard drives and any thumbdrives or CD's are overlooked or ignored by the buyers. Nevertheless, there are rings of thieves who target various law firms and companies specifically for the information their computers contain. During one set of mass tort cases, where billions of dollars were at stake, thieves working for one of the plaintiffs' attorneys systematically stole laptops from dozens of firms involved in the defense in order to gain insight regarding their motions and strategies. One of the defense firms alone lost over a hundred laptops in a single year.

The various defense firms had a common data storage system which permitted anyone with the right password to log in. Security procedures were so lax at the defense law firms, including the fact that passwords were rarely changed, that the plaintiffs' lawyers gained access to the central files and web links of their adversaries by hiring away associates and paralegals in possession of the passwords and knowledge of other safeguards.

In another case, a major New York financial institution recommended that one of its affiliates retain us after an employee had a laptop stolen from his suburban home containing 550,000 names and related financial data. Fearing that the information might be sold to identity thieves or misused in some other fashion, we immediately launched an investigation into the circumstances surrounding the theft of the laptop and set up a massive dragnet designed to recover it. Around the same time, Ameriprise, "a Minneapolis financial planning and insurance company, said an employee's laptop was stolen from a locked car at an off-site location." The laptop contained the names and account numbers of 158,000 Ameriprise clients, and the "names and Social Security numbers of 67,000 current and former financial advisers."[120] The laptop was password protected but not encrypted. But password protection is not enough. As one IT specialist told me, "It should take no more than 12 seconds to find any password [presuming you have the right software]."

Theft of laptops is not confined to in the private sector. In 2000, government officials reported that a laptop was stolen from a conference room at the Department of State in Washington. The laptop contained highly sensitive information about arms proliferation, including materials that could compromise sources and methods. It was only one of thousands of government laptops stolen or misplaced every year.

CYBERCRIME

I was contacted by the managing partner of a Washington law firm who said he thought his offices were bugged. I agreed to meet him at an off-site location, and he described to me how his firm had prepared a highly-confidential piece of legislation for a member of Congress. Just before they were to deliver it to the member, they had a technical problem which delayed them for several hours. In the meantime, they began receiving phone calls from reporters who already had copies of the legislation, even though it had not yet been transmitted to the Hill. "Our phones or offices must be bugged," exclaimed the managing partner.

---

120 Jennifer Levitz & John Hechinger, "Laptops Prove Weakest Link in Data Security," *The Wall Street Journal*, March 24, 2006.

Although we've only found two actual "bugs," or listening devices, over the past thirty-plus years, we agreed to "sweep" the offices. We told him the more likely explanation, however, was that someone had hacked into their computers, and recommended that an audit be done of their computer system.

Our sweep turned up nothing, but the computer audit found that someone was regularly hacking into their server and downloading every document and email from the law firm. And, while our computer security specialist was actually performing the audit, he caught the hacker inside the system and a furious exchange of thrusts and parries ensued with our man's fingers literally flying over his keyboard as he sought to follow the intruder back to his computer. Ultimately, he was successful and we learned that the hacker worked for a large IT company in another city and was moonlighting for the opposing law firm on the other side of the issue. In addition to the hacker and the law firm that was paying him, the hacker's employer also had certain legal liabilities because they had not exercised proper supervision or control over their employee, thus permitting him to engage in illegal activities on his office computer.

Ultimately, we reconfigured and hardened the client's computers and they took legal action against the hacker and his employer, although they couldn't go after the opposing law firm without more evidence.

If you don't take adequate steps to protect your proprietary data, you can be assured that someone unauthorized--competitors or even spies--is likely to be reading your emails and stealing your corporate secrets, often with disastrous consequences. According to one study, "U.S. companies and government agencies report losing more money from theft of proprietary information than any other type of attack on their computer system."[121]

Too many corporate executives are not sufficiently knowledgeable or involved in the details of their corporate information security (IT) programs, whether it is securing laptops or ensuring that their networks are immune to hackers and cyber snoops. If you think your computers are secure, you are probably far more likely to be victimized. The number of ways you can be attacked ranges from viruses and worms to

---

[121] "Theft of Data, Viruses Rank High in Cyber Security," Elinor Mills Abreu, *Reuters*, April 7, 2002.

back doors, denial of service attacks, taps and misinformation, strike back and other information warfare techniques. Among the results of such attacks are the theft of proprietary information, the defacement of websites and pagejacking, critical infrastructure failure, embezzlement, reputation loss, and a host of other problems.

The Internet began without security and few, if any, imagined the threats and problems that would arise in connection with its growth and daily operations. According to a panel at the Centers for Strategic and International Studies, "it will never be possible to retrofit any mechanism to effectively eliminate the threat posed by this omission."[122]

The original hackers were young, predominantly male, and initially regarded in some circles as folk heroes. But as the Internet grew and more and more people around the globe began using it, and with the development of e-Commerce, hackers and other cybercriminals became an increasingly serious problem, threatening the very efficacy and vitality of the system.

Some of the first cybergangs, composed of hackers with few legitimate opportunities to use their skills in their own countries, arose out of the detritus of the former Soviet Union, especially in places like Russia, Ukraine, Eastern Europe and the Baltic states. Initially they were involved largely in extortion schemes, threatening to attack retail and gambling sites unless they were paid off.[123] But gradually they became more and more proficient and linked up with organized crime gangs. At the outset, Mafia members were not very computer literate but as time went by they were replaced by younger men who were far knowledgeable about IT matters. As a consequence, some Mafioso "have adapted to new modes of crime, turning from numbers and narcotics rackets in the mid-20th century to Internet identity theft and denial-of-service (DOS) attacks."[124] In 1995, for example, Russian gangsters were responsible for the theft of more than $10 million from Citibank, and in recent years one gang of cyber thieves came close to stealing billions from the U.S. Treasury. Today, according to Tom

---

122 Threat Working Group of the CSIS Commission on Cybersecurity for the 44th Presidency, "Threats Posed by the Internet," (Washington, D.C., no date), p. 1.

123 Tom Kellerman, "The ShadowNet," original paper.

124 *Ibid.,* p. 10.

Kellermann, one of the nation's leading cyber security specialists, we are in the "Age of the Cyber Dons," as an increasing number of well-organized criminal syndicates arise around the globe dedicated to cyber theft and fraud. So pervasive is the problem that it was estimated just a few years ago that 4-5% of the Bulgarian GDP came from cybercrime.

Today, cybergangs are involved in massive identity theft, the theft of proprietary information, ferreting out details on IPOs and new products that could influence the stock value of companies, bank fraud, and even new forms of extortion. In 2005, for example, a British company received an email saying, "You can ignore this email and try to keep your [web] site up, which will cost you tens of thousands of dollars and lost customers, or you can send us $10k bank wire to make sure that your site experiences no problems + we will give you our protection for a year."[125]

Cybercrime has become such a large industry today that criminal gangs are running sweatshops in places like India, Russia, China, Brazil Argentina and Nigeria where lowly-paid computer operators are "working in shifts deciphering streams of characters forwarded by an unseen coordinator."[126] Thus, the grunt work is being farmed out around the world by cyberthieves eager to find new ways to compromise data and access sensitive sites.

Most criminal organizations have designed massive intrusion programs that constantly probe computer defenses at organizations of interest, looking for a vulnerability they can exploit. For example, "in 2008, the Pentagon was hit by would-be intruders 6 million times in a 24-hour period."[127] It is not unusual for major financial institutions to be hit more than a million times a day by automated computer probes. The U.S. government admits that in 2008 there were 5,488 actual incidents of unauthorized access to its computers.[128] There are

---

125 Cassell Bryan-Low, "Tech-Savy Blackmailers Hone a New Form of Extortion," *The Wall Street Journal*, May 5, 2005.

126 Byron Acohido, "Cybergangs Use Cheap Labor to Break Codes on Social Sites," *USA Today*, April 22, 2009.

127 Arnaud de Borchgrave, "Silent Cyberwar," *UPI column*, Feb. 17, 2009.

128 "US Faces Growing Cyberattacks," *USA Today*, Feb. 17, 2009.

estimates that cyber attacks cost victims more than a trillion dollars a year on a global basis.[129]

Terrorists are also using the Internet to communicate as well as to recruit members and raise money. In addition, they are "covertly and securely disseminating manuals of weaponry, videos of insurgent feats such as beheadings and other inflammatory material." They even run on-line seminars on "hacking websites."[130] Islamic extremists are known to be exploring the Internet for vulnerabilities that can be exploited, possibly even used to carry out new attacks against the United States and our allies. From intelligence, interrogations, and captured hard drives, we know that they have explored potential targets like the nation's electric grid as well as our water supplies and public buildings. They also have taken note of other attacks, no doubt to see if they could replicate them, such as the 2007 incident where alleged "pranksters" sent a spoof email disguised as an internal Apple communication to employees indicating that the launch of the much-ballyhooed iPhone was going to be delayed. When the email was leaked, "a trading frenzy of Apple stock hit Wall Street, and the company's market value plunged $2.8 billion or 3 percent, in six minutes."[131]

Al Qaeda and other Islamic jihadists are far from country rubes when it comes to computers, and they use cyberspace for covert communications. One of the techniques they employ is steganography, which is embedding messages in normal files like a video from Osama bin Laden or some other Al Qaeda spokesman, or even website graphics, to communicate with field operatives. In other words, a perfectly innocuous communication that may appear to be spam or junk mail could contain a highly sensitive message from one terrorist cell to another. An on-line terrorist manual entitled "The Technical Mujahid, a Training Manual for Jihadis," has an instructional section on

---

129 Mary Watkins, "Cyber Crime: The Rats that Gain Access by the Click of a Mouse," *Financial Times*, Nov. 8, 2010.

130 Tom Kellerman, "Cyber Terror and E-Commerce," Core Security Technologies Report, no date.

131 "A Little E-Mail Prank, and a $2.8 Billion Panic," *The Washington Post*, May 18, 2007.

steganography labeled, "Covert Communications and Hiding Secrets Inside of Images."

So pervasive is the problem of cyber crime and recreational hacking that in 2006 the Cyber Security Alliance estimated that 61% of all U.S. computers are compromised in some fashion. Similarly, the FBI has estimated that 9 out of 10 businesses in this country have been affected by cybercrime. According to the Federal Trade Commission, identity theft is the fastest growing crime in America. According to Kellerman, "In 2005 over 56 million Americans lost their identities. The average dollar amount charged in each US identity theft is $92,893, costing individual consumers an average of $1,495 and 600 hours to clear their records (not including legal fees and lost wages)."[132] Some estimates suggest that the number of Americans affected by identity theft has doubled in the last five years.

To provide some perspective on the size of the problem, consider how many databases were lost in the snapshot below in just a few weeks, and this goes on all the time. On Feb. 15, 2005, thieves accessed 145,000 names on ChoicePoint; 1,200,000 at Bank of America on Feb. 25 (lost backup tape); 25,000 at PayMax on Feb. 25; 32,000 at LexisNexis on March 10 (passwords compromised); 98,400 at the University of California at Berkeley on March 11 (stolen laptop); 120,000 at Boston College on March 12 (hacking); 8,900 at the Nevada Department of Motor Vehicles on March 12 (stolen computer); 21,000 at Northwestern University (hacking); 5,000 at the University of Nevada at Las Vegas on March 20 (hacking); 59,000 at California State University/Chico on March 22 (hacking); 7,000 at the University of California/San Francisco on March 23 (hacking); 100,000 at DSW/Retail Ventures in early April (hacking); 100,000s at the Georgia Department of Motor Vehicles (insider); 16,500 at MCI on April 5 (stolen laptop); and 185,000 at the San Jose Medical Group on April 8 (stolen computer).[133] Well, you get the idea. Database information is lost somewhere virtually ever day and it provides cybercriminals and scammers with the information they need to carry out their criminal conspiracies. One of the largest thefts in recent years was the disclosure by Heartland Payment Systems, in January, 2009, that

---

132 Tom Kellerman, "The ShadowNet," original paper, no date.

133 Stephen Spoonamore, communication to the author, June 27, 2005.

hackers had broken into the computers used to process 100 million card transactions per month for 175,000 merchants.[134]

Identity theft goes far beyond using the information to simply make a few purchases in the name of the person whose identity was stolen. The criminals use the data to acquire new credit cards, open new accounts, take out loans, wire funds and a host of other illegal activities. Because of the popularity of social networks, today identity thieves are stealing information from sites such as Facebook and MySpace in building phony dossiers that can be used to create fictional identities or to co-opt real identities. Even legitimate companies are using Facebook and similar sites as a "means of surveillance and data mining."[135]

NEW THREATS

A prominent Washington, D.C., businessman was seeking the renewal of a large overseas contract he had had for a decade. One day he received a call from someone in the media asking for his comment on a story that claimed he was attempting to bribe the president and other officials of the country in order to secure the renewal of the contract. To support its allegation, the publication printed a number of emails that the businessman had purportedly sent to officials trying to bribe them. The emails appeared to be genuine and to have come from the businessman's computer.

The businessman swore that he had never attempted to bribe anyone associated with the contract and retained us to investigate whether or not someone had been able to get unauthorized access to his office or home computers. Our IT expert immediately went to work and discovered that the businessman's computer had been "spoofed" and that the bogus messages had originated in a Washington, D.C. suburb, near the home of one of his competitors for the contract.

Because of the article in the media, we wanted to move quickly before the Justice Department opened an investigation of our client. I called a contact at the FBI field office in Washington and requested a

---

134 Melissa E. Hathaway, "Strategic Advantage: Why America Should Care About Cybersecurity," (Harvard/The Kennedy School: October, 2009).

135"Criticisms of Facebook," Wikipedia, downloaded October 27, 2010.

meeting, telling the agent that someone was engaged in illegal activity that could disrupt U.S. relations with a foreign government. There were nine FBI representatives in the room when the businessman, myself, our IT specialist, and a very distinguished Washington attorney arrived, and we described the effort to frame our client and make it appear that he was violating the Foreign Corrupt Practices Act (FCPA). We laid out the IT evidence and the Bureau team carefully analyzed it. As a consequence, no investigation was ever opened regarding the businessman and he ultimately was successful in getting the contract renewed. This case, however, is clear evidence of how a top executive can be ambushed by his own IT system and why top management must be fully engaged in their company's cybersecurity efforts.

While new technologies are convenient and improve our lives in many ways, they also have hidden vulnerabilities:

1. <u>Insider Threat</u>. In the case above, it was determined that in addition to an outside attack on their computers, someone had compromised their computers from the inside as well. Their servers, it turned out, were in an unsecured room and the door was generally unlocked during the daytime and, we feared, probably sometimes at night as well. We immediately placed the servers in locked cages and put a cypher lock on the door to the server room, and mandated that it be kept locked at all times. We also had CCTV cameras installed so anyone accessing the server room or various key offices, especially after hours, would be captured on video.

   In San Francisco a disgruntled technology administrator refused to turn over passwords to a computer network critical to the operation of everything from the city's police department to its jails, courts, health and payroll systems, and other key functions. This case demonstrates the problems inherent in IT systems where there are no checks and balances, and where a single individual can amass too much power without effective oversight and accountability. You never want to be in a situation where you lose control of your company's IT function and should take steps to ensure that it doesn't happen.

2. <u>Cellphones & PDAs</u>. According to Walter Pincus, "your cellphone or Blackberry can be tagged, tracked, monitored and exploited by a foreign intelligence service between the time you

disembark from a plane in that country's capital and the time you reach the airport taxi stand."[136] The microphone in your cellphone can be used to eavesdrop on you, even when it is off, and the ear buds of your iPod can be "converted into a recording device when not in your ears."[137] As noted elsewhere, cellphones can also be used to track your location. Since many contemporary cellphones are actually computers, various criminal organizations are targeting them and the information they hold.

3. <u>Acoustical and video spying</u>. The keystrokes on any computer can be captured from remote locations and used to steal images, data, and other information. This is called keylogging and can generally be prevented with anti-keylogging software. Your webcam and the microphone in your computer can also be co-opted by hostile forces and used against you. In some cases, the only defense against your webcam spying on you may be to cover the lens with tape or a Band-Aid. Even your video display terminal "emits unique radio-frequency waves that can be isolated and captured with a 'directional' antenna focused on a particular computer or room."

4. <u>Wireless devices</u>. "Wireless devices are the Achilles Heel of cybersecurity," writes Tom Kellerman.[138] Any time you're in a wireless environment, including airports, coffee shops, and hotels, it is relatively simple for others to spy on your activities and communications, whether you're sending an email or downloading information from your office server.

5. <u>Website corruption</u>. There has been a 5000% increase in polluted websites in recent years. Various groups, including criminal gangs, disgruntled employees, and dissatisfied customers are attacking company websites, defacing them and in some cases overwhelming them with denial of service attacks. Another tactic is the establishment of negative sites that appear to be real but contain derogatory information about

---

136 Walter Pincus, "You Cell and Your Berry: Tools of the Enemy," *The Washington Post*, March 3, 2009.

137 *Ibid.*

138 Tom Kellerman, "Cyber Terror and E-Commerce," op. cit.

the company and its products. Good examples are "GM Sucks" or "Toyota Sucks." As a part of its reputation management strategy, any company potentially in the cross-hairs should consider purchasing all of the website addresses that could be used by critics. This will make it more difficult for critics to set up new sites that are easy to find and navigate.

6. <u>Emails</u>. Remember that emails do not disappear when they are deleted. This was something NSC staff member, Oliver North, was unaware of and government investigators retrieved his emails, many of which were, at the very least embarrassing, and at the very worst incriminating, during the investigation of the Iran-Contra scandal. Similarly, Bill Gates, who clearly should have known better, lost the antitrust suit brought by the government in part because of the arrogance he demonstrated in some of his emails. "This antitrust thing will blow over," Gates said in one of his emails, infuriating prosecutors. According to David Streitfeld, "they [Microsoft] should have erased all of their e-mails -- many of which were used to devastating effect by the government in the trial."[139]

7. <u>Thumb drives</u>. In 2009, the Department of Defense and several other government agencies had to prohibit the use of thumb drives because they had been compromised by the Chinese manufacturers who built in features that allowed unauthorized access to military and other secret information. Unless proper protections are in place, thumb drives also permit the massive downloading of information by unauthorized individuals.

IT RULES AND PROCEDURES

Today good IT security involves a layered defense consisting of a combination of firewalls, virus scanners, anti-spyware, intrusion detection systems, encryption, authentication, incident response plans, active content filtering, and policy management software. Certifying information security will increasingly become a management and board of directors issue. Management can no longer claim ignorance regarding electronic data protection risks and the effectiveness of the

---

139 David Streitfeld, "Courting Defeat: Did the Giant Slay Itself?," *The Washington Post*, June 8, 2000.

company's IT security efforts.[140] Management will be held accountable by shareholders, and in some cases by the government, if the company's proprietary data is stolen, if identity data is lost, if steps were not taken to properly back up data in secure locations, and even, in some cases, if the company's website or ability to engage in e-Commerce is lost because of denial of service or other malicious attacks. As hacking related insurance costs soar, good IT security can also save a company money in terms of insurance premiums.

1. Laptops. Laptops must be well protected from theft or loss, and employees should know that their jobs could be jeopardized if they misplace a laptop. Moreover, corporate laptops should be encrypted and restrictions introduced on the amount and kind of data that employees are permitted to have on a piece of equipment that can so easily be stolen or misplaced.

2. Discarded Hard Drives. There have been numerous cases of crooks salvaging used hard drives and recovering sensitive corporate and personal data. Just as most companies have programs for document retention and destruction, consistent with Sarbanes-Oxley and other legal requirements, they need to ensure that hard drives are removed from old computers and either retained under proper conditions or systematically destroyed.

3. Emails. Accessing pornographic sites on company time or sending and receiving lewd or inappropriate messages should be noted in your employee handbook as causes for dismissal or other disciplinary action. Also, personal emails should be discouraged on company time, as well as texting, twittering, and other forms of social media that don't relate specifically to the employee's job performance.

4. Corporate Laptops, Computers and Other Equipment. "The company should have a clear policy statement in the employee handbook that lets workers know that everything at the work site is company property, including the employee's office or personal workspace, hard copy files, and all electronic devices

---

140 CORE Security Technologies, "Plausible Deniability: No Defense for Data Breach Victims," 2009, p. 3/4.

and data," according to *Security Management* magazine. "The policy should make clear that any such property can at any time be monitored, searched, or taken by the company without specific notification beyond the general policy statement and without prior permission."[141]

5. <u>Employees.</u> It should be remembered that people are the weakest link inside the electronic perimeter you have created to protect your IT systems. For this reason, all employees should undergo background checks and various monitoring systems should be put into place to ensure they don't steal proprietary data or engage in time wasting activities involving gambling, porn sites, or even updating their Facebook pages. Such systems will also make it more difficult for them to perpetrate thefts or fraud. After all, the tricky thing about IT theft is that data or information can be stolen but, in actuality, it's still there, so it is very important that IT security team have ways of detecting unauthorized entry and data theft.

6. <u>Outsourcing and Service Providers.</u> Not all companies can have closed networks or their own servers and routers. Consequently, Tom Kellerman recommends your Chief Technology Officer (CTO) should take the following actions:

> ⋏ "Verify that the legal requirements to which the service provider is contractually obligated are compatible with your organization's definition of adequate security."
>
> ⋏ "Identify who in the service provider organization is responsible for security oversight."
>
> ⋏ "Confirm that their policies and agreements regarding security breaches include customer notification on a timely basis."
>
> ⋏ "Confirm that the service provider has adequate backup facilities."
>
> ⋏ and, "Conduct risk assessments of their network security posture, and verify whether they have layered security beyond firewalls and encryption."[142]

---

141 *Security Management*, June, 2005, p. 71.

142 Kellermann, "Cyber Terror and E-Commerce," op. cit.

7. <u>Remote Access Security.</u> Special procedures should be established to ensure that those accessing the company's server from a remote location are properly vetted and are who they say they are. At the very least, companies should require two forms of identity authentication, and if possible one of them should be a biometric.

CONCLUSION

In the final analysis, weak IT security procedures at large corporations and government agencies may not only undermine corporate profits, reputation, and competitiveness but actually put the country at a huge disadvantage as it seeks to compete in the global marketplace. It is difficult to assess exactly how much of China's rapidly expanding technology economy is the result of reverse engineering, patent infringement, and intellectual property theft from the U.S. and Western Europe, but one confidential source estimates that China is five to ten years more advanced today than it would have been without its comprehensive and government supported industrial espionage activities, much of it by means of computer hacking and other forms of IT subversion.

It is vital that the U.S. Government, corporations and other organizations regardless of size constantly develop new defensive measures to protect what could be described as "the family jewels." But we're falling behind in many areas, including the training of young computer/IT specialists. One indicator of the problem is the annual international computer programming competition sponsored by the Association for Computing Machinery which is held for "talented young students from around the globe." More than 6000 teams compete for the grand prize which has been won six times by a Russian team since 2000, three times by the Chinese, and twice by Poland. The best finish by a U.S. team was second.[143]

In 2010, Iran announced that computers at the Busheha nuclear plant had been penetrated by what was believed to be a new computer

---

143 "Threat Working Group of the CSIS Commission on Cybersecurity for the 44th Presidency," op. cit. The winners year-by-year are as follows: 2000 Russia; 2001 Russia; 2002 China; 2003 Poland; 2004 Russia; 2005 China; 2006 Russia; 2007 Poland; 2008 Russia; 2009 Russia; and 2010 China.

worm called Stuxnet. The worm targets key industrial operating systems.[144] Experts worried that the worm had "infected thousands of operating systems at factories, refineries, and pipelines around the world." In reality Stuxnet had been developed by an unidentified intelligence organization to undermine Iran's effort to acquire nuclear weapons technology by targeting its gas centrifuges which are used to enrich uranium.

Corporate and governmental leaders need to prepare now for a catastrophic computer systems attack that could shut down power grids, ground aviation around the globe, disrupt communications, and do things like turn all of the traffic lights green in cities where there still is power. Whether this happens ten days from now, or ten months from now, or even ten years from now, the bottom line is that it is going to happen and when it does it will have a profound impact on national economies and global security.

---

144 Watkins, op. cit., p. 1.

- 10 -

CRISIS MANAGEMENT

"To do the right thing at the right
time is a great art."

Aesop, 6th century

AVOIDABLE CRISES

In the late 1990s, a Russian crime boss was approached by representatives of the U.S. government in an effort to settle criminal charges against him in the U.S. He had been accused of fraud in connection with the failure of a firm producing industrial magnets. He doesn't deny that he had a connection to the firm, but says that a former aide was responsible for the fraud. "They say I'm a smart guy," he once said. "Why would I commit fraud in the United States, knowing that I would be a wanted man as a consequence and that it would probably prevent me from traveling for fear of being arrested. And for what? Thirty million? I don't need the money; I have plenty of money."

The government agents said that he could cut a deal with the U.S. if he could assist on two problems. First, the U.S. was trying to recover Stinger missiles that had been given to the Mujahedeen during the occupation of Afghanistan by the Soviets, and was willing to pay $50,000 per missile for their return. Secondly, there was a terrorist living near Kandahar, Afghanistan, that was responsible for a number of attacks against the U.S., including the bombing of U.S. embassies in Kenya and Tanzania, and the attack on the USS Cole in Yemen. His name was Osama bin Laden and the U.S. agents wanted to know if the Russian could take him out.

The Russian gangster provided agents with, at first two, and subsequently nine additional Stinger serial numbers, saying he could deliver eleven missiles to the U.S. and didn't need to be paid for them, rather they were a "gift" to the people of the United States. As to bin Laden, he indicated that he could have the terrorist rubbed out. After all, he was a Jew and bin Laden was also a threat to Israel.

Unfortunately, the U.S. government decided that the Russian crime boss was so unsavory that they shouldn't deal with him and took their offer off the table. We will never know whether the Russian gangster could have eliminated bin Laden, but it doesn't seem unreasonable to conjecture that he might have, and had he done so it is likely that 9/11 wouldn't have happened. Three thousand lives would have been spared on that September day and two wars may have been prevented, along with tens of thousands of lost lives. There would have been no drive to institutionalize the global security regime that was established, in large measure, because of the hijacked aircraft that were flown into buildings in New York City and Washington, D.C. Hundreds of billions devoted to military conflicts and homeland security would not have been spent, and the U.S. economy, arguably, would have been in better shape.

Another example of an avoidable crisis started with a phone call I received in 1987 from a good friend, a prominent Washington attorney who, in his youth, had helped prosecute Nazi war criminals at Nuremburg. He said that he served on the Board of Directors of Carolco Pictures in Hollywood and that the company was preparing to film the third in the series of popular "Rambo" pictures, appropriately entitled "Rambo III," starring Sylvester Stallone as John Rambo. The screenplay revolved around John Rambo's efforts to help the Afghan resistance in its protracted war against the Soviet Union, which had invaded Afghanistan in 1979.

The question put to me was: where should we film the picture? The location scouts wanted to shoot it in Morocco and the board member wanted to know whether this was a prudent decision. We were retained by the company and initiated a major risk assessment of the country. The U.S. had recently bombed Tripoli, in retaliation for a terrorist attack in West Berlin that had left one U.S. serviceman dead, and tensions were running high in North Africa and the rest of the Arab world. Moreover, Rambo had become a popular icon in the United States and, as I wrote in my report to the company, "the personification of a resurgent and confrontational American foreign policy."

The U.S. was directly supporting the Afghan mujahadeen against the Soviets and the war was going badly for the Russians. I was concerned that Moscow might take offense at the film and could take steps to disrupt it that would put the cast and crew at risk. But the Russians were not my only concern. As I noted in my report, "[I]t is hard for some people in the Third World to understand that Mr. Stallone's roles are not an extension of U.S. foreign policy and that he is not a propaganda agent of the U.S. government."

Thus, I concluded that "an attempt to kidnap or kill Mr. Stallone would generate worldwide publicity and could be viewed as an attack on a living symbol of the United States and this Administration's policies." While I had a generally favorable view of Morocco, and noted that its "internal security apparatus...is good by Third World standards," I was concerned that, "should a terrorist group undertake a determined effort to get into the country, it would not be very difficult. Morocco's borders are fairly porous and crossed regularly by nomads. The country's lengthy coastline is also very vulnerable to infiltration. An additional problem concerns the fact that Abu Nidal's Black June organization is known to possess a large number of Moroccan passports, confiscated by the Qaddafi regime from Moroccan guest workers in Libya and passed along to various terrorist groups."

In view of these potential problems, I recommended that the film not be shot in Morocco, or in any other Arab country for that matter.

I was subsequently asked to identify alternate locations, and we ultimately focused on Israel. It had appropriate topography and extras with the right look. From a security standpoint, it was the safest place in the Middle East. My colleagues and I enjoyed good relations with the appropriate Israeli ministries and were promised the government's full cooperation with the project, in view of the money and publicity that the country would receive.

Carolco's management adopted my recommendation and it was decided that the film be shot in Israel. End of story, right?

Wrong.

Most of the picture was filmed in Israel without incident. The producers even paid for a private jet to stand by twenty-four hours a day to whisk Stallone out of the country in the event of a problem. On board the plane there was even a supply of Stallone's own blood in case he was wounded or otherwise injured. Sometime before Christmas, however, I received a call from one of the owners of Carolco. He was bordering on panic. He informed me that Stallone had become tired of Israel and decided to spend the Christmas holidays in the United States. Accordingly, the production was being transferred back to the U.S., where the climactic scenes were going to be filmed in the Arizona desert. The problem, I was told, was that the massive arsenal of Soviet-bloc weapons and blank ammunition that was scheduled to be used in the finale was blocked from entering the U.S. under provisions of the McClure-Volkmer Act. Carolco had contracted an Israeli firm to provide all of the weapons, which were of Soviet-bloc manufacture. Unfortunately, the Act prohibited the importation of all such weapons manufactured after a certain date. No one on the production staff had thought to explore the firearm importation laws before the decision was made to move the production to Arizona. And without the weapons, there would be no movie. If production was interrupted or delayed it could cost the producers millions of dollars.

We immediately went into high gear in Washington, retaining a major Washington, D.C., law firm for extra support. At first the Bureau of Alcohol, Tobacco and Firearms (ATF) and the State Department were adamantly opposed to any exception being granted in this case. They rightly believed that the company should have thought about such issues before they decided to return the production to the U.S. On the other hand, the move was a done deal and there was nothing we could do about it.

Ultimately, one of the attorneys reached a top government official who agreed to help us. He pulled President Reagan out of the first Reagan-Gorbachev Summit to explain the problem. If something wasn't done, he told the president, there would be 250 Teamster families out of work at Christmas time, not to mention the rest of the cast and crew. Reagan, a former head of the Screen Actors Guild, ordered the affected departments to find a way to solve our problem.

It was eventually decided that the weapons would be shipped from one location in Israel to another location in Israel via the United States. Thus, they would not be imported into the U.S., but would technically be in transit while in this country. To comply with other federal regulations, the sheriff of Yuma County, Arizona, was persuaded to take temporary possession of the weapons. While the weapons were in his "possession," he would be the most heavily armed sheriff in America, with an arsenal that included tanks, missiles, machine guns, and rocket launchers.

One former high official at ATF was not happy with the situation. He informed me, politely but firmly, that he had no choice but to comply with the White House directive, but warned me that, "Every weapon better make it back to Israel" or he'd hold me personally accountable.

In early January, thanks to the availability of the weapons, the final battle scenes were filmed. As the production was wrapping up, my portable phone rang. It was "Lou," who had worked with me for many years and was calling from Yuma County. He was standing by the weapons van, he said, and Stallone was demanding "his AK47." Apparently, the owner of the Israeli weapons firm had promised Stallone an AK47 and told him he could pick it up at the end of the production.

Remembering the admonition of the ATF official that I would be held personally responsible for any missing weapons, I told Lou to explain to Stallone politely but firmly that he could not have the gun.

"He's very insistent," said Lou.

"That's too bad," I told him. "Tell him he can pick it up in Israel."

I could hear loud protests on the other end of the line, then Lou reported back to me. "He says he's going to take his gun."

"No he isn't," I responded. "Inform him that you'll shoot him if he does."

"He says we can't shoot him: he's a star," said Lou.

"Tell him you've got your orders," I growled.

Lou held his ground and eventually Stallone backed off. And so ended the saga of "Rambo III."

The story just recounted illustrates, more than anything else, the fact that the most innocent, casual, or seemingly minor decisions, if not properly thought out, can have far-reaching consequences, and even result in major crises.

Another example of a crisis being caused by a seemingly minor oversight was the hydrofluoric acid (HF) release in Texas City, Texas, on October 30, 1987. A crane operator, representative of so many recent high school graduates who are incapable of doing the most elemental math, overloaded the crane he was operating at the Marathon Petroleum refinery. As he lifted a heater convection section over a tank containing 35,700 gallons (289,170 pounds) of hydrofluoric acid and 6,600 pounds of light hydrocarbons, the crane began to topple over. The operator dropped the convection section and it struck the

HF tank, shearing off both a 2-inch pressure relief line and a 4-inch loading line at the top of the tank. This resulted in the release of a cloud of the highly corrosive acid into the atmosphere. The HF tank had not been emptied, as should always be done when lifting process equipment over a tank containing extremely hazardous chemicals, nor was there an auxiliary holding tank to drain the acid into in the event of an emergency.

From the moment of the accident, everything that could go wrong, did. When the crane toppled, it struck the self-contained sprinkler system that had been designed to "knock down" an errant HF release, putting it out of action. In addition, it also rendered inoperable one of two siren systems, intended to warn plant workers and nearby residents of an emergency at the Marathon facility. The other siren system had been shut off.

It took 44 hours to plug the damaged tank, and officials estimated that approximately 20 percent of the HF and all of the light hydrocarbons stored in the tank escaped into the atmosphere, most of the release in the first two hours. Apparently, Marathon officials lacked an effective crisis management plan for addressing the emergency that arose.

According to one report, the assistant manager at the plant site referred to a DuPont manual in an effort to figure out what to do. During this time, workers at the plant report that they were not given adequate instructions regarding their own safety or properly appraised as to the toxicity of HF. One worker described the scene at the plant as "chaos." Another, Emmett Brown, said that plant employees were, "...jumping over the fence like mice. The road was filled with people trying to escape the acid."[145]

Nearly 4000 people were evacuated as the knee-high silver-colored cloud drifted through a nearby residential area, affecting an area three miles long and a mile wide. In places, HF concentrations reached 50 parts per million (ppm).

Local authorities were slow to respond to the crisis and many of their actions were totally inappropriate. Most of those evacuated, for example, were directed to a community center in the direct path of the plume, only 1.7 miles downwind. The cloud caught up with them and

---

145 Emmett Brown, interview in "Cloud Over Texas City," ABC "20/20 report, Chris Harper producer, September 15, 1989.

authorities had to evacuate everyone a second time to a school four miles away.

More than 900 people were treated at local hospitals for various injuries. Dr. Paul J. Papanek, Jr., chief of the Toxic Epidemiology Program of the County of Los Angeles, was retained to investigate the public health impact of the Marathon Oil Refinery incident. In 1990, he reviewed 121 cases of illness allegedly connected to the HF release, a large number of which involved individuals who had filed legal actions against Marathon. Among the symptoms reported were eye irritation, nose and throat problems, irritation of the upper airway, wheezing and exacerbation of asthma, skin problems, gastritis, nausea and vomiting, headaches, hypocalcaemia (low calcium levels in the bloodstream), and problems with anxiety. Indicative of the toxicity of HF, all of these symptoms occurred despite the relatively low level of exposure to which most of the victims were subjected. Indeed, nearly one quarter of those living in the plume path of the release visited a hospital emergency room.

According to Dr. Papanek's report, lawns in the area affected by the plume were seared brown and trees, especially pine trees, were scorched for a distance of 1.5 to 2 miles.[146] Corrosive damage was reported to many homes and vehicles in the same area, including etched and streaked windows on cars and buildings where dew had collected.

All of this occurred because of a relatively minor mistake, and was compounded by additional mistakes and lack of preparation by the affected company. The total amount of compensation paid out to victims is unknown, but the figure is reliably reported to be in the millions. And, as happens in so many similar crises, Marathon Oil received a huge amount of unwanted and highly negative publicity calling into question the quality of its management and raising real concerns about the company's commitment to operating its refinery in a safe and responsible manner.

The Marathon incident came only three years after 2800 (some say the number exceeds 4000) people were killed, and 200,000 injured, in

---

146 Dr. Paul J. Papanek, Jr., "Medical Effects of Hydrogen Fluoride--Some Observations from the Marathon Oil Refinery HF Release, Texas City, October 30, 1987," report to the Department of Health Services, County of Los Angeles, April 4, 1990.

one of the worst industrial accidents on record. On the night of December 3, 1984, forty-five tons of methyl isocyanate (MIC), an extremely lethal chemical used in the manufacture of pesticides, began leaking into the atmosphere at a plant operated by Union Carbide in the Indian city of Bhopal. The disaster was the result of the failure of a key valve, although Union Carbide says a disgruntled employee sabotaged the valve, and the fact that five critical safety systems were inoperable. This included the alarm itself. The man who had kept the alarm functioning had been paid the U.S. equivalent of $25 dollars a month, but he had been let go as a cost-cutting measure. When the alarm failed, there was no one to repair it.

Because of favorable weather conditions, the methyl isocyanate eventually affected a twenty-five square mile area. Some of the victims, nearly all of them poor, were permanently blinded, others suffered severe respiratory damage, paralysis, and epileptic seizures. The disaster was particularly devastating to the very young and the very old.

Once the disaster began, it became impossible for Union Carbide to communicate with its facility in Bhopal since the government had commandeered all phone lines in and out of the city and the company had not had the foresight to put in a dedicated communications system, opting to rely, in an emergency, on open phone lines. The Chairman of Union Carbide decided to fly to Bhopal to see what assistance he could be, but was arrested when he arrived in India.

According to Mayer Nudell and Norman Antokol, "The combination public relations catastrophe and massive litigation was devastating to the corporation's financial resources. The price of Union Carbide's stock dropped precipitously and the company was devalued by more than nine hundred million dollars. Crisis management had given way to damage control, and that in turn became a question of corporate survival."[147]

J.C.F. Schiller said that, "Against stupidity the gods themselves fight in vain."[148] Indeed, some crises are just so stupid that it's hard to imagine that they could have occurred. The classic case of overreaction to events, leading to a major national crises that brought

---

147 Mayer Nudell and Norman Antokol, *The Handbook for Effective Emergency and Crisis Management*, (Lexington, Mass.: Lexington Books, 1988), p. 84.

148 J.C.F. Schiller, *Die Jungfrau von Orleans*, III, 1801.

down Richard Nixon's presidency, was Watergate. It was, as the Nixon described it, a "third-rate burglary," and there is no evidence that the president knew about it in advance. But once the Watergate break-in occurred, rather than apologize to the country for his overzealous aides and let justice take its course, Nixon and his White House engaged in a massive cover-up. In the end, the president was forced from office and many of his top aides went to jail.

And it was all so unnecessary. Not only could the problem have been successfully managed, but it is difficult to imagine how it could have occurred in the first place. Nixon ultimately won the election in a landslide of epic proportions, losing only Massachusetts and the District of Columbia to Senator George McGovern. McGovern didn't even carry his home state of South Dakota. The notion that the burglary of the Democratic National Committee headquarters could, in any conceivable way, contribute to Nixon's reelection effort was one of colossal stupidity and abject overreaction.

Nevertheless, prominent individuals and corporations make mistakes like this over and over again. It is remarkable how many are willing to break the law or overreach in some way in order to strike back at some minor irritant. Another good example of this occurred several years ago when the right-hand man to one of Hollywood's barons called me and asked if we would burglarize, or in some way gain access to, the offices of a New York magazine publisher. The magazine had consistently run highly negative articles about the Hollywood mogul, I was told, using inside information available only to a small number of people. He was desperate to learn who was leaking the material and was willing to pay whatever necessary to identify the Judas on his staff.

I declined to take the job, and cautioned the caller not to pursue the matter unless his boss wanted to end up like Richard Nixon, minus the pardon. The Hollywood baron, I told him, had everything a man could desire and was wealthy beyond words. Most people regarded him with both affection and awe, so why was he willing to risk it all over some articles few people read in a magazine with a limited circulation?

Another classic example of creating a crisis out of thin air, where none had existed before, was the White House Travel Office scandal, known as "Travelgate," during the Clinton Administration. The White House travel office was set up in the 1830s to handle the travel arrangements for the White House press corps that accompanies the president on the road. Today it involves private airline charters, the cost of which is charged to members of the media and news organizations for which they work.

In 1993, the White House chief-of-staff and White House Counsel fired the Director of the Travel Office, Billie Ray Dale, who had served in the position during both the Reagan and George H.W. Bush administrations. Dale reportedly kept poor records, did not seek competitive bids from airline companies for the charters, and allegedly maintained a slush fund in one of his personal accounts to grease foreign officials in countries where it was necessary.

While the administration of the Travel Office certainly left something to be desired, Dale was immensely popular among the press corps, liberals and conservatives alike. He was known as a hands-on manager who catered to the comfort and needs of everyone accompanying the president in the press corps plane. Soon it was revealed that the Clintons had been pressured by friends and a distant cousin to fire Dale and give the business to an Arkansas-based company and a charter airline in which Clinton Inaugural Chairman Harry Thomason had a financial interest.

By removing Dale and his senior staff, the President and Mrs. Clinton outraged the White House press corps, which was loyal to Dale and quite satisfied with the service and attention they received from him. The whole episode reeked of Arkansas corruption and political patronage, and since the press corps was directly affected they turned what should have been a minor staffing change of little consequence into a major ethics scandal which ultimately painted a questionable portrait of the First Lady, in particular, who was much more involved in the firings than she had originally acknowledged, and White House Counsel Vince Foster, who ultimately committed suicide, perhaps in part because of the scandal. Mrs. Clinton was subsequently suspected of committing perjury in connection with the Travelgate matter, according to several subsequent investigations, and her reputation as a crass and cynical politician can be traced directly to Travelgate and the so-called Whitewater land deal.

The scandal ultimately resulted in several congressional investigations, a GAO (Government Accountability Office) investigation, and an inquiry by Independent Counsel Kenneth Starr. The various investigations took more than seven years to resolve and also resulted in revelations that the Clintons had misused the FBI in a clumsy effort to obtain derogatory information on Dale that could help justify his termination. In the end, Dale was indicted on embezzelement and criminal conversion charges, but he was acquitted by a jury after less than two hours of deliberation.

For Clinton opponents the whole Travelgate scandal came to represent a pervasive climate of sleaze surrounding the President, the First Lady, and many senior administration officials, and it certainly tarnished the President's historical legacy. The irony was that the whole crisis shouldn't have happened in the first place and was purely the product of White House missteps, dissembling, and bad judgment.

CRISIS MANAGEMENT

Crisis management is the art of trying to manage crises in order to produce the best possible outcomes. Crises cannot be entirely foreseen or avoided, but in many instances their impact on a particular firm or individual can be mitigated by timely and effective intervention. Waiting for an emergency to arise before getting organized to deal with it is like shutting the barn door after the horse has already escaped. To intervene successfully, corporate managers must anticipate possible crises and make appropriate preparations. Then they need to devise plans to manage the various crises in the event they do occur. Only then will they be able to move quickly to achieve control, and subsequently to assure continuing control of the crisis until it is resolved.

The failure to prepare can lead to costly failures. One of the most dramatic corporate failures in history was the Exxon Valdez affair. In March, 1989, a supertanker called the Exxon Valdez ran aground in Prince William Sound, on the Alaskan coast. The tanker, operated by an inexperienced officer on the bridge and commanded by a captain with a history of alcohol abuse, spilled nearly eleven million gallons of crude oil in the pristine sound, creating the largest oil spill ever in North America, covering 1300 square miles. It also created a public relations nightmare for Exxon, which the company is still suffering from today.

The incident itself probably would have been prevented if Exxon had been characterized by more competent management and public spiritedness. Had the Exxon Valdez had a double hull, the crisis would have been minimized if not altogether avoided. Similarly, if the company had exercised proper supervision over its crews, Captain

Joseph Hazelwood would not have been in command of the ship on the fateful day.

The title of an article in the *Wall Street Journal* says it all: "How Unpreparedness Turned the Alaska Spill into Ecological Debacle."[149] According to the article, "It took the companies [Exxon and Alyeska Pipeline Service Co.] 35 hours to fully encircle the stricken tanker with barrier booms that were supposed to restrict the spill. By then, oil was floating miles from the ship. It took much longer to mount an air attack with dispersants that were supposed to dissolve the oil. Both tactics were far too little, too late."[150]

There was a 250-page crisis management plan for the containment of spills, approved by the state, but when the crunch came the plan was of little use. It was based on flawed and erroneous assumptions, such as any tanker spill would be fully encircled within five hours.[151] As already noted, it took 35 hours to encircle the ship with booms. Because the plan had never really been exercised, many other deficiencies were discovered once the onset of the crisis had begun. According to the *Wall Street Journal*, at the time of the crisis Alyeska's only containment barge was stripped for repairs. When it was finally mobilized, it was loaded with the wrong equipment, and subsequently had to be unloaded and then reloaded with the correct equipment (barrier booms) to address the problem. Despite the fact that the plan presumed sufficient booms and dispersants for any potential spill, neither were available in the quantity required to address the Exxon Valdez spill. What dispersants the company had were ineffectively applied to the problem only after inexcusable delays, partially caused by the U.S. Coast Guard officer on the scene. Local fishermen were not mobilized immediately to assist in the containment efforts, and the equipment used by the skimmer boat "to scoop oil out of the sea was so old it kept breaking down and clogging."[152] When alerted about the problem, Alyeska's top manager in Valdez, Chuck O'Donnell, sent a

---

149 "Out of Control: How Unpreparedness Turned the Alaska Spill into Ecological Debacle," *The Wall Street Journal*, April 3, 1989, p. 1.

150 *Ibid.*

151 *Ibid.*

152 *Ibid.*

subordinate to look into it and went back to sleep, illustrating the kind of disengaged management no company needs.

The price of incompetence was staggering. An army of 12,000 cleanup workers were paid on a scale starting at $16.69 an hour. An armada of boats were chartered by the company for as much as $8000 a day.[153] The Exxon Valdez disaster has variously been estimated to have cost Exxon someplace between four and seven billion dollars. Other estimates are even higher. In addition, there were death threats against Exxon executives. Irate customers cut up their Exxon credit cards and vandals trashed Exxon service stations. The public relations cost alone was incalculable. To this day, Exxon's name is synonymous with environmental catastrophe and corporate incompetence. Exxon shareholders need only consider the fact that it cost an estimated $40,000 to save every sea otter that survived the disaster.[154] Although the stockholders may not have been dining on fresh lobster and shellfish every day, the otters were.

By the second quarter of 1989, Exxon was "spending money almost but not quite as fast as it was making it" on the disaster in Alaska. To add to its problems, by September, only five months after the disaster, 145 lawsuits had been filed against Exxon.

After an extremely rocky start, Exxon was finally able to get into gear and in the months that followed, the company did a good job of cleaning up its mess. However, the perception that the company completely mishandled the oil spill persists to this day.

ORIGINS OF CRISIS MANAGEMENT

Modern crisis management, or what used to be called contingency planning, can be traced to the airline industry in the post-war period. Commercial airplane crashes occurred on a regular basis, and usually involved loss of life, lawsuits, and bad publicity. To address the problem, airlines developed elaborate contingency plans which tried to anticipate the various needs and requirements flowing from a crash. Corporate officers were assigned different roles and organizational responsibilities for the duration of the crisis. Resources were set aside for their use during this period. Finally, the plan was exercised on a

---

153 "Alaska After Exxon," *Newsweek*, September 18, 1989, p. 53.

154 *Ibid.*

regular basis to make certain it worked and to identify problems before it had to be utilized in a real crisis. Many airlines required that all top officers carry a copy of the plan with them wherever they went so they could go into action immediately if a worst-case scenario occurred.

The U.S. Defense Department was also quick to recognize the benefits of effective crisis planning as well, especially in terms of the peaceful resolution of conflicts between the United States and the former Soviet Union that could escalate into a devastating nuclear confrontation. The so-called Washington-Moscow "hotline" was just one of the crisis-control measures that was adopted.[155]

Other industries followed the lead of the airlines and the military and adopted their own crisis management plans. Today, the ability to deal with crisis situations has become a hallmark of effective corporate management.

WHEN THE CRISIS COMES

The FIRST RULE of crisis management, as you saw at the beginning of this chapter, is to try and avoid crises before they occur. Good management and anticipatory planning will generally keep you from being blindsided by a major crisis. Likewise, the SECOND RULE of crisis management, illustrated by Watergate and Travelgate, is not to make a crisis where none exists.

With the onset of a crisis, the THIRD RULE of crisis management is not to panic. If you are adequately prepared and rehearsed, a crisis is just another day at the office. All you have to do is hunker down and go to work. Let me explain.

It was just after dawn when I reached the isolated the country estate with two former military special operations veterans--we'll call them Tom and Frank--following close behind me in another vehicle. Mist lay across the fields and hung in the trees. The sun had not yet peeked above the treetops, but there wasn't a cloud in the sky and I knew that

---

155 Dale M. Landi, Bruno W. Augenstein, Cullen M. Crain, William R. Harris, and Brian M. Jenkins, "Improving the Means for Intergovernmental Communications in Crisis," *Survival*, September/October, 1984. The "hotline" evolved from the Memorandum of Understanding Between the United States of America and the Union of Soviet Socialist Republics Regarding Establishing of a Direct Communication Link, signed at Geneva in June, 1963. In actuality, it was a 66-word per minute teletype machine.

once the mist burned off it was going to be a glorious day. Not at all like the stormy night that had preceded it, with slanted rain and howling wind.

I rolled down my window as I turned left onto the tree-shaded drive. The day was sweet and fresh, and birds were already filling the air with their songs. The gravel crunched softly beneath my tires as I drove the last half mile to the great house that lay in the distance.

When I rolled to a stop across from the entrance to the massive house, the front door swung open. Framed in it was a stunning woman, who literally took your breath away, in high heels, a white silk teddy, and a full-length ocelot coat. A member of her staff hovered in the shadows behind her.

She greeted me effusively and invited me in.

"No," I told her. "We don't know if the house is compromised or not."

I introduced her to my two colleagues and informed her that they would begin immediately to check out the house for listening devices. Until they had finished with at least one room, I continued, we would not talk business in the house.

While Tom and Frank went inside, lugging their gear, she and I walked side-by-side down the drive beneath the arching trees. Flowers bordered both sides of the drive all the way from the house to the road we had taken to reach the estate.

She told me about the breakup with her husband and her personal fears and concerns. She was particularly troubled that the publicity certain to accompany the divorce might give ideas to people, especially potential kidnappers, since she and her husband had a young child. Most people had never heard of her before or knew where she and her husband lived quietly with their child, but the media could be expected to describe the family's great estate and vast wealth, and what had been common knowledge in financial circles was likely soon to be known by every gas station attendant and grocery clerk in America. She was also concerned that the media onslaught would violate her privacy and terrorize the child. I assured her that we would take the necessary steps to protect her and ensure that no one trespassed on the property. We would secure the house, I continued, and set up appropriate procedures for her to travel safely with her child, since she had a number of public engagements coming up, not to mention the fact that she needed to meet regularly with her attorney and financial advisers.

We would also provide her with a secure communications system for calls both from the house and while she was traveling.

I made mental notes of the men and equipment we would need while we strolled and talked.

The call that had put this whole operation in motion had come in around 10:30 p.m. the previous evening. I was dining with friends at an Italian restaurant that I regularly frequented. My cell phone rang. It was a friend on the other end of the line. One of his clients needed assistance immediately, he informed me. She and her husband were about to break up and it was certain to be big news the following day. There would be lurid charges on both sides and a heavy dose of the sensational. Would I get some of my men and travel straightaway to take charge of the situation on the ground?

I agreed, although I wasn't certain how I was going to get where I needed to go. It was pouring rain outside. Some streets were flooded and flights had already departed. On top of that, I had been drinking wine during dinner and needed a couple of cups of strong coffee to clear my head.

I ordered the coffee and called Tom in North Carolina. He was already asleep. I told him to get another man and meet me at dawn at a hotel I knew in the city that was our destination.

By that time the espresso had arrived and I downed three cups in quick succession; damn the blood pressure and full speed ahead. The same thing had happened to me some months earlier at the same restaurant when I received a call from ABC's "Nightline" around nine-thirty inviting me to appear on that night's show. Apparently they'd had a cancellation. I agreed, but then needed a heavy coffee regime to negate the effects of the wine from dinner. This evening was no different and so began our efforts to contain the crisis as it unfolded, getting out ahead of the news and trying to anticipate both the personnel and resources that would be needed in the coming days and weeks.

RULE FOUR is that all crises are manageable. Some, to be certain, are more manageable than others. But this is largely a function of how well-prepared you are and how swiftly you react after the onset of the crisis. In this connection, what you and your allies do over the first twenty-four to seventy-two hours is likely to have a major impact on how well your company or client weathers the crisis. It's all about timing. As Aesop noted in the quotation at the beginning of the chapter, the key to good crisis management is not only to do the right thing but to do it at the right time. Timing is always important, whether swinging a bat at a fastball or responding to a crisis. This was illustrated a few years ago when I took a trip to one of the 'Stans. I was accompanied by our chief of investigations, Tom Kelley, a very affable and competent professional who had served for many years as the FBI's Deputy General Counsel.

We had concluded our meetings and were driven up into the rugged mountains along the Afghan border for an afternoon feast. Our hosts were cooking a freshly slaughtered lamb over hot coals near a tumbling brook, over which a platform, covered with Persian rugs, had been laid. Guests could sleep off the effects of meal and wine on the platform, lulled to sleep by the sound of the rushing brook.

Before the lunch was served, Kelley walked over to a stand of high grass near the side of the mountain to relieve himself and take in the view. This provoked a good deal of chatter from our hosts and several shouts in Kelley's direction. When Kelley returned he asked what they were shouting at him. "Oh, they were just saying beware of the cobras in the tall grass," one of the men replied nonchalantly. "Jesus," exclaimed Kelley, ashen-faced, "they might have told me before I took a leak."

As Casey Stengal, the legendary coach of the New York Yankees once observed, "Most ball games are lost, not won." So it is with crises. Most of your efforts during the first few days will determine whether you effectively cope with the challenge at hand or whether your efforts are undermined by such things as paralysis in the face of danger, a shortage of resources, and confusion. Crises can get away from you quickly and sometimes nothing you subsequently do can easily right the damage. Both the Exxon and Deepwater Horizon (BP) crises were characterized by early missteps and the appearance of confusion and incompetence. While both companies eventually managed to bring their crises under control, at great cost, their reputations suffered significantly and are unlikely to recover any time soon.

RULE FIVE is don't shoot the messenger. Not every crisis has a bearer of bad news. Some are self-evident, like a hurricane slamming into the Gulf coast. Or when you read in the newspaper about your CEO being arrested for drug possession. But other times, knowledge of an impending crisis reaches top management or the board room via the firm's general counsel, CFO, or even a whistleblower. When it comes to crises involving potential negligence, wrongdoing, or defective products, for example, you want to learn about the problem as early as possible so that you can move to address it before it gets out-of-hand, like a runaway train, taking on a momentum all its own. Thus, if you are on the board or in senior management you want to incentivize employees to bring you bad news and not shirk or ignore problems out of fear of retaliation. This happened during the early days of the mortgage crisis that was a major contributing factor to the Great Recession when senior employees of Fannie Mae did not alert, oversight agencies, Congress, or members of its board of directors in a timely fashion about looming accounting problems, especially in connection with derivative transactions and fee recognition. Why? Because Fannie Mae suffered from venal and incompetent management that allegedly punished the bearers of bad news and promoted a corporate culture that rewarded mediocrity, mendacity, denial, and in some cases out-and-out criminality. Moreover, Chairman and CEO of Fannie Mae, Franklin D. Raines, had no incentive see an investigation of accounting problems at the mortgage firm because of the way his compensation package was structured. Indeed, he received $90 million in undeserved payments on more than $9 billion in overstated profits. The way Raines managed Fannie Mae was in direct contradiction from what he told Congress in 2002, when testifying about the Enron's failure: "It is wholly irresponsible and unacceptable for corporate leaders to say they did not know--or suggest it is not their duty to know--about the operations and activities of their company, particularly when it comes to risks that threaten the fundamental viability of their company."[156]

Raines was fired, along with CFO J. Timothy Howard, in 2004 because of what is now viewed as "extensive financial fraud." While Raines ultimately made a modest settlement with the U.S. government (Office of Federal Housing Enterprise Oversight), including giving up worthless stock options, he appears to have escaped real culpability because of his relationship with President Obama and key members of Congress who were guilty of improper oversight of the mortgage giant.

---

156 James Tyson, quoting Franklin Raines in "Fannie Mae Fires Raines, Howard Over Accounting Flaws," Bloomberg, December 22, 2004.

Today, Raines receives a pension of $114,000 a month from Fannie Mae.

This brings us to RULE SIX: always verify the information before you act. In this connection, I always remember the story of a wealthy businessman in Central America during the 1970s. He decided to slip away for a weekend tryst with his mistress. The only person he told his plans to was his long-time valet. Once the businessman had departed for his hide-away at the beach, the valet produced a ransom note which claimed it was from a leftist guerrilla group. According to the note, they had kidnapped the businessman and swore, if a ransom of $50 thousand wasn't paid within twenty-four hours, that he would be killed.

The businessman's family immediately pulled together the ransom, since it was a manageable figure, and the valet "courageously" offered to deliver it to the pickup point. The valet took the ransom and was never seen again. When the businessman returned late the following day, he was taken aback by the unusually warm and excited greeting he received from his family and members of the household staff. The smile on his face, however, quickly faded when he learned what had transpired in his absence.

RULE SEVEN is, in many respects, a corollary to rule six: collect all the facts, or at least as many as feasible, before you reach a conclusion. No case better underscores this than the infamous Menendez murders on August 20, 1989.

Jose Menendez, Chairman and CEO of Live Entertainment, was spending a quiet Sunday evening at home with his wife, Kitty, in their Beverly Hills mansion. His Monday schedule wasn't particularly demanding, with only three appointments noted in his calendar, the first an 8 a.m. meeting at the Polo Lounge. But Jose never made the breakfast. Sometime around eleven, two gunmen clad in long duster-like coats made their way into the Menendez home and opened up on the unsuspecting couple with shotguns as they sat on an L-shaped couch watching television. So savage was the double homicide that the killers even reloaded and continued to blast away at the lifeless corpses long after they were dead. The crime scene was horrific. There was blood and flesh everywhere, even a piece of bloody tissue lodged in one of son Erik's tennis rackets propped up against the wall.

I was awakened from a deep sleep by the incessant ring of the telephone early Monday morning, Washington time. I groggily lifted the phone from the cradle next to my bed, upsetting the alarm clock as

I did so. It was an executive from Carolco Pictures, a company that had been my client for a number of years, and with whom I'd worked on Rambo III. The caller told me that one of their senior executives and his wife had just been found brutally murdered in their Beverly Hills home. The killings had all of the hallmarks of a mafia hit, he explained, and top company officials were worried that they, too, might be in danger. Would I get on the case immediately, he asked, liaison with the authorities, and monitor the official investigation? And, if necessary, respond to threats against the company and its key personnel? I replied that I would have investigators on the first available planes heading west.

On first glance, the facts seemed to square with the notion that Jose and Kitty Menendez had been victims of some kind of gangland slaying. LIVE Entertainment had once been IVE (International Video Entertainment), a leading video pornography distributer, and the "L" had been added to the name when the company was acquired by Carolco. LIVE Entertainment subsequently bought at least two other companies with reputed links to organized crime, and both Carolco and LIVE had directors with organized crime connections. Even more compelling was the murder of a reputed mobster in California with connections to the pornographic video industry two months earlier. And the modus operandi had been exactly the same: a shotgun-style execution.

But the organized crime theory quickly lost currency as our investigation proceeded. Whoever had killed Jose and Kitty had done so with "extreme prejudice," suggesting that it was personal, not business.

When I checked in at my hotel on Sunset Boulevard, where I regularly stayed and was well known to the staff, the desk clerk gave me a faint smile and informed me that, "I know why you're here." This was not surprising considering that the Menendez murders were the biggest story in town and he knew that I was affiliated with Carolco. But I was completely unprepared for his next comment. "I used to work for the Menendez family," he explained. "They were a totally dysfunctional family. Kitty was a drunk and Jose rarely home. The boys, Erik and Lyle, though, were real pieces of work. Especially Lyle. The family's Cuban but Lyle called all of the gardeners and maids 'spics.' We called him 'the Iceman' because he never showed any emotion. I could imagine him drowning puppies."

"What about Erik?" I asked.

"He's okay, but totally under Lyle's spell."

I was stunned. I had arrived in L.A. feeling immensely saddened and sorry for the Lyle and Erik, their parents having been ruthlessly slaughtered, in their own home, the boys having stumbled on the mangled bodies of their parents after returning home from the movies. Now I was hearing one of the sons, a 19-year old kid, referred to as 'the Iceman.' This was just the first of many revelations in the days that followed.

When I met with my investigators later that day it was clear that they were already having second thoughts about the direction the police investigation was taking, which was still focused on business rivals and organized crime as the likely suspects.

One of the investigators had managed to get a good look at the crime scene since the Beverly Hills police department had only put up evidence tape in front of the house and left the back entrance unattended. He had explored the house and even logged onto a computer, which showed that someone had accessed the same computer shortly after the time of the murders and had gone straight to Jose's will. The will, however, was missing.

Within days I spoke with Carolco president, Peter Hoffman, and expressed my reservations about the murders being an organized crime hit and our growing suspicions regarding the boys. In my report to the company in September, I wrote that, "The behavior of Lyle Menendez is extremely suspicious. Not only are his exact whereabouts on the night of the murder open to question, but his actions in the immediate aftermath of the murders are inconsistent with those one expects of an aggrieved son. Why did Lyle and his brother allegedly go to a movie that night, despite the fact that they could screen virtually any new movie they wanted at home? Why did Lyle meet with an investment counselor on Monday, and honor a long-standing engagement, and never mention the tragedy that occurred the previous evening [to his parents]? The fact that LIVE employees were brought to the Menendez home on Monday, the day after the killings, to clean up the murder scene, is also highly suspicious. Not only was furniture removed and the rugs cleaned, but according to our sources the rug in the guest quarters occupied by Lyle was also cleaned. This has been dismissed as simply the desire to clean up the house so that family members could stay there. We don't accept that explanation, especially in light of the fact that the various family members moved into hotels in the aftermath of the murders. Although we cannot state it with certainty, we have reason to believe that someone attempted to access the home computer after the murder and that the last file accessed was J.E. Menendez's will."

Police later verified that the will had been intentionally deleted in the aftermath of the murders.

Our investigation also revealed a long list of anomalies and unusual behavior by Lyle and Erik. One of the most unusual incidents was a late night visit by Lyle to his father's office to purge the files, many of which he hauled out in green garbage bags to the dumpster. We alerted Beverly Hills police, but they expressed no interest in saving the files or in the suspicious behavior of the two brothers at that time. It wasn't until March 8, 1990, that the police moved to arrest Lyle and Erik, who were subsequently convicted of the savage murders of their parents.

IMPROVISING

In a worst case situation where your company is not prepared, and hasn't pre-positioned resources, set up off-site data centers, and taken other measures to reduce exposure in a major crisis, be ready to improvise. One of the best examples of this that I know took place some years ago when South Florida was devastated by a hurricane.

Hurricane Andrew, which struck the U.S. in 1992, was one of the three most powerful hurricanes to hit this country during the twentieth century. It caused more than $26.0 billion of damage, chiefly to South Florida, and many companies were unprepared for the fury of the Category 5 storm. One of those companies was a major British holding company that owned a well-known fast-food chain headquartered in South Florida. As soon as it was recognized how serious the damage was, the company dispatched one of its executives, a former U.S. Navy SEAL, together with a number of his colleagues, to the impacted area with every piece of U.S. denominated currency that they could lay their hands on. The SEAL quickly rented motels, for cash, that could be used to shelter employee families that had lost their homes, or had no electricity, and which could be used as offices so the company could stand up operations again. With all the ATMs down and banks closed, cash loans were made available to employees, no questions asked, to tide them over through the crisis. The chief problem was that the loans needed to be memorialized on paper, but there was a dearth of dry paper available in the aftermath of the hurricane. The quick-thinking SEAL found a stack of dry Post-It notes and wrote out literally hundreds of contracts in tiny cramped lettering which were signed by those receiving loans and from whom materials and services were being purchased. In the end, the efforts by the SEAL and his team were so successful that the company lost only one day of business, while hundreds of other companies didn't reopen for weeks and some not at all.

EFFECTIVE CRISIS MANAGEMENT

As a textbook example of effective crisis management one need look no further than the 1982 Tylenol case. In the fall of that year someone in the Chicago area introduced massive amounts of potassium cyanide (more than 10,000 times the amount necessary to kill a human being) into Extra-Strength Tylenol capsules on the shelves of six supermarkets and drugstores. Within days, seven people were dead after taking the best-selling pain medicine.

Tylenol, which is produced by Johnson & Johnson, had a 37 percent market share and accounted for 19 percent of the company's profits in the first three quarters of 1982. It outsold the next four leading painkillers--Anacin, Bayer, Bufferin, and Excedrin--combined. In the immediate aftermath of the crisis, Tylenol's market share fell to 7 percent, a decline of 30 percent. Thus, the poisonings were a crisis of major proportions for Johnson & Johnson, both economically and in terms of the damage inflicted on its leading brand.

The company received a demand of $1 million to halt the poisonings and authorities traced the letter to a James W. Lewis, who had a criminal history. Although he was ultimately convicted of attempting to extort money from Johnson & Johnson and served time in federal prison, the FBI could never prove that he was the actual culprit behind the poisonings.

In the meantime, the company had to make some serious decisions regarding how to handle the crisis and, if possible, to save the Tylenol brand. A well-known advertising executive of the day, Jerry Della Famina, was quoted as saying, "I don't think they can ever sell another product under that name. There may be an advertising person who thinks he can solve this and if they find him, I want to hire him, because then I want him to turn our water cooler into a wine cooler."[157]

The first thing the company did was to decide to cooperate fully with the media. A nationwide alert was put out warning consumers not to use any Tylenol product until the extent of the tampering could be determined. Production of Tylenol was halted, along with all advertising, and the product was withdrawn from the market. The recall involved 31 million bottles, worth over $100 million in retail sales, and resulted in a seven percent decline in the company's share value. Nevertheless, by putting the public's well-being ahead of profits, Johnson & Johnson was viewed sympathetically by most people, who tended to see the company, like those who had been killed, as a victim and not negligent in any way.

The next hurdle was how to reintroduce Tylenol back to the marketplace. Consumer surveys suggested that only 40 percent of former Tylenol users would be willing to try it again. It was clear that the product needed to return to store shelves as soon as possible and in a form that would guarantee it was safe and secure. Accordingly, the company redesigned the product's packaging, introducing the triple-seal container. If any one of the seals was compromised, consumers were told, they should not use the product. 80 million coupons, good for $2.50 off any purchase of Tylenol, appeared in newspapers in November and December, and incentives were provided to retailers in the form of major discounts for restocking Tylenol at pre-tampering levels. To promote the product's re-release, Johnson & Johnson hired 2250 new sales people to make presentations to doctors, pharmacists, and other medical professionals, extolling Tylenol's safety and effectiveness.

In January, 1983, the company launched a new advertising campaign, only referring to the recent problems circuitously. Ads, for example, focused on the new packaging but without dwelling on what had precipitated the change. Loyal Tylenol users were featured describing how much they trusted the product. By adopting a very positive advertising program, coupled with the coupons, discounts to retailers, and the sales push focused on medical professionals, Johnson & Johnson was able to quickly recover and by the end of February

---

157 Jerry Della Femina, "Tylenol's Rapid Comeback," *New York Times*, Sept. 17, 1983.

Tylenol's market share had reached 28 percent, only 9 points less than it had been before the poisonings.

Business writers and business school faculty members have consistently singled out the Tylenol case as one of the best examples of how a company successfully addressed a major threat to its profitability and reputation. According to T. Berge, "The Tylenol crisis is without a doubt the most exemplary case ever known in the history of crisis communications. Any business executive, who has ever stumbled into a public relations ambush, ought to appreciate the way Johnson & Johnson responded to the Tylenol poisonings. They have effectively demonstrated how major business has to handle a disaster."[158]

CRISES AS OPPORTUNITIES

"Never let a good crisis go to waste," former White House Chief-of-Staff Rahm Emanuel is fond of saying.[159] Emanuel was suggesting that a crisis, particularly someone else's crisis, can provide an opportunity to a competitor or rival who is able to find a way of taking advantage of it. This was never more apparent than when I was working in my office in the early 1980s and was interrupted by my long-time personal assistant, Jan Baldwin, who said there was a Mr. Mroczyk in the reception area who was desirous of seeing me.

"Does he have an appointment?" I asked, inasmuch as I was crashing on a project that had a fast-approaching deadline.

"No," responded Jan. "But he said to tell you that Mr. Casey had sent him."

I looked up with a start.

"Bill Casey?" I said, referring to the then-Director of the CIA.

"That's what he says."

"Then by all means show him in."

Peter Mroczyk was a tall, good-looking man in a poorly cut suit, who spoke flawless English with a British accent. According to Peter, he had been the spokesman for Polish Solidarity until martial law was imposed in Poland and he was arrested and jailed. After a year of incarceration, he was given the choice of exile or more jail time so he

---

158 T. Berge, *The First 24-Hours*, (Cambridge, Massachusetts: Basil Blackwell Inc., 1990.

159 Rahm Emanuel; Washington, D.C.; June 17, 2009.

opted for exile.[160] His father had been a Polish ace in World War Two, who had met Peter's mother in the U.K., and had returned to Poland after the war only to see it slip behind the Iron Curtain, one tragedy succeeding another. Peter's goal was to set up a support organization for Solidarity in the West. Accordingly, we formed the Solidarity Endowment, with Peter, myself, and former U.S. Ambassador to Poland Robert T. Davies (1973-1978) as incorporators and directors. The Endowment's Advisory Board was a veritable non-partisan Who's Who of Washington with everyone from the head of the AFL-CIO and Senator Ted Kennedy on the left to Ambassador Jeanne Kirkpatrick and Jack Kemp on the right. In the years that followed, the Endowment funneled millions of dollars to the beleaguered Polish Solidarity organization, headed by shipyard worker Lech Walesca, to keep the organization going and from running out of hope, which could lead to those advocating violence taking over. We knew that the moment Solidarity took up arms it would give the Soviet Union a pretext for occupying the country and completely crushing the Solidarity movement.

CIA Director Casey had always believed that the Soviet Union was on its last legs and if communism could be rolled back in just one place the whole rotten system would collapse. Poland was the prize, he maintained, and Solidarity, along with the Polish Pope John Paul II, would be the instruments of the Soviet Union's destruction. Casey was, of course, right in his analysis and put into motion many of the forces that would see Solidarity triumph in Poland, and ultimately lead to the end of the USSR.

The U.S. clearly recognized the unfolding crisis in Poland and did everything it could to fan the flames, as it did in Afghanistan as well when it gave aggressive support to the mujahedeen fighting the Soviet occupation.

Similarly, a crisis at one company can open up new opportunities for competitors if they are prepared and able to take advantage of the situation. The economic problems suffered by General Motors and Daimler-Chrysler during The Great Recession clearly benefited Ford, which did not take government money and various foreign competitors. Likewise, Toyota's mysterious acceleration problems with

---

160 Peter's title was Chairman of Solidarity for Polish Radio and Television.

its cars provided competitors with new opportunities to increase their sales and market shares.

Drug violence in Mexico has had a chilling effect on tourism and stimulated other nations, especially in the Caribbean, to step up their advertising as alternative venues.

FAILURE

Although it seems like a truism, failure, if you survive it, should make you stronger and wiser. Not every crisis can have a positive outcome, no matter how well you prepare or how hard you try, because luck just isn't with you. And, as companies take more risks, such as encouraging innovation and opening new markets, their chances of failure also increase. Every successful company has had its share of failures, such as the Ford Edsel, Crystal Pepsi, New Coke, and Apple's Lisa. Bill Gates' first business, Traf-O-Data, was a bust, as were the first business efforts of Henry Ford, Walt Disney, and Colonel Sanders. Thus, every company or organization can learn valuable lessons from failure. Apollo 13, for example, was NASA's most successful failure, because so much knowledge was gleaned from the trouble-plagued mission that, according to some experts, it saved future NASA missions from even more catastrophic problems.

The key with failure is not to repeat it. As South Carolina Senator Fritz Hollings liked to observe, "There's no education in the second kick of a mule." Federal bureaucrats often make the same mistakes over and over again but are rarely held accountable because of civil service protections or simply the passage of time. The military is the exception to this rule because failure is carefully studied and analyzed in after-action reports and even by hearings and panels convened by senior officers and the political leadership at the Pentagon. This is not to say that cover-ups and superficial inquiries don't happen, as they surely did in the death of NFL star Pat Tillman in a friendly fire incident in Afghanistan.

Thus, failures must be studied just like successes, so that deficiencies can be corrected before they are repeated or exploited by enemies or competitors

- 11 -

CRISIS COMMUNICATIONS

"The real news is bad news."

Marshall McLuhan

An article appearing in *Corporate Legal Times* was entitled, "Well-Planned Communications Key to Managing a Crisis."[161]   The article asserts one of the greatest fallacies with respect to effective corporate crisis management, and that is that a good crisis communications program is the most important factor in a company's performance in a crisis situation.   This is just plain wrong, and is indicative of the unfortunate impact public relations firms are having in the field of crisis management. Too often today, the public relations tail wags the crisis management dog. Don't confuse public relations with crisis management; they are not the same thing.

While crisis communications is an extremely important element of a larger crisis management program or strategy, it is not the most important element.   Fixing the problem is.   Everything else is secondary to this single, overriding goal. Solutions, in other words, are more important than slogans.   How a company is judged in the aftermath of a crisis will ultimately depend on how well it performed during this period and how effectively it overcame the challenge with which it was confronted. In the Tylenol case, as noted in the previous chapter, the media campaign was critical to the resolution of the problem, but it would have gone nowhere without the company's

---

161 "Well-Planned Communications Key to Managing a Crisis"; *Corporate Legal Times*; December, 1995.

decision to pull Tylenol from the shelves and to completely redesign its packaging.

By contrast, too often companies that are guilty of ineffective management during a crisis turn to sophisticated public relations and advertising techniques to try and make it appear as though they handled the problem adroitly. There is no better example of this than the massive BP oil spill, also known as the Deepwater Horizon disaster, in the Gulf of Mexico. On April 11, 2010, the Deepwater Horizon oil rig exploded, killing 11 oil workers and injuring 17 others. Millions of gallons of oil spewed from the crippled well, causing extensive coastal damage to wildlife, the environment, tourist beaches, and the fishing industry. It took the company more than two months to finally cap the well, but in the meantime BP's stock price hit a 52 week low and by early November, 2010, the company estimated the cost of the disaster at $40 billion and still counting. The interim report on the disaster by the National Academy of Engineering and the National Research Council blames BP and its management for "an insufficient consideration of risk and a lack of operating discipline," and suggests that the company was inadequately prepared for the disaster.[162]

BP CEO Tony Haward made a series of unfortunate comments that only seemed to reinforce the notion that the company was uncaring in its response the crisis, the most famous being, "We're sorry for the massive disruption its caused to their [Gulf residents] lives. There's no one who wants this thing over more than I do. I'd like my life back." He, thus, turned an apology into an insensitive remark, disregarding the 11 men who died on the Deepwater Horizon (who probably would have wanted their lives back) and making the crisis all about him. "What the hell did we do to deserve this?" he whined to fellow executives in London, once again seeming to worry more about the impact on him than the dead and injured employees and the Gulf residents impacted by the spill. He denied that there were underwater oil plumes and suggested that cleanup workers complaining of dizziness and headaches were probably suffering from food poisoning rather than the chemicals they were being exposed to. Despite the massive size of the oil spill and the technological hurdles remaining in

---

162 Steven Mufson, "Panel: BP's Lack of Discipline Contributed to Spill," *The Washington Post*, Nov. 18, 2010.

order to cap the blowout, eighteen days into the crisis Hayward suggested that, "the environmental impact of this disaster is likely to have been very, very modest." He tried to deflect criticism of BP's slow response to the crisis by blaming a media frenzy caused by critics of President Obama who wanted the disaster to be his "Hurricane Katrina." Finally, he tried to dismiss the magnitude of the disaster by saying, "The Gulf of Mexico is a very big ocean. The amount of volume of oil and dispersant we are putting into it is tiny in relation to the total water volume."

Although communications must be viewed as simply one part of the larger crisis management effort, perceptions remain extremely important. A company that is perceived to be guilty of incompetence or misconduct, even if it is innocent of the charges, has a real problem. As noted in an earlier chapter, Exxon made countless errors and blunders in the early stages of the Exxon Valdez disaster. These made such a large impression on the public that even when the company got its act together and began to effectively address the problem, the perception lingered that it was incompetent and indifferent to the environment. And despite hundreds of millions, if not billions, of dollars devoted to positive advertising, there is a lingering impression that Exxon is not a good corporate citizen and that it totally botched cleanup efforts in Prince William Sound.

This could be called the Tet Factor. During the Tet Offensive in Vietnam, the United States fought the Viet Cong and North Vietnamese to a standstill and inflicted bloody losses on them. However, while the campaign was a military disaster for Hanoi it was a public relations victory, and one that ultimately contributed mightily to the defeat of South Vietnam. As graphic television footage from the battles that engulfed the entire country were projected into American homes during the dinner hour on the evening news, Americans became disenchanted with the war and suspicious of the many pronouncements made by U.S. leaders, especially by President Lyndon Johnson and defense secretary Robert McNamara, that the U.S. was winning the war, that the end was in sight, and that the enemy was on the run. The bitter fighting during Tet didn't look to most Americans like a victory, nor did it seem indicative of an enemy that was beaten and on the run.

As with Tet, companies can win the battle but lose the war if they don't effectively manage communications during times of crisis. After the economy went into a tailspin following the Gulf War, President George H.W. Bush's popularity plummeted. Part of the problem was that the electorate did not believe he felt their pain or that he was spending enough time on issues closer to home, like jobs and the economy. The White House permitted too many photo opportunities of Bush engaged in various sporting activities. "While George Bush putts," observed one political consultant, "America goes down the hole."[163] Or as a prominent reporter observed to this author after accompanying the president to his Maine retreat, "I don't know how a man can play five sports a day and still run the country."[164] Such observations may have been simplistic, but to Bush's dismay and the detriment of the president's reelection hopes, this was the way much of the country perceived the president. And despite Bush's unprecedented public approval rating in the polls after the convincing victory of the U.S. over Iraq in the Gulf War, such perceptions greatly eroded the president's popularity and eventually caused his defeat at the polls.

THE NATURE OF THE NEWS BUSINESS

With this introduction, let us examine the news business and draw some conclusions about the best way to deal with the media during a crisis, or for that matter, just about any time.

First of all, what is news? It is, as Matthew Green once observed, "the manna of the day."[165] Others have described news as change. We all hunger for the news, especially when there are great events taking place. This said, there has been a dumbing down of the news in recent years, with less emphasis on international and political news, and a greater emphasis on sensationalism, violence, and public personalities. All three evening newscasts on the networks have gone to a softer format, with health updates and stories that are designed to appeal to women. On the day that Pakistan tested five nuclear weapons in May, 1998, this writer was asked to appear on the local CBS affiliate to provide some perspective on the event in an interview with veteran

---

163 David Axelrod; *New York Times*; January, 1992.

164 Muriel Dobbins, remark to this author.

165 Matthew Green, *The Spleen*, 1737.

news anchor Gordon Peterson. Peterson lamented the fact that the Pakistan story ran third in the news lineup, behind stories on the progress of an investigation into a possible serial killer and the murder-suicide of comic Phil Hartman and his wife. As Peterson complained, "NBC Dateline is the future of television news." Such news magazine shows are relatively inexpensive to produce, by comparison to regular programming, and emphasize the trendy and sensational over more important and complex stories.

And if there has been a dumbing down of the news, this is, in part, a reflection of many of the reporters that cover the news, especially on television, where style too often takes precedence over substance. Although the news media is fond of invoking names like Edward R. Murrow and Walter Cronkite, few television reporters today have the experience, judgment, and background of the two veteran CBS newsmen.

Many reporters have little knowledge of the subjects they cover. All too often they are instant experts, and as such are prone to errors and misstatements. Not only do they misinterpret what they sometimes see, but too many reporters bring a subjective bias to their stories. Although most reporters work for large, wealthy corporations and earn a good living, they are inherently distrustful of corporate America and often adopt a guilty until proven innocent perspective when covering stories focusing on business.

Bad news nearly always takes precedence over good news, and the more shocking the bad news the better. Indeed, good news is generally non-news under most conditions. There is a lurid public fascination with tragedies of every dimension and news of such incidents almost always supplants good news, no matter how uplifting or heartwarming. Local television stations and even the networks, in the competition for ratings, feed this public preoccupation with violence and mayhem. This is nothing new. In the early 1980s I was asked to appear on a documentary on terrorism called "War in the Shadows" hosted by the venerable CBS newsman, Walter Cronkite. During the filming, Cronkite reminisced about covering the 1956 Hungarian Revolution. In those days, he reflected, everything was shot on film which was then flown to the U.S., where it was developed and finally put on the evening news. Generally, three days elapsed between the initial photography and the public airing of the story. Cronkite described the message he received from CBS headquarters in New York. "I was told that people were interested in these flammable devices being thrown at the Soviet tanks by the freedom fighters. They were called Molotov cocktails. So I went out and got a bottle, a rag, and some gasoline and showed all of America how to make a Molotov cocktail on television. How naive."

You can bet that if you suffer a major crisis, there is a very good chance that it is going to be fodder for the media. You're living in a dream world if you think you can suppress such stories.

Finally, if there was every any question about it, reportage of the news is not a public service. It is, no matter its format or medium, a business endeavor, and like all business endeavors, news organizations keep a sharp eye on the bottom line. Where once there were three major networks, today there are scores of cable channels and news networks, not to mention blogs and web-based publications, and the competition to be the first with a breaking news story is extremely fierce. The role of the editor has been all but eliminated in the rush to put things on the air. The public, therefore, often is subjected to live broadcasting, with little attempt to put matters into perspective or context, and to viewing raw, unedited footage that may or may not present an accurate and true picture of the events depicted.

This was nowhere better illustrated than during the 1985 hijacking odyssey of TWA 847. Islamic extremists commandeered the aircraft, which was bound for Rome from Athens, at gunpoint, on June 14. The 39 Americans on board were ultimately taken off the plane in Beirut and five of them appeared at a hastily-called press conference at Beirut international airport. The hijackers, who had already murdered one young American in cold blood, instructed the reporters not to show the heavily armed guards surrounding the five hostages or the reactions of any of the other hostages during the press conference. One of the five, identified as the group's spokesman, was an undereducated oilfield equipment executive by the name of Allyn Conwell with strong anti-Israeli views. Conwell publicly criticized the strong U.S. relationship with Israel and declared a "genuine sympathy" for his captors. He equated the hijacking of the aircraft to Israel's detention of hundreds of Shiites, and advised the U.S. against any kind of rescue operation, saying that a "rescue operation would only cause, in our estimation, additional, unneeded and unwanted deaths among innocent people."[166] Several of the other hostages tried to indicate their displeasure with Conwell's pronouncements and one even was flashing his middle finger during the proceedings, but he was out of camera range. CNN carried the feed live from Beirut without any attempt to screen it in advance or put it into perspective. The average American tuning in had little or no sense that Conwell was a hostage surrounded by gunmen or that he did not represent the views of most of the other hostages. If one took Conwell at face value, the U.S. relationship with Israel was at the root of all of the nation's problems in the Middle East.

With these observations about the news media, how should you approach the issue of crisis communications?

PRIOR TO THE CRISIS

While many companies have crisis communications programs, most are designed to go into effect only after the onset of the crisis. In reality, the steps you take prior to the crisis may have a major impact on how successful your communications strategy ultimately is received once the crisis has occurred.

The first thing any company needs to weather a crisis is a positive public image. How the media reacts to your efforts during a crisis will depend in large measure on whether you have a backlog of good will and credibility. A company which does not have a good public image or, worse, has a negative image, will have to overcome these handicaps once the crisis hits. By contrast, a company with a positive image will often be treated much more sympathetically by the media.

To cultivate a positive public image, companies should do the following:

1. Good Reputation. Companies should engage in ongoing public relations campaigns that emphasize their contributions to their workforce, their communities and society as a whole.

2. Good Relations with the Media. Your communications staff and top executives should cultivate personal relationships with reporters and news executives. Too often companies think that they can activate their relationships with the sales departments

---

166 Allyn Conwell; quoted in "Captive TWA Passengers Reject a Military Rescue"; *The Washington Post*; June 21, 1985.

of individual stations and networks to win a sympathetic ear during periods of crisis, but in reality the people who sell ads and air time have little interaction with their counterparts in the news room.

Invite news executives and reporters to company functions, provide them with regular press releases about the company, get together with them on a one-on-one basis, and design the company's advertising program to portray the company as favorably as possible. Don't operate in secret but give members of the media tours of the company and regular access to its top officers. If the company deals in dangerous industrial processes, it is often a good idea to let the media see your crisis planning and preparedness for any contingency. Loan your company spokesman to various charitable activities in the community and make him or her a recognizable public personality.

3. <u>Cultivate Allies.</u> In the event that you suffer a major crisis, it's good to have friends and allies. To the extent possible, cultivate local officials, charitable organizations, unions, and prominent citizens. They can step forward and express their confidence in the company and its leadership, and testify to its contributions to the community. Ideally, your crisis should become their crisis, inasmuch as a bad outcome could have severe economic and other ramifications on your workforce and a given locality.

4. <u>Law Enforcement, Fire Fighters, and Other First Responders.</u> Know your local law enforcement officials, fire fighters, hospital personnel, and emergency managers. Such relationships can be invaluable during a crisis.

In other words, be proactive. Once a crisis hits, it's too late to begin developing a positive public image and sympathetic allies.

CHOOSING A SPOKESPERSON

Every company should have a designated spokesperson. Generally it is best to have one individual (and one alternate) and insist that all questions be directed to that individual. The moment that some unauthorized company executive answers a question, all bets are off and virtually anyone in the firm is fair game for reporters.

The individual chosen as spokesperson should be personable, articulate, knowledgeable, and have a sense of humor. They should not be arrogant or too formal. The operational word is likeable. Someone who is inherently likeable will suggest that your company is also likeable and, therefore, not threatening or malicious. A sloppy or overweight person often will send the wrong signal, and will suggest to many that your company is similarly undisciplined and lax. By contrast, someone who is too attractive--male or female--is often threatening or distracting to others, and may have credibility problems. The same holds true for someone who is too young. A mature individual with a little gray at the temples often is better at conveying a sense of steadiness and wisdom.

Using a designated spokesperson is often better than having the CEO meet with the media because the spokesperson can more easily avoid a particularly thorny question by suggesting the need to confer with management or to seek guidance elsewhere before providing an answer. A CEO is expected to know the answers to most questions and his or her word is generally regarded as gospel and not subject to further clarification. If the CEO of the company decides to become the spokesperson, he or she may have more authority and credibility, but by the same token the risks are far greater. Tony Haywood is the poster boy for why you don't want the CEO to be the company spokesman.

The best spokesperson is someone with longevity and experience, who knows the company and its workings intimately, and has a generous reservoir of credibility built up over a long period of time and a wide range of personal contacts in the media.

WHAT DO REPORTERS HAVE A RIGHT TO EXPECT?

The news media has a right to expect certain things from you, and if you observe these rules, you will cultivate good media relations:

1. Access. If you try to stonewall, avoid, or circumvent reporters seeking comment and information on some major crisis or disaster, you do so at your own peril. The media will find someone to talk to even if it's only a janitor or a gadfly completely uninformed about what the company is really doing

to address a particular problem or crisis. That's because the media abhors a vacuum, and must fill their air time with something, even if it is someone who doesn't really possess competent insights into the company and its problem.

This was driven home to me in April, 1986, when I received a call from CBS Evening News asking me to sit on the set with Dan Rather that evening for a special report on the U.S. bombing raid on Libya. I was at the headquarters of Wackenhut Security in Florida on business and there was no way I could be back in Washington in time for the special, and the network didn't want to do an uplink from its Miami bureau. I was subsequently replaced by Congresswoman Patricia Schroeder, one of the most liberal members of Congress and one who had been a critic of using force against terrorists. Her statements on Libya were absolutely antithetical to my views, and the decision by the network to use her to replace me drove home the lesson that all the network really wanted was a warm body in the chair on the set; they didn't care whether our opinions were matched or how much Schroeder knew about the subject.

2. Responsiveness. Reporters have a right to expect you to be as responsive as possible to their inquiries. This includes background information regarding the crisis and access to the disaster site, if there is one, so long as they do not interfere with recovery operations or any criminal investigations that might be underway.

3. Courtesy. Just as you expect courtesy from the media, so too do they have a right to expect it from you.

4. Accuracy. The information you provide to the media should be accurate. If it isn't, you have an obligation to correct it at your earliest opportunity.

5. Non-Interference. You also have an obligation to let reporters do their job with the least possible interference from you or others. This means that reporters have a right to report the story the way they see it, so long as they are accurate and do not violate any undertakings as to what is background and off-the-record.

6. <u>Follow-up.</u> Reporters have a right to follow-up and request clarification of any relevant matters they do not fully comprehend.

INTERVIEWS AND PRESS CONFERENCES

The following rules should be observed when meeting with the media:

1. <u>Controlled Situations.</u> Don't meet with the media in a spontaneous, uncontrolled format. Don't answer questions shouted at you. Avoid media ambushes. Have a regular meeting place for press conferences. It could be a company auditorium or one of the meeting rooms at a local hotel. Following the Oklahoma City bombing, local authorities established a media location a short distance from the shattered Murrah building, where the press would not be in the way or contaminate the crime scene, but where they could do their standups with the shattered building in the background. Since television is a visual medium, it is extremely important that you understand that television reporters need appropriate pictures to illustrate their stories. Efforts to restrict television cameras from the action or site of a disaster will be doomed to failure as TV crews will invariably find ways to circumvent your attempts to exclude them.

    If possible, set aside space for the media to work with desks, telephones, computer hookups, and a coffee pot and snacks. While it won't guarantee that the media will treat you favorably, any consideration you show to the members of the press corps will generally be rewarded.

2. <u>Know To Whom You are Speaking.</u> Every reporter should present his or her credentials to a member of your staff, and these should be verified for authenticity. Thumbnail profiles of key members of the media are always helpful to your top executives, who might be called upon to answer questions from the media. Some companies have gone so far as to develop a system of cards similar to baseball cards, only in this case with a photograph of the reporter, the name of his or her publication, a list of the reporter's credits, and perhaps some subjective information about the reporter's views and perspectives.

In most cases, it is advisable to issue each reporter a new credential, good for the duration of the crisis. Feel free to exclude members of fringe publications and organizations that may attempt to disrupt press conferences. Also, do not credential anyone who violates the ground rules that you establish for conduct on the site and during the press conferences. At press conferences, all reporters should identify themselves and their media outlet before asking a question. If they neglect to do this, you should ask them who they are and their affiliation.

3. <u>Have a Plan for the Interview or Press Conference.</u> Every White House interview and press conference is carefully scripted. Anticipate every possible negative question and prepare answers in advance. Have appropriate statistics and other information readily available. Know what points you want to make and work them into your answers, and don't conclude the interview or press conference until you are satisfied you have made your points. It's a good idea to make your main points at the top of the interview and repeat them over and over again. Often times, an interviewer will conclude by saying, "Is there anything else you want to say?" or "Did I neglect to ask you something I should have asked?" This is your opportunity to expand on anything you forgot to say or reinforce your key points again.

If confronted with a question that you don't have an answer to, answer a question you want to answer. If the question is repeated, make another point that is important to you. There is nothing that says you must be responsive to all questions. On the other hand, try not to be evasive, and whatever you do: don't lie. Once caught in a lie, your credibility is often permanently damaged.

Don't permit outrageous accusations or misstatements to go unanswered or unchallenged. If the reporter provides incorrect information or offers up a conclusion that you know to be wrong, set the record straight. Otherwise, the error may take on a life of its own and be repeated over and over again until it becomes a truism. In rebutting inaccuracies, try to be firm but polite. Don't challenge an accusation with another accusation. And never give a reporter making a wild accusation the benefit of the doubt; if you disagree with their facts or the basis of an allegation, ask them the source of their information. As former Senator Daniel Patrick Moynihan once observed, "Everyone is entitled to his own opinion but not his own facts."

There is no better cautionary tale than that of Dan Bartlett, the White House communications director under George W. Bush. When CBS News claimed, shortly before the 2004 election, that it had memos suggesting that President Bush had received preferential treatment in the Texas National Guard, Bartlett agreed to talk to "60 Minutes" on the condition that copies of the memos would be provided to him. CBS subsequently was informed that Bartlett wouldn't challenge the authenticity of the memos, and this apparently played a major role in the network's decision to run with the story rather than continue its own effort to authenticate the documents.[167] Although the memos contained a number of obvious clues that they had been forged on a computer utilizing word processing software (that didn't exist in the early 1970s), and not typed on an electric typewriter as they were purported to be, Bartlett made no effort to independently authenticate the memos. Instead, he treated them as real and instantly gave life to a story that could potentially have cost the president his reelection bid. Bartlett later attempted to defend his inaction and gullibility by lamely complaining: "How am I supposed to verify something that came from a dead man in three hours?"[168] Of course, that's just the point: he should have refused comment until the memos had been carefully scrutinized by professional document examiners. An even greater indictment of Bartlett was that it wouldn't have taken much effort or experience to determine that the memos were bogus. As The Washington Post reported, "reasonably competent computer enthusiasts have created nearly exact replicas of the documents in 15

---

167 "In Rush to Air, CBS Quashed Memo Worries," *The Washington Post*, September 19, 2004.

168 *Ibid.*

minutes employing default settings for Microsoft Word and the widely used Times New Roman font."[169]

4. Rehearse Whenever Possible. During the early 1980's, I headed the international division of Washington's leading public affairs firm. One of our clients was the late John Denver, a thoroughly likeable and engaging individual, who approached us with a rather unusual media relations problem. U.S. cultural exchanges with the former Soviet Union had been suspended after the U.S.S.R. invaded Afghanistan in 1979. Four years later, despite the fact that President Ronald Reagan had characterized the Soviet Union as an "evil empire," the cultural exchange program was renewed and John was selected as the first American artist to perform in the U.S.S.R. since the onset of the Afghan War. He quite clearly recognized the problems inherent in his visit. There would likely to be unusual media interest in his trip, with many observers waiting for him to make some kind of pratfall or mistake, either by being too friendly to the Russians or by antagonizing them in some way. In order to steer a neutral course and to avoid the political issues separating the U.S. and Soviet Union, we carefully prepared him for the visit. He immersed himself in background papers and we introduced him to top Washington officials with responsibility for relations with the Soviet Union, including Jack Matlock, who was then at the National Security Council and would shortly become U.S. ambassador to Moscow. We capped all of this off with several mock press conferences where John was subjected to the most difficult and often devious questions we could come up with. I'm happy to say that he met the challenge, and that his trip was a success. Later, he attributed the fact that his visit came off without a hitch to the training he'd received, including the mock press conferences, prior to leaving for the Soviet Union. There hadn't been a question on the trip, he informed me, for which he wasn't prepared.

5. Regular Press Conferences and Briefings. During a crisis, communicate with the media on a regular basis. Hold daily

---

169 *Ibid.*

press conferences. Try to provide the media with as much information and, as noted above, access as possible. If you don't do this, the media will go around you and find other sources, including critics of your company or industry, disgruntled workers, and uninformed talking heads eager to see their faces on television. Remember, unless your crisis is of such compelling interest or impact that it dwarfs all other competing news stories, which rarely happens, it will only rate a brief mention on the evening news or on one of the all news channels. The average story is only about 20 second to two minutes long. Thus, it pays for you to consume as much of this time as possible in getting your message out. If you say "no comment" or don't give the media any information of value, then the story may be dominated by negative or hostile information. And make sure your spokesperson is available, otherwise a hostile reporter may say that, "We tried to contact the company for a comment, but they didn't get back to us by airtime."

6. Interviews. The following observations are offered in connection with one-on-one interviews, but many of the suggestions may also helpful during press briefings. Whenever sitting down with a reporter for an interview, especially on camera, make certain that you are in a comfortable environment and not one that is cold or threatening. Removing your coat can sometimes convey a warmer and more approachable persona. It is always advisable to engage the reporter in informal conversation before the interview, so long as you steer clear of subjects that will be discussed during the interview. This way you can establish a personal rapport with the reporter, which usually makes the interview less tense and confrontational. Smile at the reporter, maintain eye contact, and keep your answers succinct. Don't ramble and don't volunteer more information than necessary. In this respect, interviews are like depositions. Remain calm no matter how rude or aggravating a reporter's questions. Offer up statements that capture the essence of your case or position in as few words as possible, and make those words quotable. As many PR experts advise, speak in headlines or sound bites.

7. <u>Be Positive.</u> While you should always be realistic, you are under no obligation to take the most negative view of the crisis. You may want, for example, to emphasize how well the recovery efforts are going rather than dwell on the disaster itself. Feel free to find the silver lining in the cloud. For example, during the darkest days of the sectarian strife in Northern Ireland, the Northern Irish Tourist Board emphasized the low prices for accommodations and the fact that there were 74 championship golf courses in the six counties, with no wait for a tee-time. Beirut was promoted similarly during the early 1990s. A water shortage in Puerto Rico a few years ago was countered with advertising emphasizing how many continuous sunny days San Juan had experienced.

8. <u>Internal Communications.</u> In 1979, confronted purportedly by intimidation tactics on the part of the Teamsters trying to unionize his workforce, Edward J. Daly, President and Chairman of the Board of World Airways Inc., released an open letter to his employees, with copies to his board of directors, shareholders, legal counsel, and public relations representatives. In it, Daly wrote that, "The Teamsters assumed that they were taking on a pigeon because of the gutless types in the top management of many large corporations throughout the Country, who do not have the courage to stand up and fight...We have people in this management who are not passive, who are not permissive, who do not run scared, and who will not be intimidated." Continuing, he referred to the Book Leviticus, Chapter 24, Verse 20, which says, 'If a man injures his neighbor, what he has done must be done to him--broken limb for broken limb, eye for eye, tooth for tooth.' I disagree with this brilliant man and his 'Mosaic' law." If there is "any more intimidation," he went on to say, "I can assure you that it will not be one for one--it will be two for one, in favor of World Airways and Daly...Further, if there are any more threats upon my life or that of my family and anyone associated with World Airways, or threats to do damage to my personal property--not meaning

to be poetic, I will search that son-of-a-bitch down and he will end up in the ground."[170]

While Daly's letter to his employees is surely one of the most unique internal communications in memory, it is highly advisable to communicate regularly with your employees and shareholders during a crisis, otherwise they will get their information, along with the general public, from newspapers and magazines, television, blogs, and web-based news sites. Many of these reports may be inaccurate or highly biased against the company and its management. Management needs to ensure that employees and shareholders hear about the crisis, its impact on the company, and the steps being taken to resolve it from those most knowledgeable about the events in question and most engaged in efforts to bring it under control.

CONCLUSION

Perhaps one of the worst managed crises in recent memory, certainly from a public relations point-of-view, was the Ford rollover controversy involving Firestone tires. 6.5 million Firestone tires, mostly on Ford Explorers, were recalled after blowouts caused the vehicles to roll over, resulting in an estimated 148 deaths and more than 500 injuries.[171] Firestone and Ford each blamed the other for the problem, but the Japanese leadership of Bridgestone/Firestone initially sought to deny any responsibility for the rollovers while Ford took a much more solicitous and empathetic approach that paid off in the end. According to one writer, "it [Bridgestone/Firestone] began with a strategy of denial, and only when faced with new and dramatic evidence did it begin to become more truthful in its responses."[172]

"I come to accept full and personal responsibility on behalf of Bridgestone/Firestone for the events that led to this hearing," the

---

170 Edward J. Daley; open letter dated October 28, 1979; copy of original; p. 2.

171 Congressional Research Service, "Firestone Tire Recall: NHTSA, Industry, and Congressional Responses," January 24, 2001, p. CRS-2.

172 Keith Michael Hearit, *Crisis Management by Apology: Corporate Responses to Allegations of Wrongdoing*, (London: Lawrence Erlbaum Publishers, 2006), p. 136.

Chairman of Bridgestone/Firestone, Masatoshi Ono, told lawmakers, but he denied that the public recall of 6.5 million tires by his company could be construed as an apology before Congress and was any kind of admission of guilt or that there was anything wrong with their products. "This was a sympathy expressed for those individuals who operated vehicles using our products and got into accidents," said Ono later. "If we are deemed responsible for the accidents, that is another matter. However, there are maybe outside causes that had caused the accidents. then I wouldn't say we're responsible for those accidents."[173]

By contrast, Ford's President and CEO, Jacques Nasser, told lawmakers that "his company moved aggressively at the first indication of a widespread problem."[174] Nevertheless, both companies dissembled and evaded direct answers, each trying to point the finger of blame at the other. But Nasser was the most forceful: "Because tires are the only component of a vehicle that are separately warranted, Ford did not know--I'll repeat that--Ford did not know there was a defect (in the tires) until we virtually pried the information from Firestone's hands. We then demanded, insisted, that Firestone pull the tires from the road."[175]

Nasser also appeared in print ads and on television in commercials designed to reassure Ford customers that the company was doing everything possible to get to the bottom of the problem. "You have my personal guarantee," Nasser to the public, "that no one at Ford will rest until every recalled tire is replaced."[176]

Ono was forced out of his job in October, 2000, just a month and a half after he testified before Congress. In that short time he had managed to alienate, Ford, his largest customer, open the door to scores of wrongful death lawsuits, and virtually destroy the public

---

173 Dan Ackman, quoting Masatoshi Ono in "Bridgestone's Ono Out of the Fire," *Forbes*, October 10, 2000.

174 Thomas Fogarty, "Congress Grills Ford, Firestone, NHTSA," *USA Today*, 2000.

175 John Chartier, "Firestone, Ford Under Fire," CNN Money, September 6, 2000.

176 Jacques Nasser, "Your Safety," Ford Motor Company, 2000, p. 21.

image of his company. As a result, Bridgestone/Firestone's profits fell 80% in 2000.

- 12 -

CLOSE TO THE EDGE

"If you are not living on the edge,
you are taking up too much room."

Jayne Howard

WORKING ON THE EDGE

The windows were rolled down and I could hear voodoo drums echoing through the stillness as we climbed the narrow asphalt road, leaving Port-au-Prince and its misery behind us. Trees lined both sides of the road and a full moon the size of dinner plate hung in the dark sky in front of me. We came to a stretch of the road where spider webs, like archways of spun sugar, connected the tops of the trees on either side of the road and, silhouetted against the moon in front of me fist-sized spiders languidly made their way across their webs.

I was in the backseat of a late model black sedan driven by a Tonton Macoute driver, still wearing his wrap-around shades despite the fact that the sun had gone down some time ago. I had asked him to take me to a small restaurant in Petionville, which was located in the hills above the Haitian capital where the breezes were fresher and there was still foliage that hadn't been chopped down to make charcoal. Most government officials and the small circle of wealthy business families lived there, along with senior members of the aid community and a handful of successful Haitian folk artists, in lordly splendor high above the pollution and daily struggle for survival by the teeming masses below.

When I reached the restaurant, I was greeted effusively by the owner and shown to my table. There was only one other couple in the dining room and much to my shock and surprise it was my colleague from Washington with whom I had traveled to Haiti, and the absolutely stunning wife of the nation's dictator. They were obviously enjoying themselves and he had his arm around her. I said hello to them perfunctorily and then beat a hasty retreat back to the hotel Oloffson, where I was staying, to give them some privacy. We had been the only two non-Haitian travelers to arrive on our flight that day and I marveled at the thought of my colleague having an affair with the dictator's wife in plain sight in a country where there were no secrets.

As eerie and potentially dangerous as that night may have been, it left an indelible memory on me and one I'll carry for the rest of my days. In retrospect, I wouldn't have traded that evening for a thousand nice, safe, and secure suburban evenings in front of television following dinner at the Olive Garden. That night in Haiti was part of a complex crazy quilt of experiences I've accumulated over decades working at the margins of our complex and conflict-riven world on problems that generally defy easy resolution. "I want to stand as close to the edge as I can without going over," Kurt Vonnegut Jr. once observed. "Out on the edge you see all the kinds of things you can't see from the center."

While there is no real need for most companies to do business in places like Haiti, and frankly there's very little business to be done there, nevertheless U.S. companies must learn to compete throughout the world, especially in the hard places, near the edges, because that's where the new markets of the future are emerging, where competition for oil and gas, along with strategic minerals and water, will be the most intense, and where many of our critical supply chains will be anchored. We mustn't shrink from visiting and working in those places.

We've gotten fat and complacent as a nation, and too often avoid doing business anyplace there are substantial risks or problems, or for that matter which lack American hotels, restaurants, and other amenities. I had a U.S. businessman tell me a few years ago that he wouldn't travel to any country where he couldn't get hotel or airline points. What kind of attitude is that?

This is not the way that great trading nations succeed. Rather, it is a surefire formula for the decline of our competitiveness and ultimately our eclipse by younger, more energetic powerhouses like China, South Korea, India, Brazil, and Malaysia, to name only a few. Far too many young men and women today live vicariously, divorced from reality, through television, computers, Play Stations and theme parks. The wanderlust that once called to generations of young Americans, beckoning them to travel and experience life in all of its diversity and wonderment, is absent.

While the world is full of problems and challenges which will test our preparations, strength, and ingenuity, we must not shirk from taking risks but instead need to develop a new and even more aggressive risk-taking culture, similar to the one which built this nation in the 19th and 20th centuries. Indeed, most great accomplishments have involved risk. As Neil Simon observed: "If no one ever took risks, Michelangelo would have painted the Sistine floor." Risk is, and should remain, the essence of our capitalistic society, and every young man and women should be encouraged to take risks in their lives; not foolish risks but rather careful, well-thought-out risks that provide them potentially with great rewards, not the least of which may be unforgettable experiences that are an affirmation of character and a challenge to their intellect and resourcefulness. As George Patton said, "Take calculated risks. That is quite different from being rash."[177]

CLIENTS WHO DON'T LISTEN

No matter what you do, no matter how good your advice, the client will sometimes reject it, usually to their regret. The failure to accept good, solid advice, backed up by careful research and painstaking work, can even have tragic consequences.

The best example of this was the 2007 assassination of my friend Benazir Bhutto, who had twice served as prime minister of Pakistan and had been twice overthrown. Ultimately, she returned to Pakistan to seek power a third time.

I learned of her intention to return some years earlier when I met her in Dubai at her home before taking her to dinner. The sun had gone down and the room was dim when she greeted me wearing a long sari and cradling a cat upside down, stroking its stomach with the backs of her long fingers as the creature's head lolled backward and its tail curled. We departed for dinner at her club with a female chaperone, but no security detail.

We reached the club and dined outside on the terrace in the pleasant evening air, with a light winter breeze blowing lazily off the Gulf.

---

177 George S. Patton, "Best Quotes and Poems," http//www.best-quotes-poems.com/risk-quotes.html.

"Excuse me for bringing up the subject," I told her, "but I didn't see any security at your house, not even an alarm system. And now we're sitting in the open, exposed on all sides, without the benefit, unless I'm missing something, of guards or any kind of security detail."

"The government of Dubai looks after me," she replied.

"Yes, but you're an easy target and you have enemies, serious enemies. I'm not sure you should be relying on the local government to provide you with security at their discretion. You should have your own round-the-clock security apparatus, loyal only to you, and a good system at your house as well."

"Perhaps," she answered dismissively with a wave of her hand.

As I spent more time with her in the years that followed I came to realize that Benazir believed emphatically that she had a grand destiny and that nothing would interfere with that destiny, certainly not a gunman or suicide bomber. That someone might try to kill her she accepted as a possibility but she totally rejected any notion that they might succeed.[178] She also apparently had failed to understand or fully comprehend the changes that had taken place in Pakistan during her exile, and the vicious and unbending nature of the new adversaries she faced, who would stop at nothing to prevent her from regaining power, in part because she was a woman.

We spent many hours in the intervening years discussing her security, but always without any progress. I would warn her repeatedly, as would others, of the risks she was confronting but she adamantly refused to take meaningful actions to enhance her protection. These included wearing body armor, having American special operations veterans guard her and train locals in the art of executing protection, setting up counter-surveillance and intel operations wherever she went, manipulating radio frequencies to detonate explosive devices in advance of her convoy, and modifying a vehicle along the the lines of the Pope-mobile so she wouldn't be so exposed when she greeted crowds and moved through the city streets of Pakistan.

---

178 Israeli Prime Minister Yitzhak Rabin also rejected any idea that he might be assassinated or that he should increase the security around him. "He (Rabin) believed that something like that could never happen," Minister of Planning and Economy, Yossi Beilin, said in an interview. Rabin was killed by a right-wing gunman after a peace rally in Tel Aviv. See: "Rabin Believed He Would Never be Killed," *Newsweek*, November 18, 1995.

When she finally returned to Pakistan on October 18, 2007, she was met by a massive crowd at Jinnah International Airport and along the streets leading into Karachi. Ten hours later her convoy was still moving slowly into the city when two bombs were detonated, killing 136 people and injuring nearly 500. More than a third of the dead were members of her security detail. While she was unhurt, the bomb blasts seemed only to contribute all the more to her sense of fatalism.

Parliamentary elections were scheduled for January, 2008, and she announced that she was running for a seat in Karkana as leader of the PPP Party. As she left a party rally in Rawalpindi on December 27, she was riding in a hardened car, standing up through the sunroof and waving to the crowds, when a bomb went off nearby. Whether she was killed by shrapnel or by the blast effects of the device, which caused her to hit her head on the car, is still a matter of dispute, but she succumbed to her injuries shortly after arriving at a local hospital.

Benazir's tragic death is one of the more glaring examples of someone who didn't listen to advice which, in this case, might have saved her life. While the consequences were not so severe, another example of someone who disregarded extremely sound advice and counsel was a client based in New York City, who ran a hedge fund. Although he had only limited international experience, he became a global traveler in his effort to raise money for his fund. Somewhere along the way he met a Chinese firm that allegedly desired to purchase scrap metal from the United States. In seeking to put the deal together, he located a man in Florida who claimed he could provide the scrap metal at the price and in the volume he required.

Prudently, he hired me to perform due diligence on the individual from Florida. The first thing I told him was that the scrap metal business is often controlled by the mob, but he was only interested in whether or not the man could supply him with the product the Chinese wanted. It didn't take long to discover that the man was a convicted swindler who had spent time behind bars in Florida. Far from being a wealthy businessman who drove a Rolls Royce (he was behind the wheel of a Rolls when he met the client), the man lived in a crummy leased apartment located in a marginal neighborhood and drove a ten-year old Toyota. The Rolls had obviously been borrowed or rented.

We concluded, therefore, that the man was crook and not to be trusted and conveyed our assessment to the client, who thanked us and paid his bill without complaint. I assumed that the matter was closed so I was extremely surprised when the client called a year later and asked if I could assist him in connection with the scrap metal issue we had previously investigated. It turned out that greed had got the best of him and despite my warnings he had given the man $1.5 million for shipment of scrap metal and now he wanted help in getting his money back. The man had kept his money and, showering him with excuses, had failed to ship even a single pound of scrap metal to China.

"Why did you do business with him?" I asked incredulously. "We warned you he was a crook and didn't have a pot to piss in."

"I know, I know," replied the hedge fund manager, "but if I could have fulfilled the order I would have made a fortune."

Hence, the first rule of all deals: if something seems too good to be true it probably is. I've been in business for almost four decades and I can say unreservedly that there are very few "inside" deals where, due to discrepancies in the marketplace, one party can make exceptional profits because the other party doesn't know the real price of goods or where to find the product. This is particularly true with the advent of the worldwide web and the ability to track global commodities in real time. The hedge fund manager lost his money and he should have known better but, even with accurate up-to-date information about his source, he couldn't bring himself to abandon the deal for fear that he would lose a fortune.

CONCLUSION

I end with stories of failure rather than success because that's the nature of life. No one can triumph over every problem, but it's the journey that is often most important, not the result. My journey has been full of sights, sounds, tastes, people and experiences--not all of them good--that I would not have given up for anything. Along the way I've been able to help a wide array of clients with an even wider array of problems and challenges, most of which were novel and without exact precedent. That was the fun part, and it meant that we never knew what the next day would bring, only that it was unlikely to be boring.

Every young man, and an increasing number of young women, needs to "kill their lion". I have, I'm proud to say, killed mine.

ABOUT THE AUTHOR

Neil C. Livingstone is an internationally renowned crisis manager and problem solver, who has handled hundreds of one-of-a-kind problems for corporations, governments, celebrities and other private citizens. He has worked in over 60 countries and some of his recent cases have involved kidnappings, the introduction of transparency to Russian companies, industrial espionage, blackmail, fraud and missing assets.

He has headed a number of major companies, including one which he founded in 1998 and took public in 2005. He serves on numerous advisory boards in the security and related industries.

He is the author of ten books and more than 250 articles on terrorism and national security that have appeared in leading newspapers and journals around the world. A familiar face on network television, he has appeared on more than 1600 television programs and 1100 radio shows.

Much in demand as a public speaker, he has delivered more than 500 major addresses around the world on national security issues, including speeches at the United Nations, the House of Commons, and the Herzliya Conference in Israel.

Livingstone holds an A.B. (with honors in Government) from the College of William and Mary, three Masters degrees and a Ph. D. from the Fletcher School of Law & diplomacy.

Made in the USA
Charleston, SC
05 February 2012